Victor

THE SPIRIT OF MUSIC

Victor L. Wooten, a five-time Grammy winner, is a founding member of the supergroup Béla Fleck and the Flecktones. Victor has also become widely known for his own Grammy-nominated solo recordings and tours. Among other accomplishments, he is a skilled naturalist, teacher, author, and magician and has won every major award given to a bass guitarist, including being voted Bass Player of the Year in *Bass Player* magazine's readers' poll three times (the only person to win it more than once). In 2011, *Rolling Stone* voted Victor one of the Top Ten Bassists of All Time. In 2015, *The Huffington Post* listed Victor as one of "50 Iconic Black Trailblazers Who Represent Every State in America." Wooten represented his birth state of Idaho. He lives outside Nashville, Tennessee.

ALSO BY VICTOR L. WOOTEN

*The Music Lesson: A Spiritual Search
for Growth Through Music*

THE SPIRIT
OF MUSIC

THE SPIRIT OF MUSIC

The Lesson Continues

Victor L. Wooten

VINTAGE BOOKS

A DIVISION OF PENGUIN RANDOM HOUSE LLC

NEW YORK

A VINTAGE BOOKS ORIGINAL, FEBRUARY 2021

Library of Congress Cataloging-in-Publication Data
Names: Wooten, Victor, author.
Title: The spirit of music : the lesson continues / Victor L. Wooten.
Description: New York : Vintage Books, 2020.
Identifiers: LCCN 2020028516 (print) | LCCN 2020028517 (ebook) |
ISBN 9780593081662 (trade paperback) |
ISBN 9780593081679 (ebook)
Subjects: LCSH: Wooten, Victor, author. | Music—Social aspects.
Classification: LCC ML419.W68 A3 2020 (print) |
LCC ML419.W68 (ebook) | DDC 781.1/7—dc23
LC record available at https://lccn.loc.gov/2020028516

Vintage Books Trade Paperback ISBN: 978-0-593-08166-2
eBook ISBN: 978-0-593-08167-9

Book design by Nicholas Alguire

www.vintagebooks.com

Printed in the United States of America
10 9 8 7 6 5

You Are Not Lost
Keep Going

Is anyone working on a bomb that makes people love each other?

We already have it. It's called Music.

—Michael

CONTENTS

ACKNOWLEDGMENTS

The biggest Thanks, Gratitude, and Love to GOD and Her staff for allowing Life and Music to flow through me. A big THANKS to everyone at Vintage Books for presenting this journey to the public. A special thank-you to Keith Goldsmith for believing in me and helping to shape these ideas into a cohesive manuscript. Susannah Noel, Kim Ingenito Thornton, John Vorhees, James Meader, Edward Allen, Jessica Deitcher, and Melissa Yoon, you are all special to me. I thank you for everything you've done to make this book a reality.

Special thanks, kisses, and hugs go to:

Holly and Kaila Wooten, Dana Parker, Daniel Levitin, Béla Fleck, Jennie Hoeft, Rolland Brunet, Dave Welsch, Steve Bailey, Bob Franceschini, Rod Taylor, and Keith Goldsmith for reading, reading, and reading again as *The Spirit of Music* continued to grow.

My wife, Holly, and my kids, Kaila, Adam, Arianna, and Cameron, for loving, teaching, inspiring, and helping me to be a better me. I love you!!!

My parents for continuing to teach and guide me through Life and my brothers, Regi, Roy, Rudy, and Joseph, for teaching me about Music and for allowing me to share your wisdom in these pages.

My manager, Danette Albetta, for continued friendship, guidance, help, and support.

I love you all.

And a special thanks goes to Music, Michael, and all the characters for allowing me to write about you and to my musical instruments for allowing me to express through them.

To everyone:
Thank you for reading and listening,
for sharing your Spirit, and for accepting mine.
I love you for that!

Peace,
Victor L. Wooten

THE SPIRIT
OF MUSIC

A New Beginning

I need your help. Are you with me? May I have a show of hands?

There is an intense epidemic happening all around us, and for the most part, it's accelerating unnoticed as if we've chosen not to notice.

Allow me to elaborate.

Could Music as a whole ever be threatened? Could Music get sick, die, or, even worse, be killed? Could we wake one morning to find Music removed entirely from our existence? Is any of this possible? If so, would you do anything to stop this tragedy from happening? It sounds crazy, like a conspiracy theory, right? Well, my friends, it may be more than just a theory.

If I were to tell you that Mother Nature is dying, it would make perfect sense. The message would be clear. But although it is important and true, it is a message we've heard before. What we haven't heard is that Mother Music is also dying. Yes! That is also important and true.

You see, like Nature, who is aware of all her children, Music is a living consciousness who is aware of each musician. She chooses us in the same sense that we choose our instruments. In fact, we *are* her instruments. We might consider it an absurd thought if our instruments believed they were making music instead of us. It may be just as absurd for us to think that we are making music instead of Music herself. Understanding this truth not only makes our music better, it also enhances the musical experience. Without this understanding, Music and we (as a people) suffer.

Some years ago, I wrote a book called *The Music Lesson: A Spiritual Search for Growth Through Music.* In that book I told about a dream I'd had one night that contained a beautiful but disturbing conversation between Music and me. Her voice, like that of a wise and concerned mother, reverberated through my mind, telling me that she was sick and dying because she was losing touch with humans. According to her, we do not feel her as completely as we used to, and because of that, she currently has a more intimate relationship with computers than she does with people. That is a bit scary to me. In my book, I referred to it as a dream because I was afraid to tell the truth. But now, I am not afraid to tell you that it was not a dream at all.

I've spent many hours shedding tears while contemplating her message. I eventually moved beyond my tears and made a vow to do something to help. Today, I am mortified by how little I've accomplished. Like a vivid dream that stays just out of memory's reach once you've awakened, the urgency to act gently faded away. Maybe it was because I could find very few people who believed me. I felt alone.

No! I will no longer live that lie!

This time around, I will be completely honest. The truth: I wasn't up for the challenge. I was scared. Now, I don't care who believes me. Even if I have to act alone, I will do all that I can to help Music. Now is the time!

A few years ago, an unusual man named Michael helped to transform my way of thinking. He would say that he did nothing. No, he would not want the credit or the blame for that. But when he showed up at my house, unannounced and uninvited, my way of approaching Music changed forever.

Michael often spoke of Music as if he were talking about an actual person, using a capital *M*. To him, Music is someone with whom you can converse—like a friend. I didn't get it at first, but now I understand. And now, after my conversation with Music, I often refer to her in the same way.

Michael was my teacher, although he claimed that he could teach me *nothing*—that he could only *show* me things and that I would have to teach myself. That totally confused me. In the modern world, it is often stated that knowledge is power. In Michael's world, knowledge, alone, is powerless. It is the teacher's role to point the student toward knowledge, but it is the student's role to learn it. Then and only then can the student add power to the knowledge. The teacher can never accomplish that for the student. It took a long time for me to understand. Keeping me thinking was Michael's way.

I used to think I was dependent on a teacher for answers. Michael helped me realize that if I asked more questions, more answers would show up. For him, having the correct answers wasn't as important as having the correct questions. "Once the question is asked," he'd say, "you are in an arm's reach of the answer." I'd previously made a habit of assuming I didn't know anything, waiting for a teacher to give me answers. Michael made it clear that I needed to make new habits.

Now, I need your help. I need you to ask questions and to feel the answers in your heart. You see, feeling is the key. Music needs to be felt. *Feeling* and *sincerity* are essential for her to remain whole. I am sure, like me, you are thinking, *I can feel Music.* Well, I am sure that you can, but what you may not have considered is that, currently, there is increasingly less and less Music to be felt. Music is not reaching us in her entirety.

Questions? I will help you with that.

How can Music be sick? How can Music die? Only living things die, right? I used to ask myself the same questions. Even as a musician, I believed Music only existed on an instrument, in a voice, or on a piece of paper. Now I realize that those are only tools used to express Music, and that we should never mistake the tools for Music herself. I used to focus so much on the tools that I often lost sight of the experience. Like most people, I never realized that Music was a living entity—not like a human, a plant, or an animal, but living nonetheless. Think of her like a spirit. That may make it easier to comprehend and accept.

Here's another thought. If a human body becomes riddled with a disease such as cancer, the affected area can become so contaminated that the whole body dies. In other words, the whole body does not have to be infected for the whole being to die. Think about that. I believe this is exactly what is happening to Music. She is being diseased a little at a time. The craziest part of all is that we are the ones doing it.

In *The Music Lesson*, I divided Music into ten equal parts: notes, articulation, technique, emotion, dynamics, rhythm, tone, phrasing, space, and listening. Think of these topics as arms, legs, hands, feet, or other parts that make up the "body" of Music. Now ask yourself: Is it possible that some of the individual parts can become so infected that the whole body of Music can begin to deteriorate? It is an outrageous question, I know, but it is also one worth looking into. Let us delve deeper.

Before the invention of recording devices, in order to hear Music, one would have to listen to live musicians or play it oneself. Obviously, that is no longer the case. Presently we have many different choices when it comes to how we experience Music. Is it possible that these choices are unwittingly undermining quality with convenience?

Here's an analogy. If we use 12 inches to represent the sonic quality of listening to live music, a vinyl record could be represented as approximately 8 inches. A compact disc (CD) is usually made from .wav files, putting it at around 6 inches. An mp3, which is only one-tenth the size of a .wav file, would equal .6 inches. Listening to an mp3 through tiny earbuds or computer speakers could reduce it to approximately .25 of an inch or less. That scares me.

Literally, we are not receiving the same amount of Music that our parents did. The frequencies we hear today have been drastically diminished in just a few short years. Think about it: our kids are growing up with a mere ¼ inch as their musical norm.

Gus, a recording engineer near Boulder, Colorado, is one

of the creators of the DAW, or Digital Audio Workstation. DAWs allow musicians to make records without the use of big machines and expensive rolls of tape. This makes them very convenient, and I've recorded many records using this technology. Guess what? Gus does not like the DAW and wishes he had never created it because, as he says, "We didn't get it right."

As a result, Gus continued experimenting and has come up with a new digital recording platform that meets his satisfaction. It's called Sonoma. While the most popular digital devices record 192,000 pieces of information per second, Sonoma records close to three million per second. The difference in sound is undeniable.

I brought a violinist friend to Gus's studio one afternoon, and while listening to a recording of Joni Mitchell singing with the London Philharmonic Orchestra, she removed her shawl, stating that she could feel Music caressing her skin. She was speaking literally. Listening to Music in Gus's studio is a life-changing experience. Music can actually be felt in a way that, for most of us, has long been forgotten. Fighting back tears, I realized that I'd been a musician my whole life but had forgotten what Music was supposed to feel like. I am sorry.

Dr. Diamond is a stress doctor in upstate New York who uses Music to help his clients manage their anxiety. With the arrival of the compact disc in the 1980s, Dr. Diamond was excited at the prospect of having a more durable means of playing Music for his patients. According to the specifications, a CD would never degrade the way his cassette tapes were constantly doing.

One day while at his home in Colorado, Gus received a

phone call. Dr. Diamond was on the other end complaining that, for some reason, his patients were getting *more* stressed instead of less. After intense investigation and experimentation done over time, Gus and Dr. Diamond concluded that there was something in the sound quality of the CD that was negatively affecting his patients. Dr. Diamond now uses Sonoma to treat his patients, and they are much happier. As Gus once told me, "It doesn't really matter if you can hear the difference. It's what you feel that counts."

There is a similar concern surrounding the food we eat. Genetically modified organisms (GMOs) are living organisms whose genetic material has been manipulated in laboratories using genetic engineering. I haven't followed the research on GMOs, but one thing I know for sure is that it is very difficult to improve Mother Nature's recipe. I believe she got it right the first time. I feel the same about Mother Music. If we currently have to label some foods as GMO, should we also have to label some Music as GMM (genetically modified music)?

Although we have made tremendous technological advances in modern times, many of the current methods of experiencing Music may have serious side effects. They have literally changed the way we think, as well as the way we socialize, or not. While Music used to be experienced in groups, currently, listening is mostly a solo experience.

In decades past, purchasing a new vinyl record was a social event. Friends and family bonded together and listened to the whole album as a group. Even the album credits were read and shared together.

Listening to or purchasing an album in its entirety is no longer the norm, and reading liner notes is a thing of the past. Downloading individual songs and listening to them in our own chosen order is the current standard, which totally neglects the vision of the artists, composers, and producers. It is equivalent to purchasing our favorite scenes from a movie, watching them out of order, and fallaciously thinking we've seen the whole film. As my mom would say, "Now ain't that some foolishness."

Music is recorded very differently than it used to be, and many of the current recording techniques have caused us to become comfortable with less rather than more. I know that positives can be found in everything, but in this case the negatives may be gradually taking over. In other words: the glass may be becoming half-empty. The bigger problem is that most of us do not realize it. Like the arrogant hare and the tortoise, if we are not careful, we may regretfully find that we have lost the race.

Auto-tune and pitch correction are currently used in the recording world to digitally correct notes that were played or sung out of tune. Most contemporary singers heard on the radio have been auto-tuned, some to the extreme. Because of this, we are no longer hearing all of the available pitches. Some of my favorite singers, such as Billie Holiday, Sarah Vaughan, and Chaka Khan, wavered in and out of tune in a way that created sultry and soulful feelings and emotions. Those delicate nuances actually caused us to feel their performances in a much grander way. Today, if these singers were digitally "corrected," I seriously doubt the technology would make them sound better. Actually, I am sure it wouldn't.

Quantizing is another "correction" technique that is currently in the mainstream, but this one is used to digitally correct rhythms. It works like this: when a musician plays a rhythm that is imperfect and slightly out of time, the engineer runs the musician's recording through a digital processor that magically corrects the rhythm. Used properly, this tool has the ability to improve upon a less-than-par performance, but it also runs the risk of making it sound too perfect. I cannot imagine artists like the Beatles, the Rolling Stones, or James Brown being quantized. It would literally remove much of the soul from their Music.

Compressors and limiters are additional technologies that digitally remove, adjust, and balance the dynamics of a song or an instrument. They work by making soft things louder and loud things softer. These tools can work as the musician is playing in real time. In either case, good or bad, they change the performance from what it naturally is.

All these tools and techniques are designed to make Music better, and when used well, they work. But if the result leaves us with only one-quarter inch of Music, shouldn't we be concerned? Don't misunderstand me. I am not totally against these tools. I actually use them myself (sometimes). Plus, now that they are here, I do not think they are ever going away. But, I pose the question: Can we use them in a way that does not destroy or even diminish the spirit of Music? I think we can.

I remember when music video channels first emerged on cable television. The thought of having a channel devoted to Music twenty-four hours a day was not only thrilling but also groundbreaking. Now, just a short time later, these channels resort to showing everything except music videos to stay on air. Game shows and "reality" shows (which are very often everything but reality) have taken Music's place.

Think about it: music video channels don't play Music anymore. Do you recognize a problem?

Before the 1980s, "Pop" was not a style of Music; it was simply an abbreviation for the word "popular." Regardless of style, pop radio stations played the songs people most wanted to hear. You could hear Janis Joplin, the Jackson Five, Led Zeppelin, Sly and the Family Stone, Louis Armstrong, and more, all on the same station. Currently, more and more radio stations are excessively formatted and financially driven. The few remaining disc jockeys who are brave enough to play Music they are excited about in order to expose their listeners to new sounds face a continuous struggle to find funding.

Cutting off funding to the arts is similar to cutting off the blood supply to the human body. Much like blood being constricted by plaque in our veins and arteries, there is a steady lessening of blood flowing to the heart of Music. The organisms we call Music are malnourished. If this plaque buildup continues to go unnoticed and uncared for, Life, as we know it, could cease to exist. It is not just about the ear and how it sounds; it is about how and if the flow reaches the heart.

A boa constrictor squeezes its prey until it can no longer breathe, cutting off its blood supply in the process. Each time its prey exhales, the snake squeezes a little harder, making it more difficult for the prey to inhale. The process is repeated over and over until the victim is rendered lifeless. In many cases, the prey doesn't even realize its fate until it's too late. Using this as an analogy, are we also being constricted? Are we someone's prey? If so, who is doing the constricting, and how much time do we have?

Beautiful plants such as wisteria, kudzu, and certain varieties of honeysuckle are also good examples of silent destroyers. These rampant vines cause damage by constricting, smothering, and destroying everything around them. The interesting (and quite dangerous) quality of each is that, like the boa constrictor, these vines are sneaky. They are in no hurry. They slowly grab on with one tendril, then another and another. Before you know it, many of the surrounding species of plants are dead, leaving the vine the only one remaining. Lured by their beauty, caretakers often don't recognize the problem until the damage has been done. The result is that the ecosystem of the area is critically impaired.

Music's ecosystem has also been critically damaged. The good (and bad) part is this: You don't have to be a musician to be part of the problem or the solution. Whether you play an instrument or not, we all have a biological relationship with Music. We are born with her. Our vibrations are connected. She is in our DNA.

A young child does not have to learn how to respond to Music. If the right song plays, a child will sing, dance, conduct, or simply smile. Adults are the same but mostly when we are alone. We sing in the shower or in the car. We smile when we play "air guitar" and we dance when no one is looking. These are natural responses. They are our birthright.

I think of classical music as vibrant, emotional, and alive. It is one of my favorite genres. It was also the soundtrack of the cartoons I watched in my youth. One day, while riding in a car with Michael, I noticed a procession of people walking out of a church. They were dressed very nicely, most of them wearing black, and their faces were somber. I asked Michael if he knew who had died. His response was shocking. "Music!" he answered. What I thought was a funeral was actually people exiting a classical music concert. I didn't understand. Michael told me that the musicians had probably lost touch with their own emotions while trying to resurrect those of a two-hundred-year-old composer.

"There is a way to do it," Michael told me, "but not by neglecting the present. Audiences don't like that. A copy, even if done better, is never worth as much as the original." I'm still trying to understand that one.

A banjo player introduced me to the world of bluegrass and to the many wonderful musicians who inhabit that world. I have learned that some of the world's best musicians play that style of Music. I attended a bluegrass festival and was struck by the sight of little kids sitting under a tree learning fiddle tunes from their elders. It seemed such a natural process—education at its best. "Bluegrass isn't taught in schools," one of the fiddle teachers told me. "It's taught under a tree."

It is indisputable that there are far fewer trees than there were five decades ago, and in a sense, as I've shown above, there may be less Music than there was five decades ago. If Bluegrass is taught under a tree, how long will it be before there are no trees left for children to sit beneath?

There's a Chinese proverb that states: "The best time to plant a tree was twenty years ago. The next best time is now!" I wish my journey to save Music had started twenty years ago. I guess "the next best time" will have to do.

A few years ago, I made a vow to save Music. I wish it were as easy as planting a tree. Fortunately, I had an eccentric teacher to help me find my path. But it was Music herself who summoned me through the archway and into a new world, a world that was always there but not always easy to see. Once the veil lifted and I chose to see with wide-angle vision, I could feel her as if she'd been with me all that time deep in my soul.

I know now that I was recruited to help her. I wish Michael had told me that in the beginning. "I can teach you nothing" were his original words. Those words have begun to take on a whole new meaning. Maybe nothing is what I'm supposed to know. Maybe that's where I'm supposed to be—**a new beginning**.

Michael said that I called him. Music definitely called me, and now . . . I am calling you. I'm not sure where to go from here, but the one thing I am sure about is that I cannot go alone. Follow me back in time so that I can catch you up. Hopefully, somewhere along the way, you will become our ally—our Music-ally. That is a choice you will have to make. Yes, there will be risks, but if you choose to join us, you will find us standing on the path alongside you. Just look for the marker. Together, I know we can make a difference. If you are with us, keep reading! If not,

Definitely Keep Reading!

Parents Know Best

◈

*Never say what you're not going to do because that
is your first step toward doing it.*

There's a joke that asks the question: "How do you get a
musician to complain?"

The answer: "Give him a gig."

Somehow, I'd fallen into the trap of disliking most of my
gigs, and the previous one had left me feeling a bit unsettled. I didn't know what was causing it or how to make the
feeling go away. I wasn't sure if it was Music or me who kept
refusing to show up.

I knew there had to be more to my musical life, but I
didn't know what *more* meant or where to find it. After many
months of struggling with myself, I decided to turn to the
only two people who had always been there for me, who
would definitely help me feel better, and who would not
allow me to continue lying to myself.

Mom and Dad have always been the fixers-of-all-things. Almost two years had passed since I'd seen them and I was longing for their company. A visit would be good for my soul, and a home-cooked meal would be good for my stomach. The ten-hour drive would be good for my mind. Yes, I was running away from something—something I was trying to ignore—something I knew I would eventually have to face.

I'd never paid close attention to my alarm clock. It would go off (too early), I would hit it, and keep sleeping. That was the normal routine. But on this particular morning, the harsh sound of the note *G* repeating in my ear caused me to sit up right away. I didn't know why I recognized the actual pitch. It had never happened to me before. Regardless, hitting Snooze was not an option. I did *not* want to hear that sound again. I quickly stopped the alarm and hopped to my feet. A few minutes later, an irritating note emitting from the microwave informed me that my food was ready. The out-of-tune *C* ruined my appetite. I picked up the phone to call my parents. Even the sound of the dial tone irritated me. I placed it back down without making the call. I tried to avert my attention, but my ears acted on their own and my brain colluded by not allowing me to ignore any of the sounds. By the time I made it into the car, musical tones were speaking to me from every direction. Because the car was rented, all the sounds were unfamiliar to me. The fact that I could name every pitch was surprising and should have been a good thing, but I was not ready to listen.

I turned on the radio, hoping it would bring some order to the chaos. Even that became a challenge. The morning cacophony of sounds seemed to be ganging up on me. Every note competed for my attention. I couldn't make them stop. I felt a headache coming on and turned off the radio, hoping the silence would bring a bit of solace to my journey. It didn't work. Even the silence spoke loudly.

The tires played a duet with the road; the engine whined a horrible tune, and the wind kept me company by whistling through the window directly into my left ear. Every fragment of noise had a pitch, a rhythm, or both.

Just as I was reaching my peak of frustration, a truck passed by on my left side. A message written on its back grabbed my attention. *Nature's Choice.* For some reason, I read it as: *Not ure Choice.* My brain retaliated. I screamed at the truck.

"It *is* my choice. You can't tell me—"

My eyes fixed the mistake. I felt foolish. Without signaling, the truck merged too closely in front of me. I slowed and regrouped. I took the next exit and parked on the side of the road, not waiting to find a parking lot. I turned off the engine and laid my head on the steering wheel. As soon as I closed my eyes, an unsolicited thought entered my mind: *There's an ear in every heart as it beats in every breath. Listen and be silent.* Having no idea from where the thought had come, I listened and obeyed.

"It *is* my choice," I whispered to myself.

I sat up straight and made a firm decision. *From this point on, I will have a different attitude.* I pulled back onto the highway with a smile on my face and a clear head.

This time, what I'd previously considered separate fragments of noise merged into a cohesive coalition of beautiful symmetry. The patterns were intricate and entertaining. The rhythm of the road provided a pulse that complemented all the other sounds.

Once I turned the radio back on, the songs seemed to welcome each extraneous noise, creating thought-provoking compositions. Even my turn signal had a groove. Changing lanes became a musical adventure. And even though it wasn't raining, I rode with my windshield wipers on for a few minutes just to experience the complex polyrhythms they added. Music was with me and I was listening. We were both smiling.

Time passed rapidly. I stopped for gas just a few exits from my parents' home. There, Music didn't stop speaking. A beautiful tone scolded me for opening my door before turning off the engine, and it was a pleasure to hear that I'd left my lights on. The rhythm of the gas pump added an interesting cadence to the music playing through the speakers at the gas station. Although I liked the song, the harsh tone of the speakers caused it to sound horrible. *Why install bad speakers in a public place?* I paid for the gas and left as quickly as I could.

My excitement grew as each mile drew me closer and closer to my destination. It had been way too long since I'd seen my parents. I'd finally allowed myself to admit that I needed this visit, but whether I would be completely honest with them was a concern. Either way, dishonesty or half-truths would never deter my mom. She'd get to the heart of the issue no matter what. She speaks her mind and can see through any façade.

Mom is a wise woman who cares about everyone as if all people were her children. Demanding a hug instead of a handshake, she has a way of making everyone feel welcome.

Friends from all around make their way to her home, hoping to gain warmth and wisdom from her words and delicious Southern cuisine. "I'm not telling you this because you're gonna like it," she'd say. "I'm telling you because you need to hear it."

Dad is the hardworking, quiet type. He was in the army and the air force and fought on the ground in the Korean War. Dad is capable of dealing with just about anything. He once told me that growing up in the thirties and forties made fighting in the army seem easy. On a typical day, he would come home from a long day of work, grab a plate of food, and watch television while reading the newspaper. He would quietly sit, seemingly oblivious to all the commotion going on around him produced by a house full of kids and friends. Over the years, I'd never heard him complain about any of the noise. Whenever he had something to say, everything stopped so that we could pay rapt attention.

I'd been thinking about my parents a lot. Many of the life lessons I'd learned from them only became apparent as I grew into adulthood. Gradually, I'd learned to recognize and appreciate the abundant knowledge found in all their sayings. I never enjoyed writing as a child, but increasingly, I'd begun to see the value of taking good notes. **Parents know best,** I thought. *One day, I will write their words of wisdom down.*

They were sitting on the front porch when I pulled up in front of my childhood home in Newport News, Virginia. Their smiling faces, illuminated by the setting sun, were like a dose of good medicine. Dad had parked his car on the street, leaving the driveway clear for me. *That's my Dad. Quiet and thoughtful.*

I pulled up close to the garage door, just as I'd done many times before. A surge of energy ran through my veins as I shifted into Park. I exited the car so quickly that my parents barely had a chance to step off the porch. I'd known that I needed to see them, but until that moment, I was unaware of how much. I was their baby boy, and it had been too long since I'd acted like it.

After rounds of hugs and kisses, I was ushered into the kitchen while Dad emptied the car. Three place settings were already on the table. A tall glass of orange juice sat next to one of them. I smiled and took my seat.

As soon as I sat down, music playing on the television caught my ear. At the same time, the cuckoo clock began announcing the time with a succession of seven repetitive chimes.

"Dinnertime! My favorite time!" Dad sang as he walked in the house, the screen door making a high-pitched squeal.

"Wash your hands first," Mom's caring voice rang out.

Their voices, blending beautifully with the sounds from the television, screen door, and clock, produced a short musical cadence that grabbed my attention. I sat there replaying it in my mind.

"Wash your hands, I said!" Mom repeated, breaking my musical muse.

"Right," I answered.

The floor squeaked as I stood up. The pitch grabbed my attention as if it were deliberately speaking to me. The sound continued, matching my steps as I continued down the hallway. I entered the bathroom and was surprised by the fact that even running water produces a pitch. Something was following me around, trying to get my attention, and although I knew what, or more precisely, who it was, I stood at the sink in a daze, not ready to give in. *What do you want from me?* I thought, shaking my head.

"I want you to wash your hands and stop wastin' water!" My mom's voice echoed down the hall.

My mouth fell open. I was sure I hadn't spoken out loud, and even if I had, I didn't think she could hear me from the kitchen. I walked back and scrutinized my mom with an inquisitive stare. She faced the stove but didn't look back. A sly grin adorned her face. She was stirring a large open pot of water that had a tree limb sticking out of it. I smiled. I'd seen it many times before.

"I'm making Pinetop Tea," Mom said, obviously reading my thoughts again. "You seem to be snifflin' a bit."

The pot had been simmering on the stove since I walked in. Inside was a branch from a pine tree, complete with bark and needles. It was a remedy she'd learned as a child. The oldest girl of thirteen children, she cooked and cared for the younger siblings from an early age. I was reminiscing and preparing myself for the bitter taste when it hit me.

"Wait a minute! Mom, how did you know I had a cold? I mean, even before I got here?"

The expression on her face was enough to let me know I'd asked a stupid question. She had always known what her kids were up to, even if we were hours away. I was probably a teenager before I realized that her uncanny ability was not commonplace. Again, I shook my head.

Dinner conversation was normal, but as soon as I finished my second piece of cake, Mom began her inquiry.

"So, what's on your mind, Baby Boy?"

As if on cue, Dad stood up, took his dishes to the sink, and retreated to the living room.

"What do you mean?" I asked.

"Who you talking to?" she rhetorically replied. I knew exactly what she meant.

"Okay, Ma," I responded, knowing she would not allow me to get away that easily.

I took another sip of tea. I added more honey, paused, and looked at her. Her gaze was persistent. She was calm and patient.

"Well," I began, trying to find the safest words. "I just . . . I don't know . . . it's like . . ."

I looked up at her. She gave a reassuring smile, the kind only a loving mother can give. I relaxed.

"If we could find a way to bottle your smile, we could heal the world," I told her.

She responded with a gentle nod. I was still avoiding something and she knew it.

"I don't know, Ma. It's just that I moved to Nashville to play music. Yeah, I'm doing it, but I'm not enjoying myself. I'm gigging some weekends and I'm paying my bills. The gigs are fun and I love the people I'm working with, but . . . I found a used car I want to buy. I almost have enough saved to get it. So, it's not about money. It's . . . I really don't know what it is."

"You sure you don't know?" she asked.

I looked up at her but didn't answer. Mom continued.

"You've been playing most of your life. You know you can stop anytime you want. The choice is always yours."

She put the responsibility back on me. It was a bold thing to say.

"I don't think I want to do that," I responded.

"Then what good is complaining 'bout it gonna do?"

Of course, she was right. I didn't offer an answer.

She backed away from the table and walked toward the stove. Her hair was braided close to the scalp, making it appear as if she were wearing a crown. I was sure she'd braided it herself. She had that gift. She did whatever needed to be done whether she knew how to do it or not. If she didn't have the skill, she would acquire it from somewhere, sometimes seemingly out of thin air. The fact that she never tried to hide or dye her graying hair reminded me of how content she was.

Using the same ladle she'd used since I was a child, she refilled my cup and placed it in front of me. I took a sip.

"How's the tea?" she asked while taking her seat.

"It's bitter but good," I answered.

"What?"

"It's bitter but good," I repeated.

"Exactly!" she replied. "Bitter but good. Oftentimes, the best things Life has to offer are just that . . . bitter but good. Think about that!"

I closed my eyes and nodded. She was always right.

Mom had spoken the word "Life" very deliberately, as if it were a person's name. My unusual teacher, Michael, and his acquaintances were the only other people I'd ever heard speak that way. It was refreshing. My eyes opened on their own. I looked up at Mom.

"Pete and I gave birth to five children," she continued. "Now, the pain of pushing you boys out wasn't the most pleasant experience in the world. I ain't never been one of them women who could just pop 'em out. But . . ." She closed her eyes and shook her head slowly back and forth, obviously reliving the experience. She grabbed my hand and held it tightly in both of hers. "I wouldn't trade it for nuthin' in the world." She opened her eyes and leaned in close, her gaze caring but penetrating. "Now, tell me what's really going on."

I chuckled at her directness. I took a deep breath, lowered my head, and began.

"Well, something's been tugging at my insides for a while now—for a couple years actually. I don't know what it is, but . . . I don't quite know how to put it."

I looked up at her. She sat back and folded her arms. With a wrinkle in her forehead, she pursed her lips, which let me know I was pushing her limits.

"Okay. I think it's Music. She's been, I mean, *it's* been talking to me, well, trying to talk to me, I think. It's like, it wants to tell me something." I paused to see how she was accepting my words.

Mom kept silent, waiting for me to continue. So, for the first time, I told the complete truth. I knew, as well as she: I needed to talk.

"A few years ago, I had a conversation, an important conversation with Music." I looked up. Her face was calm. "I know, I know," I continued. "You can't really have a conversation, but, I mean, it was like she was actually there. I know it sounds crazy. That's why I haven't told anyone about it. It may have been a dream, but . . . she was real! Actually, she reminded me of you. I mean, her voice, it was gentle and even musical, but also sad. She told me she was sick . . ." My eyes welled up with tears as I recalled the feelings.

I related the whole experience, talking longer than planned. I may have been talking *to* Mom, but I was talking *for* me. And although she mostly remained silent, it helped having her there as a sounding board.

The more I talked, the more I let go of the need for her to believe me. I spoke from my heart, which was what I knew we both wanted. "Speaking from the heart is a cleanser of the soul," Mom once told me. "It doesn't matter who or what you talk to. You can talk to a tree if you want. Trees are better listeners than most people anyway."

Mom listened intently, barely moving a muscle as I spoke. She had a special gift of making one feel as if they were being heard without being judged. When I finished, she corroborated my story.

"Yeah! You're right. Music *is* sick. I can tell you that for sure."

Her response shocked me.

"Really? You believe that?"

"It's more than a belief," she answered. "I noticed it long ago when they started letting them bands play in church. My mother dreamed about it and told 'em not to do it. She said bad things would happen if they let them folks play. Ain't but singing 'spose to be in Living Hope Church."

"Why didn't Grandma want instruments in the church?" I asked. "Is there something wrong with instruments?"

"Ain't *nuthin'* wrong with instruments. The problem is the people. When people sing, they sing from the inside. When they play instruments, they play from the outside. That don't belong in Living Hope. Mother always say, 'If you wanna play outside, then stay outside.' I agree with Mother."

"Well, I can't argue with that," I replied.

"Well, you best not argue with anything I say," she countered with a chuckle.

My mom grew up in the eastern part of North Carolina, and her speech reverted to that vernacular every time her mind went back there.

"If Mother dreamt it, you best listen! All us kids knew that and never questioned it. Young folks today, y'all don't like to listen," she concluded. I hoped she wasn't referring to me.

When my mom was little, their family was governed by her mother's dreams. And when her mother's warnings weren't heeded, the consequences were never good.

"But what about Music talking to me? Isn't that kinda strange?" I asked.

"That ain't nuthin' but the Good Lord talking to you. He comes in all shapes and sizes. You just know how to listen to Music better than you listen to anything else. That's why you hear Him that way."

"Really? You think so? I never thought about it like that."

"You questioning me?" said asked with a smile.

"No, Ma. Definitely not." I laughed. "What should I do, then?"

"Listen, child! Listen to Him, or Her, or whatever title you want to use. That don't matter. Just listen to what Music is telling you!" she answered emphatically. "That's why your stomach is churnin' all to pieces. You ain't been listenin'! And you know as well as I do that you need to start."

Just then, my dad walked back into the kitchen. Apparently, he'd been listening the whole time.

"And since you made a promise to do something 'bout it, you best get to it," he said as he placed his empty dish in the sink. He pulled up a chair and joined us at the table.

"But why me?" I asked. "Why is Music talking to me?"

"Because you's a musician, son," my father answered, grabbing Mom's hand. "Don't seem to be many of them left." I looked up at him. His expression was serious.

"What do you mean?"

"I mean *musicians*," he answered. "Real musicians! Yeah,

we gots lotsa people playing instruments these days, but ain't many of 'em playing Music."

That sounded familiar.

"How do I know if I'm a real musician?" I asked.

"Be what you are," Mom answered. "To be a real musician, you can't just play; you also have to listen. Listen to everything, but most of all, listen to your heart. That's the best way for Music to reach you, through your heart, not just your senses."

"He ain't got to worry about that, 'cause he ain't got no sense!" Dad joked.

This time he was smiling. My dad was a jokester, and his timing couldn't have been better. I needed that release. I'm sure he could sense it.

"Listen, Baby Boy." Mom leaned forward and spoke quietly as if she was sharing a secret. "Music has given you everything. She's always been there for you. Now, it sounds like you want something from Music, but have you given her anything? In this life, you can't get without giving. That's just the way it works. You want more opportunity? Give someone else some opportunity. Maybe that's it. Have you done any teaching since you've been in Nashville?"

"I haven't had time," I answered, knowing it was a weak excuse.

Mom knew it, too. She didn't offer an answer, just an unsatisfied look. She rose from the table, taking my cup with her. I heard the clicking of the stove as she turned it back on. Time for more tea, I presumed.

"What I'm hearin' is foolishness," Dad chimed in. "Maybe that's why Music ain't got no time fo' you. You ain't got no time for her."

He wasn't pulling any punches. I offered a weak counter. "Times have been tough, Dad. I mean, I have a few gigs and everything, but I've been struggling just to—"

"Times ain't tough!" he interrupted. "Not fo' you, anyway. You ain't had to pick no cotton. You ain't never even mowed a lawn. You definitely ain't been drafted. You ain't married. You ain't got no kids, and you sho' 'nuf ain't had to walk to school in the snow, uphill both ways with one worn-out shoe and—"

"Okay, Pete. You made your point," Mom interrupted with a chuckle. Dad nodded but wasn't finished.

"Listen, son. Here's the way I live my life. I give it my all. I make up my mind what I really want to do, and when it is made up, I cannot fail at it. The basic rule to success, I think, is when the going gets tough, that is a positive signal to keep chargin'!" He slammed his fist on the table and stood up.

"Thank you, Dad."

With a smile, he patted my head and walked back into the living room. I'm sure he was imagining me as the little boy who used to ride on his shoulders.

"Listen," Mom continued, placing another cup of warm tea on the table. "I think you should start teaching when you get home." She closed her eyes for a second and opened them again. "Yes, that feels right. Find yourself a student. There's one out there probably waiting just for you." She laughed. "He might find you before you find him." She chuckled. "Don't worry; you'll know when the time is right."

"I'm so glad I came home. I really needed this." I stood up and gave Mom a squeeze. "I love you!" I said in earnest.

"I love you more!" she responded.

My parents are the best. They always know what to say as well as how to say it. Their words brought clarity and made me feel much better. But there was one thing Mom was absolutely wrong about. I would never be a teacher.

◈

*"Never say what you're not going to do because
that is your first step toward doing it."*

The Teacher

✚

When the teacher is ready, the student will appear.

Dreams tormented me throughout the first two nights of my visit. I awoke on the third morning hoping my feeling of foreboding had vanished for good. It hadn't. Music had awakened before me and was looking for company. She was ready to talk, but I wasn't completely ready to listen. She was determined, but I was hesitant, reluctant to face the fact that I hadn't upheld my end of the deal. I should have been smarter than to think I could outrun her.

I remember that day clearly. I'd risen with the sun and decided to go for an early morning jog. Running was never a habit of mine but had always proven successful whenever I felt the need to declutter my mind. The first half of my journey was uneventful. The second half was a voyage all its own. Unbeknownst to me, a new path had been chosen. A mixture of yellow brick road and never-ending rabbit hole, my life would be changed forever . . . again.

My morning run quickly became my morning walk. On the way back home, I attempted to take a shortcut through an empty parking lot but became disoriented. Finding myself in an unfamiliar location, I decided to explore. I was tired and had no plans for the rest of the day, so I took my time and enjoyed my surroundings until I could find my bearings.

As I approached a busy intersection, a beeping sound caught my attention. It came from a crossing signal up ahead. The sound was pleasing. I walked toward it shaking my head. I could feel Music tugging at me, but for some reason, I wasn't ready to give in. I stood motionless, contemplating what to do until I realized I'd missed my opportunity to cross the street.

Just as the light changed, I saw what looked like a bicycle leaning against a garbage bin. It was in the opposite direction from where I was headed, but I decided to check it out anyway. If the bicycle was salvageable, I'd ask my dad to fix it. I was sure he could find a neighborhood kid to give it to.

As I neared, I was delighted to find that it was not a bicycle but a unicycle instead. *Imagine this,* I thought. The rim was bent, but I took it anyway. If my dad could fix it, I'd keep it for myself.

I thought back to my younger days when I used to ride one all the time. Other than walking, a unicycle was my main mode of transportation. I rode to school, to friends' houses, and even to the grocery store. A young kid zooming around town perched atop a one-wheeled contraption generated a lot of attention.

On occasion, some friends and I would dress up in improvised costumes, grab our unicycles and a basketball, and crash the local holiday parades. We'd perform stunts and Harlem Globetrotters–style tricks while riding. We were always a crowd favorite. No, we were never invited to the parades, but we never received any complaints about our impromptu appearances.

I felt motivated. I grabbed the battered unicycle and fantasized about riding again. Out of practice since my move to Nashville, I was excited to find out how easy it would be to pick back up. *It's just like riding a bicycle.* I wondered if the familiar saying would still hold true? I would've found out right then, but because the rim was bent, I carried the unicycle instead.

It was a beautiful day and relatively warm for that early in the morning. The sun was low and not a cloud could be seen. I was happily surprised by a gentle puff of air on my left cheek. As quickly as it appeared, it was gone. I looked around. The leaves on the nearby trees hung motionless. *Strange.* The wind didn't appear to be blowing at all. Five steps later it happened again. I stopped. Something was different about this breeze. It didn't just blow on my face; it caressed me. I turned my head in its direction and offered a smile. I had convinced myself it was just my imagination, but then it happened again, this time on the other cheek. It was as if a cool moist finger had gently stroked the right side of my face.

I turned in a complete circle, searching for the source. I thought someone may have been playing with me, possibly with a toy air gun. I remembered them from my childhood. These toys made a definite popping sound when the trigger was pulled. If the shooter's aim was good, you would feel a puff of air a full second or two later. On that day, there was no one in sight and no noise preceded the delicate blow.

Curious and amused, I decided to continue on my way. But before I could take another step, a stronger gust hit me straight on. I was stunned. I took a step back. The unicycle slipped out of my hands, falling to the ground. The sensation was pleasant but weird. Shifting my weight to my rear foot, I folded my arms and pondered what was happening. The breeze was taunting me.

"Okay, I'm listening. What do you want?" I asked out loud, not expecting a response.

I felt silly speaking to the air. I threw my hands up and chuckled to myself. To my surprise, the breeze responded. Starting at my legs, it began spiraling around, working its way up my body, playfully poking and prodding like a childhood friend. Then, as if beckoning me to follow, the wind drifted off ahead. As I stood, watching leaves and debris dance across the pavement, a curious thought entered my mind:

> *The Wind, like Music, is invisible.*
> *Although we can feel them both,*
> *we can only see their presence*
> *by the motions of the things they touch.*
> *Notes to Music are like confetti to the Wind.*

I followed the wind willingly, not knowing where we were headed. We approached a newly built apartment complex adjacent to the parking lot. I stood in front of the building, watching as the wind swirled higher and higher, leaves and debris dancing synchronized pirouettes in front of me. Then, a sweet melody reminiscent of a wind chime blew through the air. The delicate sounds captivated me. It seemed to come from all directions at once, as if Mother Nature played the melody herself.

While glancing around, searching for the source of the sound, a quick flash from the third floor of an apartment building caught my eye. I stood for a moment, waiting to see if it would happen again. It didn't. I probably should have continued toward my parents' home, but for some reason, I ascended the stairs in search of the flash—unicycle in hand.

At the top of the stairs, I found myself staring down a long vacant balcony. The emptiness was the only unusual thing about it. A row of doors lined the wall on the right, and except for the numbers, they appeared identical. I slowly made my way down the corridor in search of anything that would've grabbed my attention from the ground. Nothing stood out. Not knowing what I was looking for, or why, I abandoned my search.

As I turned to retrace my steps, the sun caught my eye as it glimmered off one of the doorknobs. I moved forward to get a closer look. Something about the knob looked inviting, so, like a curious child, I turned it. To my disconcerted surprise, the door swung fully open.

Why did I turn the knob? I didn't have an answer. All I knew was that I shouldn't have done it. A surge of uncertainty filled my body, but for some reason, I stood in the open doorway as if I was right where I belonged.

The sun, still low in the sky, projected my elongated shadow into the room and across the floor. I stood motionless, allowing my eyes to adjust, and as they did, I saw a young man reclining on a couch with a bass guitar in his lap. *Fascinating!*

I couldn't tell from my position, but the kid appeared to be in his midteens. It also appeared that he lived alone, which would make him a bit older. He wore dark pants and a T-shirt and had stringy brown hair down to his shoulders. A small lamp cast a circular glow on the empty table to his right and a piece of sheet music lay on the cushion to his left. The bass guitar rested facedown on his legs. Everything in his sparsely furnished apartment seemed to be perfectly placed, suggesting a high level of organizational skills. I was envious.

Caution whispered from my right shoulder; curiosity screamed from my left. Siding with my left, I moved in for a closer look. The kid opened his eyes. I froze and held my ground. His face was full of wonder, mine uncertain. He rubbed his eyes as if trying to figure out whether I was a dream or a reality. He lay there looking up at me for a full minute before either of us said a word. I stood above him, wearing a Cheshire cat grin on my face.

By chance or design (I'm still not sure), I was wearing a bizarre outfit consisting of blue running tights, a yellow raincoat, white tennis shoes, and a brown gardening hat. The sun, backlighting me, caused me to appear as a glowing silhouette. To add to the effect, I pulled the wide brim over my eyes and lowered my head.

Maybe it was the broken unicycle that kept him from calling the police. I'm sure it added to his confusion (and mine). He had every right to be suspicious. I'd entered his home illegally, uninvited, unprepared, and overdressed. He didn't know who I was or why I was there, and frankly, neither did I. We both remained motionless. As I was about to give in and break the silence, he spoke.

"Who are you?"

He wanted to know who I was, and I didn't have an answer. Years earlier I'd found myself in the exact same situation, except it was I who was lying on the couch looking up at a strange intruder who had mysteriously appeared in my house. Like the young man now in front of me, I should've been scared but was not. I also recall asking my trespasser the same question. He'd told me that he was my teacher. I didn't know anything about this young kid, but I was sure back then that I hadn't asked for a teacher.

The tables were turned and I wasn't sure how to answer the youngster. I could tell him anything I wanted. Would he believe me? Should he believe me? I could tell him the truth, if only I knew what that was.

Again, the kid spoke. "I asked a simple question. Who are you?"

There was nothing simple about it. Not knowing how to reply, I went with my gut. Well, actually, it wasn't my gut. I copied my teacher by replying as he had to me.

"I am your . . ." I paused, uncertain whether I should continue. Against my better judgment, I continued, "I am **the teacher**."

Wow! It felt good to say that. I caught myself about to copy my teacher verbatim, so I had changed one word in an attempt to be original.

"Oh really? The teacher?" he asked. "*The* teacher!" he repeated, emphasizing the first word. He reclined and crossed his legs. "Hmmm. What are you gonna teach me?"

My answer was immediate. "Nothing! I can teach you . . . nothing." I paused for effect.

The words felt good, but I wished I hadn't said them. Again, I answered as my teacher had answered me. I lowered my head in an attempt to hide my embarrassment. What was I getting myself into? And how was I going to get myself out?

"That doesn't make any sense! What do you mean, 'you can teach me nothing'?" His voice was stern.

Attempting to match his brashness, I retorted, "Exactly! Nothing! I can teach you nothing because there is nothing to be taught. But . . . I can *show* you things." Emboldened by growing confidence, my sly grin returned.

"Okay then. Show me *Music*!" He answered without hesitation, saying the word in a surprising way.

"Yes! I can do that, but not as well as Music herself can."

"What do you mean, 'herself'?" he asked.

"You will see . . . or not," I answered with a furtive flare.

He wrinkled his forehead before questioning, "How'd you get in here? How did you even find me?"

"I followed the wind and you let me in."

"The wind? I let you in? Yeah, right. Did I give you a key?"

"I don't need a key."

For some reason, he asked similar questions to the ones I'd asked Michael years before, and for some reason, I responded with the same answers. It was as if we were following a script. The kid tilted his head in thought for a moment before looking up at me and continuing.

"What instrument do you play?"

"I play Music, not instruments."

"What's that supposed to mean?" he asked.

It was as if I was improvising, even though I knew that I wasn't. Yes. I was plagiarizing, but I understood what I was saying. I was totally sure of myself. So, I kept going.

"You asked if I had a key. Music *is* the key. Your search for Music created the spark that brought us together. My use of an instrument, any instrument, allows you to hear how musical I am, but I express my musicality *through* the instrument, any one I choose. Again, I play Music! And once you stop playing your bass, you might start playing Music, too."

"Hmmm," he replied from his laid-back position on the couch.

As much as I'd like to be brilliant, I was practically stealing all my answers from Michael. I admit, I wasn't as eloquent as my teacher, but I was doing pretty well. Fortunately for me, the kid was asking the same questions I'd asked. The best part of all is that I didn't have to think before I spoke. The words seemed to be already in place, as if my lines were being fed to me.

"You say that you can teach me *nothing*," he remarked. "That doesn't make any sense. Your outfit is cool, I'll give you that much, but I can tell you're not really a teacher. So, who are you? What's your name?"

Looking down at my clothes, I thought before I answered. *What should I tell him?* I wondered if Michael had given his real name when I'd asked for it. For lack of a better answer, I raised my brim and told the truth.

"Victor. Call me Victor."

Again, he didn't hesitate. "All right, Victor, you say that you are musical without an instrument? Well, let's hear it. Play!"

He pointed at me and clutched his bass to his chest, making it clear I was not allowed to use it. I shuddered.

This kid moved faster than I had when I was in his place. He was also bolder, much bolder. He went straight for the jugular, and my defense was lacking. I'd just spoken a bunch of mumbo jumbo about how musical I was, and now I was being challenged. He doubted me. I doubted myself. I was tired and sweaty, and all I had was a broken unicycle. I took a seat in the chair across from him and smiled a nervous smile. He held his position.

I didn't know what else to do, so I placed the unicycle in my lap and spun the wheel. It made a quarter turn before the bent rim got stuck. Embarrassed, I removed my hat, looked up, and raised one eyebrow trying not to show my looming lack of comfort.

How had I gotten myself into this situation? I considered waltzing back out the front door. That would, at least, minimize the damage. I had no idea what to say or do, so I waited. We waited.

I thought about Joe, a wonderful musician I'd seen on numerous occasions. He is comfortable playing multiple instruments including violin, mandolin, percussion, and anything else he can get his hands on.

On one occasion, I witnessed Joe play an amazing solo using only his shoelace. With his shoe still on his foot, he placed a microphone near the floor, stretched out his lace, and began plucking it like a guitar string. Tightening and loosening the lace caused the pitch to change. I watched him effortlessly execute this incredible performance in front of a few thousand people. It was unbelievable! The audience went crazy and gave him a well-deserved standing ovation. Joe proved that anything can be made into a musical instrument. Was he improvising? Was he prepared? Or both? Joe obviously had remarkable skills. Me? I wasn't so sure.

I closed my eyes and took a slow, deliberate breath, making sure to retain the excited feeling I'd experienced while reminiscing about Joe. Almost immediately, a row of lines formed in my mind. I didn't understand the image until the lines fanned out into a circle. Glancing down at the crooked contraption in my lap, I knew exactly what to do.

I raised both arms high in the air, took three more deep breaths (for effect), lowered my right hand (in slow motion), and plucked one of the spokes. The kid raised his head. To his surprise (and mine), the spoke produced a pitch. I immediately plucked another, then another, each one producing a different tone. I kept plucking until a rhythm and a melody emerged. Increasing my energy, I bobbed my head and rocked in my seat, adding to the display. The groove, growing stronger and stronger inside my body, provided the needed confidence to continue. My sly smile telegraphed my braggadocio. For the first time ever, I felt that, like Joe, I could make Music with anything I touched.

I rotated the wheel back and forth like a hip-hop turntable artist and produced a harp-like glissando by gliding my fingernails across the spokes. It wasn't a conventional instrument, but I made that unicycle sing. The vibrations coursing through my body felt wonderful. I reveled in the sound and played until I was satisfied. I concluded with a big inhale, held it for a dramatic pause, then slowly placed the instrument on the floor with one hand, raising the other in the air.

I looked the kid in the eyes and let out a slow, deliberate exhale. For the first time he sat up. For the first time I sat back. He stared at me with a look of astonishment. Control was in my court, so I held my position, seizing the moment while I had it.

After a minute, I leaned in close, staring firmly into his eyes. An unexplainable energy emanated from my body. His face softened as he held my gaze, giving way to what I was about to say.

"Listen to me, Jonathan! Now you know. Music is everywhere. You do not have to create it; you just have to feel her and become one with her. Then, anything you touch can and will become your instrument."

Although I'd heard Michael use similar words, the entire meaning had previously eluded me. He had told me over and over that he could teach me nothing, but not until I was sitting in front of that kid did I completely understand. Michael couldn't teach me. No one could teach me. Michael could only *show* me the way. I had to walk the path and teach myself. And the best way to completely teach myself was to teach someone else, or more accurately, *show* someone else. *I* had to become the teacher in order to complete the cycle. Finally, I felt ready—ready to continue the Music lesson.

"When the teacher is ready, the student shall appear."

Filled with certainty, I stood up, took another deep breath, and walked toward the door. The kid, more composed than I was at that age, spoke with a look of bewilderment.

"Hey! How did you know my name?"

Artism

✦

Sometimes, confusion is the doorway to clarity.

Confusion spoke louder than confidence. As soon as I left Jonathan's home, my body was overcome with emotions. Thoughts raced through my mind in all directions. *What did I just get myself into? This isn't fair to him. I can't ever go back to his house. I am not a teacher!*

The sun beamed down, following me like an unwanted spotlight. I felt it was mocking me, pointing out to everyone that I was a fraud. Although the sky was clear, the clouds in my brain cast shadows over any remaining confidence, making my path difficult to travel. And my colorful attire was not helping my self-esteem at all.

But, I had surprised myself. How *did* I know Jonathan's name? Had he mentioned it? Had I noticed it written somewhere in his apartment? It's possible. Or maybe . . . maybe, I just knew. Michael used to do these sorts of things all the time. He would just *know*. I'd learned to be okay with it when he performed those feats. Now, because it happened with me, I felt less interested in the mysteries—I wanted answers.

✦

"Sometimes, confusion is the doorway to clarity."

Jonathan wanted answers also. He wanted to know who I was. I'd told him I was his teacher, and we both knew that wasn't true. Michael always appeared to be extremely confident when he was teaching. I, on the other hand, had to fake it. I wondered if Michael had faced the same internal battles when he first appeared in my house. I knew how I felt about my teacher, but how was Jonathan feeling about me? Regardless, I'd gotten myself into the situation and was determined to stay the course and see where it led.

My childhood house was in view before I realized I'd left the unicycle lying on Jonathan's living room floor—blatant evidence of my unsolicited intrusion. My head hung low in disgust. I'd hoped to walk into my parents' home unseen, but my dad, as if on cue, opened the front door just as I arrived.

"Why you so dressed up?" he asked with a chuckle.

I didn't answer. I hurried past him down the hall and straight into the bedroom, closing the door behind me. It wasn't the nicest response, but I had other things on my mind. I collapsed onto the bed. It was the same one I'd slept in as a child. There was a calming ambiance in that room that didn't exist in my house in Nashville.

Along with that comfort was the familiar childhood guilt

I felt whenever I knew I'd done something wrong. I'd displayed an attitude toward my dad that was less than pleasant. I was wrong and knew that I'd be unable to relax until I apologized.

I found my parents sitting at the kitchen table waiting for me. They wore gentle smiles but neither said a word. An empty chair was pulled away from the table and a tall glass of orange juice had already been poured. My parents always knew. I took my seat and took a drink.

It was then that I realized my cold had vanished. I'd had a stuffy nose when I first arrived at their house, but I'd woken the next morning without a sniffle. I hadn't realized it, but the Pinetop Tea had worked. Maybe I should have continued drinking that instead of orange juice. I wondered what other remedies my parents knew. Growing up with very little money, they rarely visited a doctor. They needed to have knowledge of plants, trees, and other things they could use to cure common ailments. I wanted that knowledge. I hoped it wasn't too late for me to learn.

My mind was wandering. Actually, my mind was avoiding. I knew it, and I'm sure my parents did also. I wanted to talk, but starting was always the most difficult part. I looked at my parents. They calmly looked back.

Silence is a powerful tool and patience is a virtue. My parents displayed both. I quickly emptied my glass and started to get up to refill it. With a gentle touch, my mom kept me in my seat. Without saying a word, her message was clear. I was stalling and she knew it.

"I was rude to you, Dad. I'm really sorry."

He nodded. I wanted to say more but didn't. I returned to silence.

"What else is on your mind?" Mom asked.

I summoned up the courage.

"I met a bass player this morning. He's young. I might try to teach him. I'm not sure."

"Not sure about what?" she asked.

I wasn't sure how to answer. I was unsure about a lot of things, my teaching ability being one. Mom would not accept that as a valid excuse. I *was* sure about that. I paused for too long, so she continued.

"You don't think you're good enough. Is that it?"

"I just don't want to let him down."

"Is it really about him?"

Mom was smart. My main concern was about letting *myself* down and she knew it. I knew that I could find something to teach Jonathan. That wasn't the real issue. I was scared, and although I had no immediate responsibilities back in Nashville, I hadn't decided how long I would stay in Virginia. I didn't want to start something I couldn't finish.

"Listen," Mom continued. "I suggest you go back to his house tomorrow. Try it out. See what happens. See what it feels like."

"I did try it and it actually went well. It felt great . . . until I left his apartment. The whole time I was walking home, I was trying to convince myself that I should never go back. Even though I kind of want to, I'm not sure I can do this. I don't think I should even try."

Dad had kept quiet until then.

"Now you talking foolishness. You just scared, that's all, and that ain't never a good reason to quit anything."

"All of life is governed by your feelings and your thoughts," Mom added, raising her index finger to her temple.

"That's right," Dad continued. "A happy person thinks

happy thoughts. A rich person thinks rich thoughts. The opposite is also true. Poor thoughts, sad thoughts, sick thoughts—they all the same. Change your thoughts, change your life. It's as simple as that!" He pounded his fist on the table and continued. "Feelings? They can be difficult to change, but thoughts can change as quick as you can change your mind. Your thoughts shout while your feelings whisper. Pay attention to both. That's what you need to do." He nodded his head and leaned back in his chair.

Mom sat quietly, clearly enjoying hearing Dad express himself. Sensing a break in his speech, she sat forward. Her gentle voice was enchanting.

"Life is always on your side, Baby Boy. When your goal is to truthfully help someone, you will be given the opportunity to do so. Their truth will be opened up to you and you will know exactly what to do with it. It saddens me that some people, especially teachers, will take advantage and undermine a person's truth just to replace it with their own. But you're not that kind of teacher. I know you're not." She smiled. I sat up straight. "Your intention is to expand, not to diminish. Because of that, you will see into that young boy's truth. That's how it works: the more people you intend to help, the more truth you will see." She sat back in her chair and grabbed Dad's hand.

Hearing them talk was soothing. Where had their wisdom come from and what took me so long to start listening? They gazed at me with gentle smiles on their faces, allowing their words to take root. Like spiritual gardeners, they'd been sowing seeds in the soil of my soul longer than I was aware. And like spiritual vitamins, their mindful medicine helped maintain the purity of my spirit whether I realized it or not. Right then, I could feel their seeds sprouting throughout my body, but it was up to me, and only me, to make sure there was a healthy harvest. With my energy recharged, I listened intently as Dad continued.

"Understand this, son. Fear just means that you about to grow. So, recognize your fear and keep charging." He leaned forward, his face serious. "In the military, we like fear. Like pain, it let us know we's still alive." He raised his hands in front of his face and looked at them front to back.

It felt good to hear my dad be so vocal. He was usually the quiet one, but whenever he spoke, everyone listened. His voice was powerful and commanded attention. Placing his hands back on the table, he looked at me and completed his thought.

"Fear is always ahead of us, reminding us that we have time—time to prepare. You see, we don't fear what's happening; we only fear what *might* happen. I know you afraid of disappointing that boy, but that boy ain't here right now, is he? So, take this time to prepare. Come up with a lesson for him. You already started. Just continue with it, but don't leave nuthin' undone. Like I always say, 'if you leave something on the floor, pick it up.'"

Wait a minute! What did he say? I'd never heard him say that before. I had left a broken unicycle on Jonathan's floor, but Dad couldn't have known about that. I gave him a curious look.

Mom continued, "Life won't ever steer you wrong, but you have to do your part. Treat Life right, and Life will treat you right. You know that."

That was one I'd heard her say many times.

"So," she continued, "go to your room and get yourself together. Tomorrow, you go back to that young boy's house and teach him something. You'll know what to do. I guarantee! But don't forget, there's always a lesson in it for you, too."

I hugged them both and returned to my room, but not without another full glass of juice, courtesy of Mom.

The next morning, I had begun my journey to Jonathan's house when trepidation began to attack me. I hadn't formulated a lesson plan, choosing instead to improvise the way I had the previous day. But now that idea was making me nervous. Because I've never made plans or schedules for my own practice, I hoped I would be okay. Jonathan and I could just talk and get to know each other if nothing else came to mind.

The one thing I *did* put great thought into was my choice of clothing. I made sure not to make that mistake again. Michael, my teacher, was an odd one and dressed bizarrely every time I saw him. I eventually became comfortable with it. Even the one time I saw him in ordinary clothes, it seemed out of place. "Ordinary teachers produce ordinary students," he once told me. I didn't consider myself a teacher yet, so I dressed as ordinary as I could.

The sun was bright and the air was pleasant during my walk. The sound of birds chirping in the trees created an audible backdrop that calmed my nerves. A thought appeared. *The birds don't sing for money. They sing because the sun comes up.* It was an eye-opening thought, one I could learn from.

As I approached his apartment building, I met Jonathan coming down the stairs. He waved and ran toward me. His energy was vibrant. I liked him. I realized that I hadn't paid much attention to him the day before. I was so nervous and concerned with my own situation that I hadn't really found out who he was.

"How is my teacher doing today?" he asked.

What? I'd already made up my mind that I liked him, but that question caught me off guard. I felt my body tense. I'm sure my facial expression didn't hide my angst. My response blurted out.

"Teacher? I am not your teach— Oh, um, sorry. I'm okay, I guess. It's a beautiful day, don't you think?"

He reacted as if he didn't notice or care about my apprehension, so I tried to forget about it, too. Jonathan was on his way to a record store. I decided to tag along. *Perfect!* We could get to know each other during our walk, then go back to his apartment and listen to our purchases. Maybe I wouldn't have to teach anything. A plan was emerging and I liked it.

At the store, Jonathan's actions were exceedingly precise. He spoke pointedly when asking questions. He seemed to know exactly what he was looking for and didn't spend time browsing at all.

Jonathan told me that he had been diagnosed with autism. I didn't really know what that meant. He expressed himself clearly and easily and seemed to be comfortable around people. He joked with me and the salesman, displaying a sense of wit that was well beyond the norm, and his knowledge of Music was impressive. If this was what autism was, I was cool with it. In my eyes, Jonathan was blessed with **artism**.

Doctors had warned Jonathan that he would never be able to live alone, work with his hands, or drive a car. Jonathan had his own ideas about that. Dismantling the doctors' words, Jonathan lived in his own apartment, had been playing bass guitar and singing in bands for years, and drove a car he bought with his gigging money. He told me that he liked it when doctors told him what he couldn't do. That, he said, let him know what to work on next.

I noticed right away that Jonathan never avoided eye contact. He addressed everyone directly and seemed to deliberately never avert his gaze when speaking with someone. In my experience, that was atypical for a young person and, apparently, unusual for someone diagnosed with autism.

When I finally got up the nerve to ask Jonathan about it, he told me that I was correct. He'd grown up with the inability to make direct eye contact with anyone. Realizing this trait, he decided to overcome it. While gigging in bars, he would converse with drunken people. In this way, he could practice making eye contact. "I knew they wouldn't care," he told me. I was already figuring out he was a smart kid, but that idea was brilliant! The more time I spent with him, the more I grew to love him.

During our time at the record store, Jonathan remarked about the lack of Music. I hadn't previously noticed, but he was right. Music usually plays constantly in a record store, but on this day, all was silent. When Jonathan asked if he could preview a record before purchasing it, the owner told him that his record player was broken and that a repair-person was on the way.

Almost immediately, a man walked through the front door wearing a suit and carrying a toolbox. He wasn't dressed like a repairman, but the owner greeted him and brought him over to the broken record player. The man immediately got to work, which made us hopeful, but a few minutes later the repairman left. The owner told us that the record player could not be fixed.

"But he didn't even try," Jonathan complained.

"That's what he told me," the store owner replied.

It was obvious that the repairman had made a feeble attempt to fix the machine. Maybe getting paid without doing any work was his mode of operation. Jonathan wasn't satisfied and ran over to him, blocking his exit from the store.

"Hey! What's going on? You didn't do your job. I was watching."

Jonathan stared straight into the man's eyes as he spoke. Without answering, the repairman placed a pair of headphones over his ears and walked around Jonathan and out the front door. Jonathan turned to me and shrugged his shoulders.

It was very strange. There was no apparent reason for the man to be that rude. The store owner apologized to Jonathan and gave the record to him for free.

The sun was almost directly overhead. We left the store and walked toward Jonathan's apartment in silence. To break the mood, I made a comment about the birds.

"When the sun is overhead, animals are less active. That's why the birds are so quiet."

Jonathan replied, "Correct. They conserve energy. Europeans call it a siesta. I don't know what the birds call it. I wonder if they got the idea from the birds?"

I chuckled. I'd never thought of that.

"I think that record player was also taking a siesta," I added.

"I don't think so." Jonathan didn't laugh. His reply was literal, as if he'd missed my joke.

Back at Jonathan's apartment, we listened to his new record and took turns reading the liner notes. Sitting with him brought back good memories. When I was younger, listening to a new record was a social event, and, because money was scarce, it was also a rare event. Whenever a new record showed up in my household, we would gather as a family to listen to the whole thing. In some cases, the local musicians would gather to study the recording together. That was how we learned.

Things had changed since I moved to Nashville. CDs had already taken the place of vinyl and mp3s were on the horizon. Listening to music had gradually become an individual experience. It was difficult to remember the last time I'd sat with a friend and listened to a whole album.

I was surprised at Jonathan's choice—an album called *Live* by Donny Hathaway. Hathaway is a Grammy Award–winning singer who wrote many R&B hits in the seventies including "Where Is the Love" and "The Closer I Get to You," both made famous by the legendary Roberta Flack. He also wrote and performed the ever-popular Christmas song "This Christmas." He has always been one of my parents' favorites. As long as I can remember, *Live* has been a part of their record collection.

I remember the tragic day in 1979 when Donny Hathaway committed suicide by plunging to his death from his room on the fifteenth floor of a hotel. He had spent the day recording with Roberta Flack and was reported to have been in good spirits. At only thirty-three years of age, his death came as a surprise to everyone. I was one of the devastated fans. I was only fourteen.

If I remember correctly, Hathaway didn't do drugs and

hadn't had much to drink on the day of his death. I wonder what could have driven him to do such a thing. I know that the life of a musician can be challenging. It often seems like a gamble. Our personal laundry is laid out for all to see. We always have to be at the top of our game, and if we falter, even a little, that becomes the public's focus. What it must be like to be a *famous* musician—I could only imagine. If one is lucky enough to attain that status, the pressures drastically increase. Even at my low level, I was facing struggles. I hoped I would never succumb to them the way Mr. Hathaway and many others evidently had.

We listened to most of the record in silence. Jonathan kept his eyes closed, rocking back and forth to each groove, only pausing in between songs. I alerted Jonathan as the record approached the end of side two.

"Here it comes. This is my favorite part."

"What is it?"

"Just listen," I whispered.

The last track on the album is called "Voices Inside (Everything Is Everything)." This soulful song is over thirteen minutes long and includes a classic well-known bass solo. Jonathan's eyes widened as the solo began. He leaned forward with anticipation. I knew that he was reaching for his bass.

"Leave it for now. Just listen," I instructed.

Jonathan sat back, grabbed the album jacket, and perused the album credits. Although I already knew who the bassist was, I allowed him to make the discovery on his own.

"Willie Weeks."

"That's right," I concurred. "He's a legend."

"Wow! He's amazing—very articulate!" Jonathan exclaimed, his eyes wide.

"I agree. Listen to how he takes his time building the solo."

"Simplicity at its best," Jonathan added.

We listened over and over before I motioned to Jonathan to grab his bass. I spent the next hour helping him learn the solo. Basically, I sat back and watched. Listening to it repeatedly solidified it in his mind. The groove, feel, and structure were already set. He just had to locate the notes on the instrument.

In my opinion, listening first is the best way to learn any piece of music. Learning how to play it on an instrument before you've internalized it is more difficult and a much slower process. Separating the two tasks has helped me numerous times in the past. I felt proud to share this approach with my new student.

I could vividly remember also learning Willie Weeks's solo by listening to the record over and over. Learning in this fashion caused me to consciously and unconsciously internalize more. Every time I picked the needle up and placed it back on the vinyl record, I had to listen closely to find the right spot. It required me to pay attention to minute details, not only to the bass part, but also to all the other instruments, as well as the structure of the song. Learning in this way developed my musical ear quickly and thoroughly. I was appreciative to have grown up in a time when this was one of the main methods of learning. I was also happy to have Jonathan relive it with me. He was a joy to spend time with. He felt like the little brother I never had.

"You see, Jonathan, when I was younger, using a record or a cassette tape was the only way I could learn a song like this. Unless someone had already gone through this process and could help me, I had to do the work myself. Because you've learned the solo the old-fashioned way, you've learned more than you realize. Your goal was to learn only the solo, but you've actually learned the whole song, including the lyrics."

His smile was big.

To make sure I didn't overwhelm him, we called it quits and made plans to continue the next day. I stood up and walked toward the door, mentioning how impressed I was with him.

"I've never had a teacher like you," he told me.

I smiled. My confidence lifted. For the first time, I felt really good about myself. Something had changed inside me.

"I've never had a student like you," I replied in earnest.

I doubt he knew how literal my comment was. Jonathan was my first student and I was excited to see where our relationship would take us.

After I closed the door behind me, I looked through the window and could see Jonathan continuing to play. A smile covered his face and he bounced happily. I left him just as I'd originally found him—with a bass guitar in his lap.

Me? I had a broken unicycle.

A Brother from Another Motherland

✦

All dreams are important!

A broken unicycle was not a comfortable travel companion. It was a dead weight, bringing my emotions down as I descended each step. As soon as I closed Jonathan's door, I had the feeling that I'd forgotten something. The further I ventured from his apartment, the more I realized what it was. The day before, I'd left my unicycle. On this day, I'd left my confidence behind. I was still uncertain of my role, but there was something about being with Jonathan that brought a certain amount of purpose to my existence. I felt good while I was with him, but as soon as the door closed behind me, I began to question myself once again.

Although doubt had returned, I decided to stay in Virginia so I could spend more time with my new student. I didn't have a curriculum or a plan, but I felt the need to follow through with my teaching experiment. As fond as I was of Jonathan, the desire to stay was more for me than it was for him.

We spent the next few days playing together and sharing ideas. I really wanted to become a competent teacher. Jonathan made it easy for me. He progressed quickly and asked great questions, oftentimes seeming to know more than he let on. Sometimes, I felt as if he was deliberately holding back.

My role became much easier when I remembered to stop trying to teach. Michael had repeatedly reminded me that he could teach me nothing and that he could only *show* me things. That was easier to understand when *I* was the student. Now that my position had changed, I needed to realign my perspective. If I could consistently remember to relax and *show* Jonathan where to look, he would *teach* himself what he needed to know.

During one of my sessions with Jonathan, I shared Michael's concept that music could be divided into ten different parts, and that by using all the parts equally any musician could instantly sound like a seasoned professional. Many musicians run into difficulty because they focus too much on playing notes. Notes are important, but because there are only twelve, concentrating on them too much can be limiting, like trying to speak a language using only twelve words. If notes are only one of the ten elements, I asked Jonathan if he could come up with nine others that were equally important.

As luck would have it, Jonathan came up with the exact same elements I had chosen years earlier: articulation, technique, feel, dynamics, rhythm, tone, phrasing, space, and listening. It didn't take him as long as it had taken me.

Not long after my time with Michael, I realized that the elements were related and intertwined. For example: The dynamic of a song can be changed by altering any of the other elements. Adding or reducing space changes the dynamic as well as the phrasing. Altering the rhythm can change the complete style or feel. Choosing different notes can change the emotional feel. And most importantly, to know how to properly use any of these elements, we must first listen.

Jonathan described each level as having sublevels. It was a remarkable revelation, one I wished I'd come up with on my own. Together, we explored the idea and were surprised at what we discovered. For example:

Notes can be subdivided into pitches, scales, harmony, chords, and key signatures, as well as taking notes (the physical act of writing things down). This was an eye-opener.

When referring to music, articulation usually refers to the length or attack of a note, but the clarity of Willie Weeks's solo also caused Jonathan to use the term "articulate." Like an articulate speaker's language, his solo was clearly executed and easily understood.

Techniques can refer to tools, fingerings, or methods. One can even have techniques for learning techniques. Playing the same piece of music while changing techniques can change everything. That was also a revelation for me.

In the past, I would have described rhythm as a pattern of sounds, tones, or beats. But that day, I realized that it could also pertain to sports. I've heard many athletes speak about finding or losing their rhythm. The state of being in the zone means that one's rhythm and technique are in a highly synchronized working order.

Phrasing is a way of grouping things. It can be a group of words to form a sentence or a verse, and it can also be a group of notes and rhythms to produce a melodic line or solo. A verse is but a longer phrase made up of shorter phrases. A group of verses creates a poem or a song. A group of songs can be placed on a record to create an even longer phrase. Actually, someone can group together events and/or strategies to phrase their whole career or even their whole life. Anything that can be grouped together can be purposefully phrased.

Jonathan and I both described Willie Weeks's bass solo as dynamic. Usually, this word is used to describe the increase and decrease in the audible volume of a sound. In this case, Weeks's solo didn't change in volume but did change in intensity, causing us to realize that dynamics could relate to energy as well as power. This was a valuable insight.

We explored each element and expanded them further. I was having fun. Even though I was supposed to be the teacher, I was learning just as much as my student (and maybe more).

A flamboyant, pretty little lady named Isis once gave me an in-depth lesson on space, drawing my attention to the importance of silence and rest as it pertained to Music and Life. "Nothing Is Everything" was her motto. "What you don't play is always more important than what you do play," she once told me. Even though I understood her then, the more time I spent with Jonathan, the more *nothing* was starting to make even more sense. I could see him improving on his own right in front of my eyes, and I felt like I was teaching him nothing.

A musical groove, which is the result of accurately executing all the elements simultaneously, is synonymous to the word "pocket." In some circles, musicians who groove well are said to have "deep" or "heavy" pockets. A pocket on a pair of pants would be useless if it couldn't hold anything. It has to be oriented in such a way that it creates a cavity capable of carrying things. Metaphorically, a musical groove needs to be constructed in the same way, providing a vessel that all the musicians can fit comfortably inside. I explained the concept to Jonathan.

"We use the elements together to create a musical fabric, and that fabric must be strong enough to hold the whole band. All the elements, especially dynamics, need to pulsate like boiling water so that the music will groove instead of sounding flat. When it works, we call it a pocket."

"Right!" Jonathan responded. "Or you can explain it like this: You can't hold no groove if you ain't got no pocket!" We both laughed. It was an accurate description of something that had previously been difficult for me to describe.

Jonathan progressed rapidly, causing me repeatedly to question who was teaching whom. He had shown me as many things as I'd shown him. I played it cool and didn't mention this, since I was supposed to be his teacher. I didn't mind; I was having fun. I hoped he was, too.

The only physical item I had acquired from Michael was a fourteen-measure piece of music he'd handwritten just for me. He told me that the ten elements could be found within those measures and that once I was able to perform the whole piece, I would be well on my way to understanding all the elements completely.

Having (secretly) run out of things to offer Jonathan, we agreed to end and resume the following day. I made a mental note to bring a copy of Michael's measures. I felt they would be challenging enough to keep Jonathan occupied while providing time for me to come up with something else to share. Jonathan reclined on his couch and bade me farewell.

I stood before Jonathan's door and hesitated. An unfamiliar sensation formed in my chest. It was as if there was something I wanted to say, but I didn't know what it was. Although my brain felt empty, the urge to speak was strong. Not knowing what else to do, I turned to face Jonathan and started speaking. Unfamiliar words flowed fluently from me. So, I listened.

"Jonathan, we are more than musicians. Music breathes through our bodies and expresses herself through our souls. The word *musician* indicates that we are *Music shamans*. Our role is to summon her spirit and bring her to life. You see, Music exists without us, but on Earth, she cannot take form without us. We create Music's vibrations, but we do not create Music, no more than a mother creates the spirit that exists inside her baby. But like the baby who cannot exist without its mother, Music cannot physically exist without us. That gives us power and responsibility. Music Shamans! That is who we are."

"Some people may be scared of this power."

Jonathan's response surprised me. I didn't know what he was talking about, but I didn't know what *I* was talking about either. "Music Shamans"? Where had that come from? I decided to hurry up and leave before my mouth decided to say something else.

As I opened the door to leave his apartment, I felt a sudden chill. Everything was quiet. No birds were chirping. I walked down the balcony, noticing a man standing at the bottom of the stairs three floors below. His appearance was unassuming, but for some reason, his presence disturbed me. He stood motionless, looking in my direction as if he wanted something from me. I felt as though I'd seen him before, but I couldn't recall from where.

I nodded. He continued staring but didn't respond. His body, partially hidden by the staircase, added to my suspicion. I considered delaying my departure, but the door had already closed behind me.

Looking closer, I noticed he was wearing headphones. Maybe he couldn't hear me and that's why he didn't respond. I relaxed and began a slow stroll down the stairs. I could feel the temperature drop, which caused my heart rate to increase once again. I glanced over the railing every few steps and tried to calm myself. *A man listening to music is no cause for alarm.*

When I reached the bottom floor, he was gone. That should have put me at ease, but on the contrary, I felt even more on edge. I looked around but didn't see anyone. Making a wide arc, I checked behind the staircase. It was vacant except for a few bicycles. I took a different route home as a precaution.

Later that night, I pulled a photocopy of Michael's measures from my bag in preparation for sharing it with Jonathan. To my surprise, there was a measure missing. The tenth measure, the one relating to space, was gone—completely gone. There was an actual blank space in the middle of the page where the measure was supposed to be—not as if I'd forgotten to write it down, but as if it had been erased.

My mind wouldn't let it go—like a riddle that wouldn't

allow me to rest until it was solved. I could see faint markings where the measure used to be. I pondered whether one of my parents had erased it, but why would they have done that? *Can a photocopy be erased?* I went to sleep with the mystery on my mind, and for the rest of the night, I was tormented by delusions and half-awake dreams that made little sense.

I found myself standing alone in a large, open field. All was still and quiet. As the sun crested over the horizon, a flock of light blue birds began to appear. They came from all directions and circled above me. A single bird came close, hovering in front of my face as if it wanted to communicate. As soon as we locked eyes, it opened its beak.

I woke up confused. It was still dark outside, but the images from the dream were bright. Since I dream in color so infrequently, I knew this one was special. But what did it mean? I couldn't stop thinking about it. Although it was much earlier than I was accustomed to being awake, I got out of bed and dressed.

It is interesting how dreams can slowly fade away once we have awakened. I sat watching the sky illuminate as details from my nighttime visions receded into darkness. During breakfast, a previously forgotten scene popped into my mind.

The whole dream had happened in silence. As the birds circled around, each one continued to face me as if I was the focus of their attention. Their beaks were moving, but I never heard a sound. It wasn't until the one bird hovered in front of me that I remember trying to hear. I didn't realize the significance of that until later.

I began clearing my breakfast dishes in an attempt to also

clear my mind. My mother walked in, surprised to find me up and active so early. Always perceptive, she asked if there was something I wanted to talk about. I started to tell her about the dream but decided against it. I told her, instead, that it wasn't important.

⊕

"All dreams are important!"

Somehow, she always knew. She kissed me on the cheek and walked away, leaving me alone with my thoughts. For a while, I stood motionless in the kitchen, wondering if I'd made the right decision.

I procrastinated until the afternoon to start my walk to Jonathan's apartment. About halfway there, an uneasiness crept into my body. At first, I thought it was just my nervousness about teaching, but the stillness in the air and a faint sensation in my abdomen told me otherwise. I tried not to worry. I glanced in all directions, searching for anything out of place. A flock of birds circling overhead caught my attention. I tilted my head to listen. Their soft chirps were a welcome sound.

I relaxed, trying to push my nerves aside, but the sensation persisted and grew stronger as I neared Jonathan's apartment. I had no idea what I was feeling but knew to pay attention. I was definitely on edge. Not knowing why, I ran to the front of Jonathan's building and bounded up three flights of stairs.

Once I reached the door, everything stopped. Except for the sound of my breath, all was silent. The sounds of birds were nonexistent just as they were when I left Jonathan's apartment the day before. This same silence had also been the soundtrack of my previous night's dream. I didn't like it. I stood transfixed in a vacuum, focused only on the doorknob in front of me. The sensation in my gut grew stronger. Something wasn't right. I hesitated. My legs, weary from the ascent, trembled as I stared at the door.

Slowly, my right hand extended toward the knob—the same doorknob that had propelled me into this adventure. I tried to retract my hand but it had its own intentions. I looked behind me. I appeared to be alone, but my senses told me otherwise.

I gently turned the knob. It was unlocked. Then I realized that I was technically breaking into Jonathan's apartment for the second time. Not wanting to leave any fingerprints, I wrapped my hand in my sleeve and gave a quarter turn more. The door crept open a few inches and stopped. The eerie squeaking of the hinges announced my presence as it echoed through the room. I retracted my hand, paused, and listened. The lack of sound spoke loudly. I leaned forward and edged the door open a few inches more. I took a cautious step forward and gasped at what I saw, or more accurately, what I didn't see.

Jonathan's apartment was completely empty, as if no one had ever lived there. The only remaining items were the closed curtains covering the front window. I pushed the door totally open and took two steps inside. I whispered Jonathan's name, not expecting a response. I stalked forward a few more steps, calling a second time and a third. I stood motionless, trying to figure out what to do.

Guilty thoughts raced through the air in front of me.

Jonathan must have grown tired of me. He realized I was a fake. Yes! That must be it. I left early yesterday. That gave him time to remove all his things. Or maybe something happened to him. It's my fault! He doesn't know how to reach me. I'd made sure of it the same way Michael had with me. I felt it would add to the mystery. *Jonathan left me! Who do I think I am?*

Fear receded, replaced by despair and embarrassment. I was not Michael and I felt ashamed at my dismal attempt. The curtains, animated by the breeze, performed a sardonic dance, taunting my presence. My head dropped toward the floor and I let out an audible sigh. Overwhelmed by the heavy feeling of failure, I fell to my knees and covered my face with both hands.

I felt foolish. But crying on the floor in the middle of an empty apartment felt even more foolish, so I tried to be rational. *This is getting me nowhere,* I thought. *If Jonathan left because of me, it was his choice.*

I found some courage and rose to my feet, but as I turned to leave, I noticed a pair of black headphones resting defiantly in the middle of the open doorway. Fear gripped me once again. My body froze but my mind raced.

Where did they come from? Is someone following me? Maybe they belong to Jonathan? I should return them. No! Don't touch them!

I couldn't decide which thought process to follow. I took a breath and shook my head back and forth, trying to convince myself I was just being silly. Fear was winning.

I summoned up enough nerve to advance slowly toward the door. I knelt down at the threshold and poked my head outside, looking left and right. All appeared clear. From my crouched position, I stepped over the headphones and made my way out of the apartment, leaving the door ajar. I crept down the stairs, checking behind me every three steps.

At the bottom, I cautiously looked under the stairs and hid behind parked cars on the street, checking first beneath them. While on my knees, I inched my way to the front bumper of one of the cars and looked around it. Still, there was no one in sight. I didn't have Jonathan's number or a way to call him. I knelt beside the vehicle, trying to think of what to do.

A small bird landed on the ground next to me. Its color was light blue. Startled, I fell back against the car. The bird tilted its head, flicked its tail, and hopped toward me. My mind raced.

I waved my hand to scare the bird away. It took flight past my head and landed on the trunk of the car. I shifted my position, following it with my gaze. Flapping its wings wildly, it turned its head back and forth. Although the bird's actions were animated, all was silent. Its beak was moving but no sound emerged. Mom's words floated through my mind.

⊕

"All dreams are important!"

I eased up and glanced over the rear of the car. Quickly, it all became clear. My blue feathered friend was alerting me. The same man I'd seen the day before was staring at me from across the street. This time I recognized him. He was the repairman from the record store. I could see him clearly. His appearance was normal, but something about him didn't feel right. This time, he wasn't wearing headphones.

The bird, perched next to my head on the trunk of the car, let out a loud shriek and flew away. I panicked, jumped up, and started running. I didn't know where I was going or why, but I knew I had to get away fast. Adrenaline, coursing through my body, caused me to sprint faster and farther than normal.

I ran several blocks before I stopped. I looked behind me and saw no one. "What happened to Jonathan?" I whispered aloud. I knew that the strange man had to be involved, but I didn't know how or why. I wanted to help, but what could I do?

I longed for the security of my parents' home—the old familiar world where comfort and safety were never questioned. The fastest way there was in the direction of the stranger. That was not a good option. Instead, I circled around, taking the long route home, attempting to stay out of sight by staying low behind parked cars. Travel was slow and tedious.

I crossed the street and headed for the public library. There I hoped to rest and allow time to pass. The sun was still high and it was hours before dark. Waiting inside felt like a good plan.

The parking lot was mostly empty, but fortunately the front door was unlocked. I entered cautiously and closed the door silently behind me. Staying low, I eased over to the front window, searching to see if I'd been followed. The streets were clear. The library also appeared to be empty. I walked to the counter and whispered. No answer. Continuing to stay low, I searched for a telephone.

In the next room, I spotted an open book lying facedown on a table. Something about it drew me closer. It was well used and the cover was missing. Apprehension moved aside as curiosity took its place. I picked up the book and flipped through the pages. It fell open to a chapter titled "Music in the World's Religions." I was curious and began reading. I'd become engrossed in the material when a man grabbed me on the shoulder from behind. I dropped the book and screamed (in reverse order).

"Whoa! No problem, my brother. Keep reading. It is okay."

His voice was kind and with a definite accent. I didn't know who he was and hadn't heard his approach. I stared at him with my mouth open. I'm sure my expression and my posture showed no kindness.

He had referred to me as his brother, and for a moment, I was a little bit baffled. He could easily pass as one of my relatives—like **a brother from another motherland**. His darkened skin and facial features made it clear he was of African descent. Which country, I couldn't tell. Although he looked friendly, I was sure we'd never met, but unsure whether to trust him.

He appeared to be slightly older than me and just a bit taller. Although his eyes were friendly, they also appeared tired. His black hair was short and unkempt and still held the impression of the hat sitting next to his backpack on the table. His blue jeans and black jacket appeared as if he'd been wearing them for a long time. I took a step back and tried to gather my composure. With a smile on his face he offered his hand. I didn't accept.

"Hello, my brother. Are you okay?"

"I'm sorry. The door was unlocked and I . . . are you still open?" My voice was shaky.

"Yes, I mean, no. I don't work here," he replied with

laughter as he retracted his hand. "You okay? You look like you saw a ghost."

I was breathing heavily through my mouth and sweating profusely. Still a bit cautious, I was unsure how to respond.

"Um, I'm okay," I answered.

It was a lie. I wasn't okay. I reached down to retrieve his book from the floor and realized my hands were clenched. I opened them and dried my sweaty palms on my pants. I picked up his book, took a breath, and tried to appear calm.

"I just . . . uh . . . well, I was running."

"From a ghost?" he replied with a chuckle.

His demeanor was super friendly, which helped me relax. He offered his hand again. I relaxed a bit more. I faked a smile and accepted his greeting. I didn't know how much to tell him.

"No. I mean . . ." Feeling embarrassed, I lowered my head and hesitated.

"It is okay," he said again. "I am your friend."

Without looking up, I responded, "I'm sorry to bother you. It was just a man I saw. I thought he was following me. He was wearing headphones. Well, no, I mean yes! He was wearing them but not today. I mean, he had them, but he left them upstairs. I think they were his, but they may have been Jonathan's. But he wasn't home." I realized how confused I sounded and shook my head. "I don't really know why I was running."

I sounded silly even to myself. How ironic that I was cautious of him, when I'm sure I was the one who sounded untrustworthy. I offered the book with both hands. His hands dropped toward the floor and his smile slowly faded.

Without a word, he grabbed his belongings off the table and walked toward the door. I didn't understand.

"Um, sir, your book?"

He paused but didn't turn around. He appeared to be thinking. I remained quiet. He continued forward at a slow pace and stopped in front of the window. After looking in all directions, he turned and walked back to me.

"Tell me! Who do you see?"

"What do you mean?" I replied, tilting my head.

"The man—the man with headphone." His face became stern as he leaned forward.

"Now *you* look like you've seen a ghost," I commented.

"The man! Tell me!" he demanded, shouting in a whispered tone.

"I don't know. He was looking at me. I got scared and ran. I don't know why. It was dumb."

"Was the headphone black with red light?"

"Yes. Maybe so, but I didn't really pay attention. He wasn't wearing them the second time. I think he left them upstairs. I thought they might be Jonathan's, so I left them on the floor. The sun was in my eyes and—" I was rambling. He interrupted.

"His headphone was on the floor? Did you put it on?" he asked, again grabbing my shoulder.

"No."

"His eyes. Did you see?"

"I don't know. He was kinda far away."

"You are a musician, yes?"

"That's right," I answered. "How'd you know?"

"You were smart to run."

I wasn't sure what he meant.

"Did he follow you?" he asked.

"I don't know. I don't think so. What's going on?"

He sat down, placing his head in his hands. He was visibly distressed. I didn't know what was troubling him and decided to give him a moment before asking. Just as I was about to speak, he murmured something I didn't quite understand.

"Essah say: 'Action is to fear as food is to hunger.'"

I was confused by his response.

"We must go!" He spoke in a firm voice and quickly rose to his feet.

"Wait a minute!" I replied. "Tell me what's going on!"

He pointed toward the door. "They are here, my brother. We must go!"

He turned to walk away. This time I placed my hand on *his* shoulder.

"I'm not going anywhere until you tell me who you are talking about!"

"We must go!" he repeated. "Victor, my brother, trust me. We must go . . . now!"

He pulled away from my grip and gave me a look I could not deny.

"Okay," I answered. "Let's go!"

Nothing was starting to make sense.

MEASURE FIVE

A Surreal Trip

✛

*There are no wrong turns when you don't know
where you are going.*

I don't like running, but we'd practically run from the library to my parents' house. My new friend refused to talk on the way there. The few words he had spoken were to let me know I was not running fast enough. If he'd known the route, I'm positive he would have left me behind.

Once we reached the house, I saw my parents sitting on the porch as if waiting for me. It was then that I realized I didn't know my companion's name. Fortunately, he was kind enough to cover for me by introducing himself. I was the only one who seemed uncomfortable about it. I had decided we needed to leave Virginia immediately, and telling my parents about my unexpected departure was the most difficult part. I avoided saying why I was leaving, and my parents were considerate enough not to ask. I quickly collected my belongings and said good-bye, electing not to tell them about our situation.

"Hold on a minute, boys. You look a little hungry."

Mom, always thoughtful, fixed a care package filled with leftovers: a little rice and beans, cornbread, two pieces of cake, and a large thermos of Pinetop Tea. Dad put it all in the car. As I closed the car door, I looked at my parents standing on the front porch, calmly taking in my abrupt departure. I sensed they had already known I would be leaving. Maybe that was why they were already on the porch. Whether they actually knew or not, they accepted it.

With a flash of inspiration, the term "parents" took on a whole new meaning. Parents are a pair of adults who rent their kids from Life but must return them at some point, hopefully better, stronger, and more prepared than when they first arrived. I'd never looked at it that way. All parents know that their children will grow up and eventually move out of the house. My parents were prepared for that. They'd done their job, and now their rental period had ended.

I exited the vehicle, ran back to the porch, and gave them each a big hug. I also thanked them for unconditionally being there for me. "That's what parents do," my dad replied. They waved from the porch as I tearfully drove away.

I was driving toward Nashville, which was ten hours away, with a literal stranger in my car. He'd introduced himself as Ali, but I didn't know if that was true. There was a lot I didn't know. Maybe I should have driven to the police station, but instinctively I chose to trust him. Ali hadn't eaten all day, so he enjoyed the food. I drank the tea.

The drive was pleasant, but I had trouble concentrating. Blurred images mixed with confusion filled my brain.

Although I knew his name, I really had no idea who the guy sitting next to me was. To add to the weirdness, as soon as Ali finished eating, he climbed into the back seat and quickly fell asleep without saying a word.

I gathered my thoughts in an attempt to put together this bizarre puzzle. No matter how hard I tried, I couldn't make sense of it. I had pieces, distinct pieces, but getting them to form a clear picture was a problem.

I was traveling with a man I didn't know. We'd connected to each other because I'd seen a man I didn't know. And now, I was driving one of those men to Nashville for reasons I didn't know. Although it was playing out like a fairy tale, I knew that we were taking **a surreal trip** of some sort. Little did I know what kind it would be.

⊕

"There are no wrong turns when you don't know where you are going."

As I pulled onto Interstate 64 West toward Richmond, I glanced back at Ali. His sleeping face was animated. I wanted to know what he was dreaming about. I wanted to know a lot of things. I felt the urge to wake him and start my interrogation, but I decided not to, hoping he would be in a better talking mood after getting some rest.

My mind was still racing as the setting sun painted the sky in front of me. To turn off my brain, I turned on the radio. The pleasant sounds were no match for the disrupting sounds in my mind, so I switched to a country station.

A few years ago, Michael tricked me into learning a bluegrass song. Since that day, I've been a fan of both bluegrass and country music. Now, when I'm in the car, I often listen to them in particular when I want to practice music theory.

I was enjoying a relaxing time naming chord progressions: C major, F major, A minor . . . , when I heard Ali begin to stir. As soon as I spoke the next chord name, my friend, still in a slumber, responded.

"Jesus?" he asked, leaning over the front seat.

"G sus," I repeated.

"Sweet Jesus!" he shouted.

Not understanding why he was repeating me, I responded again.

"Yes. G sus is sweet."

"Are you praying, my brother?" he asked.

"No. I'm naming the chords of the song."

"Same thing."

He reclined again. I was confused.

"I think you might still be dreaming," I said. Then it dawned on me. "Were you talking about Jesus?"

"No, my brother; *you* were talking about Jesus."

"No, I wasn't. I was talking about music: G sus."

"Same thing," he repeated.

"Same thing? What do you mean?" I asked.

"Your religion is based on music," he answered. "You just don't know it. Or maybe . . ." He sat up again. "Your *music* is based on religion. Hmmm."

I chuckled, although still confused. "What are you talking about? Are you still dreaming? I was talking about the chord G sus. Not Jesus from the Bible."

"What is G sus?" he asked.

"A chord, not the Lord," I responded, trying to make

him laugh. It appeared he didn't understand music theory, so I continued. "'G' is the name of the note and 'sus' is the type of chord. 'Sus' is an abbreviation for 'suspended.'"

"Suspended!" he repeated. "Wasn't Jesus also suspended?"

I swerved into the next lane, almost hitting an adjacent car. The driver beeped at me. I flashed an apologetic smile and regained my composure.

"Um, yes. Jesus was suspended on a cross," I responded.

"Maybe that is why we use a cross as the symbol for an augmented chord," he answered. "To augment means to add more. Wasn't Jesus more?"

"Cool, a neat coincidence. That's pretty clever."

"Clever?" he asked, again leaning over the front seat. "My brother, it is much more than that. It is—"

"Wait!" I interrupted. "It's much more than what? What are you talking about?"

"The Elders! They teach me. Your teachers do not. I study your religion, and from the beginning, Music is always a part of it. Today, everything is separate. Music not supported by the government. I don't know why. Maybe you not supposed to know."

I was intrigued. "But what you said about G sus—that's just a coincidence, right?"

"Oh no," he answered. "Musicians, singers, instruments; music is everywhere in your book. Your angels play instruments. A trumpet tells the end of time. And now you see, even Jesus, the dominant figure of your religion, is symbolized by a G sus, the dominant chord of your music."

I flashed an inquisitive look at Ali, unintentionally changing lanes again. His expression was serious. Fortunately, there were no cars in the other lane.

"Are you joking?" I asked.

"Oh no!" he answered. "'Revelation' mean to 'reveal a tone.' Why you think your book is written in verses? Is all music! You see, G sus, the dominant chord. The purpose? To show you to the one, C major—no sharps, no flats, the pure chord."

I was hooked and wanted to know more. "Keep going," I said, realizing I'd underestimated his knowledge of music theory.

"Yes, my brother. Do you know how to make a suspended chord?"

"Of course," I answered. "You take the third note and raise it . . ." My eyes opened wide. The revelation hit me like a ton of bricks. Ali smiled as I continued. "You make a sus chord by raising the third. Jesus was raised on the third day."

"Yes, my brother. Many, many 'coincidences,' as you say."

"You seem to know a lot about music and religion. Did you learn it from the book in the library?"

"I read many books and I study many religions. This way I learn more."

"I read books, too, but I've never learned any of this stuff."

"Maybe because you not supposed to know. Maybe I not supposed to know either, but Essah taught many things I not supposed to know. That is why our school is secret. Like the umbilical cord that carry nutrients to the unborn child, Music carry food to the soul. Maybe that is why we not supposed to know. We feed souls in ways no one else can do."

I understood completely. Ali connected dots I didn't know existed. I knew that music and religion were related but singing in church was about as far as I'd ever taken it.

"This is amazing! Did you learn all this stuff in your secret school?" I asked.

"Some of it, but sometimes, Music tell me. When you tune the note A to equal 432 hertz, everything become clearer. At 432, C in the second octave become equal to 512 hertz. You see, religion always hide things. Read your book and use the numbers: Old Testament Second Chronicles: 5:12. This verse tell how harps, cymbals, singers, psalteries, one hundred and twenty priests sounding with trumpets, and other musical instruments were used to fill the house with a cloud. According to the Elders, these are the instructions how to activate the Ark of the Covenant."

"You found that verse by listening to Music?" I asked.

"Yes. The church have always known about Music. They name your classical music ensemble an orchestra. Listen: 'or-chest-ra.' Sound like 'arc-chest-ra' to me. Think about it: an orchestra position itself in an 'arc' with the conductor in the center. The Ark of the Covenant was known as a golden 'chest' with great power in the center. And 'Ra'"—he smiled—"is another name for God. Coincidence? I don't think so, my brother."

I didn't know how to respond. "Wow!" was all I could come up with. He was beginning to speak with more force and I was enjoying it, so I let him continue.

"Many years ago, the church say diminished chord is bad. Priest say the chord have the 'demon-in-it.' Maybe 'demon' mean to 'demonstrate' and 'devil' mean to 'de-veil.' I don't know. I *do* know that 6 by 6 by 6 equal 216. That is half of 432. Bring us right back to A. Maybe someone don't want you to know that."

I'd never heard anything like what Ali was telling me.

I didn't quite know what to think. It was strange information, but I liked it. Plus, there were too many coincidences not to consider it. Ali paused for a moment, so I took the opportunity to jump in and try to lighten the mood.

"This is crazy stuff, Ali. If diminished chords were forbidden, imagine if they heard Jimi Hendrix."

I laughed but Ali didn't. He continued, fueling my appetite by feeding my mind.

"Jimi Hendrix was a powerful man—much more than a musician. Some people like him, some do not, but all young people love him. He represent the times, and he give young people power and freedom when he play. He light his guitar on fire, and he play your country's song in his own way. He also help unite races. It is interesting that he have one of the first interracial bands in your country."

"Yeah! I remember seeing him on a television show. He really spoke his mind," I added.

"Yes, my brother. But some people don't like that. He make young people feel free. Young people want change. Jimi show them the way. We have musicians like that in my country, too. Their music is powerful, and like Jimi, they are much more than just musician."

I'd heard similar things about musicians from Michael, but I was surprised to hear Ali speak about it. He said he'd learned from his Elders. I wondered where Michael had learned. Michael claimed that knowledge was in the air. I was only beginning to understand that concept. Then an enlightening thought hit me, seemingly arriving from the air.

"Musicians have power that other people don't. Imagine: if a policeman tells people to raise their hands in the air, or a politician tells them to do it, people might refuse or feel forced to respond. But if a musician tells everybody to raise their hands, everyone will do it willingly."

"Yes, yes, my brother." Ali smiled broadly. "People respond to musicians on their own—no force. That is *real* power. My Elders call it 'female' power. Jimi Hendrix have a song about a foxy lady. Most people don't know what he really sing about."

"It's about his girlfriend, right?"

"Maybe, but not a human girl—a guitar girl."

"A guitar?" I asked.

"Yes. You see, a guitar is a soprano voice, like female. It have head, neck, curves, slim waist, and a womb in the middle where vibrations grow. The human body have chromosomes. Guitar have chromatic zones. The body have twenty-four vertebrae. Guitar have twenty-four braided frets. The body have chakras. Guitar have harmonics. Your guitar have two E strings, one low and one high. That refer to your eyes, two low and one high."

"The third eye!" I exclaimed in shock. "The invisible one in the middle of our foreheads."

"Exactly! And when you play with guitar the right way, she make very beautiful sound." He glanced at me and winked.

I liked what I was hearing; Ali's information led me to think. But I couldn't stop my skepticism from kicking in.

"Okay," I responded. "These word similarities, they're very interesting, I must say, but they're just coincidences, right?"

"No!"

His head snapped in my direction. It was obvious he believed everything he'd told me. I wanted to know more.

"Are there similar references in other languages or religions?" I asked.

"Of course!" he said. "You think your religion is the only one that contain Music?"

He laughed. I frowned. He continued.

"Your language say 'do-re-mi,' yes?"

"Exactly!" I answered confidently, trying to reassert some credibility in our conversation. "It's called solfège."

"Yes. If 'do-re-mi' equal 'one two three,' what is name for number six?"

"La," I answered immediately.

"Very good, my brother. In the pure key of C, what will the sixth note be?"

"A," I answered just as quickly.

"So, 'ah' . . . equals . . . 'lah.' More coincidence?" He slowed his speech for my benefit, allowing it to really sink in.

"Ah . . . la," I repeated to myself. "Allah!" I spoke with force.

I was dumbfounded. My driving reflected it. The driver in the next lane raised a deliberate finger. I flashed another smile. I didn't know what to say. Ali continued.

"Maybe that have something to do with why your country don't like them. Your music based on major—G sus. Their music based on minor—A la. They both related, you know."

He laughed. I didn't. He kept talking. I kept quiet. Trying to think *and* drive straight caused my brain to work overtime. I lifted my right foot, allowing the car to slow down. Ali plowed ahead, picking up speed.

"You see," he continued, "in my land, people live in tribes. Your country don't like that. To you, we are primitive, but that is your heritage, too. We *all* come from tribes. You"—he pointed in my direction—"even though you live in big city, your soul remember tribes. Your spirit long for it. Your country don't have tribes like us, but you do have different kind. You have concerts. You think the concert is for the music, but it is not only for that. It is also for what the music do. It bring people together. You feel each other. You accept each other. At the concert, you find your tribe again. Maybe, somebody don't like that."

"What do you mean?" I asked. "Somebody doesn't like what?"

"Maybe somebody want us to be separate—not find our tribe again."

Whoa!

I thought about an Australian musician I'd met years ago. His name was Tjupani. His whole family, relatives and all, had been separated when he was only a child. Decades later, as an adult, while playing a didgeridoo concert in a town hundreds of miles away, Tjupani was recognized by a long-lost uncle. Tjupani thought the man was joking when he asked him for the name of his mother. But when the man pointed out the similarity of their facial features as well as the tribal song Tjupani was playing, Tjupani was convinced. Together, the two men were able to reunite family members who had been separated for over thirty years.

Music *is* more powerful than most realize, and it really does bring us together. That continues to be proven to me over and over. I've witnessed Music do things I previously thought were impossible. I've seen her heal a man right in front of my eyes. I've seen her reach unconscious people who were thought to be unreachable. Every day, Music peacefully brings together people from different cultures, backgrounds, and religious, political, economic, and social statuses. As Ali said, it is what Music does to us that keeps us coming back.

Lost in thought, I was startled by red flashing lights in my rearview mirror. I looked over my shoulder and noticed a dark-colored vehicle with tinted windows rapidly approaching. I immediately glanced at my speedometer. I was traveling at seventy-one miles per hour. The speed limit was only sixty-five.

I slowed down and merged into the right lane, hoping the police car would pass. It didn't. Instead, it eased up to my rear bumper. Disappointed, I pulled onto the shoulder and stopped the car, keeping the engine running.

Recalling childhood lessons from my father, I retrieved my driver's license and placed it on the dashboard in clear view. Next, I rolled down the window and positioned both hands on the steering wheel at ten and two. I took a deep breath and waited. Ali wiped his eyes and looked back as the dark car sat behind us.

"Maybe they didn't like what you were saying," I joked.

He didn't respond.

A well-dressed man stepped out of the vehicle. He didn't appear to be wearing a police uniform. *Peculiar.* I suspected he might be an undercover agent of some sort. Ali, still gazing out the back window, gave explicit instructions.

"Drive!" he whispered, his voice firm.

"No way. I'll take the ticket."

Ali turned and pointed at the dashboard.

"Was the radio on?" he asked.

"The radio?"

"Yes! Was it on?" he nearly shouted.

"Yes, it was, but—"

"Did you turn it off?" he interrupted.

"No. I guess I didn't."

"Drive!"

He leaned forward and thrust the weight of his body into the back of my seat. I remembered turning the radio on, but I didn't remember turning it off. *No! It couldn't be.* I watched the officer's approach through my side mirror. Something wasn't right. He looked similar to the man I'd seen standing outside Jonathan's house. As he approached in the dark, I noticed a blinking light hanging around his neck. My adrenaline skyrocketed.

"Ali. Headphones," I whispered.

"Go! Now! Drive!" he screamed.

Running from the police was never my first choice, but as the man drew nearer, he placed the headphones over his ears. At that point, I instinctively slammed the car into gear and fled, leaving behind nothing but smoke and tread marks. My hands were trembling. The man stood motionless as I pulled away. I expected him to chase after me, but he didn't. In my rearview mirror, I saw him slowly remove the headphones. I drove faster and faster. A few seconds later, the radio faded back in. I looked back at Ali. He was staring out the back window. I was now just as confused as I was scared.

Apparently, a strange man was following me across the country. Who was he and what did he want? Also, there was a stranger from Africa riding in my back seat who mysteriously knew my name. How did he know? If I hadn't pulled the same feat with Jonathan, I would've . . . well, I don't know what I would've done. I needed answers.

Why was I taking Ali to Nashville? I never asked if he wanted to go, but we'd already driven too far to turn back. It was possible that the strange man was following him instead of me. I considered pulling over and putting him out on the side of the highway right then and there, but I knew that I couldn't. Just then, Ali climbed into the front seat and fastened his seat belt, making it clear that he was along for the whole ride.

"I think he's gone. Where are we now, my brother?" he asked.

I wanted to make it clear to him that I was not his brother, but something held me back.

"We're still in Virginia on 81 South near Abingdon."

"Where is Appy-ton?" he asked.

"A-bing-don, in the western part of Virginia near the Tennessee border. We're getting close to Interstate 40, which will take us into Nashville." I still wasn't totally sure why I was driving him or being polite.

"How much further until we reach the City of Music?" he asked.

"You mean Music City," I answered, trying to maintain some supremacy. "We still have five hours."

"Good. That'll give us plenty of time to prepare."

"Prepare for what?" I was trying to be assertive. "You haven't told me anything yet. You ate all the food, then climbed in the back seat and fell asleep without saying a word. It sounded like you were having a terrifying dream, like someone was chasing you. I thought someone was following me, but now I think he may be following you. Somehow you knew my name and you seem to know where we're going when I never told you. It's time for you to start talking. You need to tell me what you know about this man right now!"

His answer caught me off guard.

"Okay, my brother. It is time. I will tell you everything I know." His tone was polite.

Ali readjusted himself and leaned his head back. I waited in anticipation, hoping he would tell me something that would bring a bit of clarity to my increasingly frightening predicament. I also hoped he couldn't see through my acting. I wanted to be mad at him, but for some reason, I wasn't. I looked at the man in my car and nodded, letting him know I was ready to listen. He turned toward me and began.

"As you know, I am Ali." He touched his chest. "I come from small village in Africa. It is there I learn about Music. It is also there I learn she is under attack. It is here I will save her."

He emphasized the name "Music" in a way I was familiar with, but I didn't want to let on too soon.

"You're crazy!" I made my best attempt at appearing oblivious. "Under attack? By who?"

"You have seen them, so you must know."

"I don't know anything," I replied. "I mean, she told me she was sick, but I never imagined that people would actually try . . ."

I stopped midsentence and looked at Ali. He smiled, letting me know that my cover was blown. He knew that I wasn't telling him everything I knew. I decided to give in and open up.

"Okay. Music is sick and may be dying. She told me that. But, is there someone who actually wants her to die?"

"I think so," he answered.

"That's crazy!" I said. "Who is it? Is it one person? A group? A government? Why would anyone want that?"

"I don't know." He leaned back and took a deep breath.

The fact that we both referred to Music as "she" grabbed my attention. I hadn't heard many people speak about her like that. Hearing him say she was under attack made me uneasy. To anyone else, our conversation would've sounded totally ridiculous, but I could feel the truth in everything Ali said. I needed to know more.

"That sounds ridiculous." I tried to play dumb again, but he didn't fall for it.

"No!" He looked at me and narrowed his eyes. Then he pointed a stiff finger. "If they are following you, *you* must know more, too." He sat back and folded his arms.

"How do you know they're following me and not you?" I asked.

"I know they follow me. They follow both of us. But you act like you don't know." His stern facial expression conveyed that he could see through my charade.

"Okay," I replied. "You tell me everything and then I'll tell you what I know. I don't know much, but together we may be able to make some sense out of this. First, tell me how you knew my name. It's been years since I've lived in Virginia and nobody knows my name here anymore."

"I don't know how. I just know what I know," he answered. "Your name come to me and I say it. That is all. It happen more and more now."

"Yeah! I know what you mean. I've been—" I stopped myself for some reason. I guess I still wasn't quite ready to open up. "Tell me more."

Ali smirked at my apprehensiveness and continued talking. He told me that he'd been having the same nightmares repeatedly. They'd started sometime after the strange men began showing up. He said that his culture respected dreams and dissected them for deeper meaning. While with the Elders, Ali dreamt that he had taken a trip across the waters to a Western city filled with music and religion. He had no idea where this place was located, but when he eventually learned about Nashville, Tennessee, he sensed that this was where he needed to go. Ali had learned many things about dreams except how to make the bad ones go away.

Although most of what he told me was disturbing and confusing, listening to him was also comforting. I was not alone. Much of his story was similar to mine. I felt more relaxed as my earlier distrust subsided. I knew that fate or even Music herself had brought us together. His next comment struck a definite chord with me.

"When I was young child," Ali reminisced, "everyone was musician. Everyone in my village would play. In times now, only some play, and those who do, they try too hard. To play right is okay, but to *feel* right is much better."

That sounded familiar. I'd heard those words before, as if we'd been taught similar information.

"Go this way." He pointed toward the approaching exit. "There we can have rest and share tales. I think it will help us both."

"Do you think we are safe?"

"Yes, for now." He looked over his shoulder. "Keep the radio going, but keep it low. If the music stop, we go!"

I took the next exit and pulled into a truck stop. I parked in an area off to the side where we couldn't be seen from the highway. After searching for signs of anything strange,

I locked the doors and lowered the radio volume. Tired, I reclined my seat and closed my eyes. I was anxious to learn more about my new friend. I nodded, indicating I was ready to listen.

I wasn't prepared for what I was about to hear.

Opposites Attract

✦

I no longer believed him. I knew he was right.

Ali sits alone in his church office. Clouds fill the sky, but a curious ray of sun slithers in through the window, casting a small rainbow on the worn wooden floor. Feeling a bit apprehensive, he closes the curtain. As he pulls his robe over his head, an undeniable chill lets him know with full certainty that it is not going to be a good day.

Ali lived his early years in a small African village with his family, but his late teens were spent with a group of people referred to as the Elders of Higher Learning. Led by a woman he called Essah, the Elders shared secret information on magic, meditation, and mysticism, among other topics. Already excelling in music, Ali was shown the inner workings of how it related to all aspects of life, and how it could, therefore, be used to affect it. Because he was an exceptional student, Ali's reputation rapidly grew as a musician and a minister.

When he was twenty-one, Ali moved to another region in Africa far away from family and friends in an unfamiliar place consumed by civil war, hoping to build a church that would bring more love, peace, and music to the area. He acquired a small plot of land and began construction. Scared and alone in the midst of turmoil, he clung to his dreams; but a few short weeks after the church doors opened, his hopes began to dwindle as doubt and loneliness crept in.

Should he have moved so far from home into this war-torn area? He knew that living there would be challenging, but the continued vandalism caused him concern. Feeling alone and helpless, Ali realized, for the first time, what the comfort of family, friends, and elders really meant. He searched his soul for meaning, the harsh realities having all but robbed him of his original desire.

Ali felt alienated from the very community he'd fought so hard to build, and he continued to question his place in this new land. Feeling underappreciated and bitter, he found it hard to practice the art of forgiveness he so often preached. These and other mounting issues meant less and less time devoted to music and prayer. He struggled to find peace.

The money Ali had saved to move and build the church had quickly been depleted. The funds generated by his congregation had always been used to help sustain the church. This left him with little time or money for himself. It would only take a little bit of either to bring a smile to his face.

On this particular morning, Ali sits alone in his church office and unlocks the bottom drawer of his desk. He finds himself staring at the collection money from the past week's service. He checks to make sure the window shade is still drawn, then reaches into the small pile of money and fondles one of the bills. Holding it in his hand, he ponders his character and agonizes over what he is about to do.

He is a good man and tries hard to be honest, but the face on the bill stares back at him as if it is testing his will. A tear slides down Ali's cheek, landing like a heavy weight on the money resting in his palm. The guilt is strong, but not strong enough. He drops the bill back in the drawer and picks up a smaller one instead, placing it in his pocket. Ali hurries out of his office, glancing left and right before proceeding down the hallway. He checks his watch just in time to see the display change.

Time to begin. As usual, Ali waits just outside the chapel door for the morning bell to ring. There is something about the sound that makes his entrance appear more holy. He waits. The silence conveys to him that something isn't right. He checks his watch and listens. Still, there is nothing. Walking back into his office, he glances at the clock on his desk.

Wondering if the bell is malfunctioning, he walks outside to check. The clouds dance above him, but the air is still. The usual morning sounds are absent. He looks at the top of the church and observes an alarming sight. The bell is swinging, but no sound is produced.

Confused and afraid, he goes back into his office to say a quick prayer. Ali sits behind his desk and lowers his head, noticing the open drawer. The pile of money catches his eye, sending a chill down the length of his spine. The large bill with the still visible tear mark seems to stare back as if mocking him. He tries to wish the image away. It doesn't work. A putrid feeling permeates his gut. He slams the drawer closed and hurries out of the room.

Ali strolls slowly down the hallway in an attempt to clear his mind. Unsuccessful, he opens the door to the chapel and is dismayed to find only twelve people seated in the pews. Two of them are strangers wearing dark jackets and dark glasses. Ali is usually happy when new people attend his services, but something about their bearing causes concern. And he questions what they are listening to in their headphones.

Ali wants to walk over to personally welcome the men and also get a closer look at who they are, but his legs won't move. He stands motionless, gazing down at his feet. Something is definitely wrong. Did the bell ring? Had anyone heard it? He checks his watch again.

The stares of the small congregation cause Ali to feel self-conscious. He reaches under his robe, feeling for the bill, which slices into his finger, giving him a sharp pain. Ali knows he is being punished. In reverence, he lowers his head and silently asks for forgiveness. Sweat seeps in, stinging his eyes. It is not a good sign.

Ali turns his thoughts to the opening song, hoping it will give him solace. He walks toward the pulpit and nods. The small choir rises to their feet and awaits his next command. Ali regains his composure and raises his hands. The room is silent. The air is still. Ali is anxious.

Following the motion of their conductor's hands, the choir members breathe in and exhale in unison. Ali's movements come to a halt as his eyes widen. A chill suddenly courses through his entire body. He falls helplessly to his knees, covering his face with both hands. Once he eventually looks around, something is different. The twelve members have become ten.

He'd heard the stories but believed they were only myths. The dreaded day had unexpectedly arrived. As the Elders had foretold, there would be no Music that day. It was time for him to act. *I must do something!* he thought.

~~~~~~~~~~~

Ali's story was fascinating. He suspected that the two men had somehow blocked the choir from singing, but he didn't know how or why. Feeling defeated, he closed the church the following day. Peace was what he'd hoped to bring to the African town. Despair and disappointment were all that remained.

The gentle sounds from the car radio were a welcome comfort. They also provided a nice backdrop to Ali's story, which sounded more like an embellished fairy tale, although I knew that it wasn't. He sat silently with his eyes closed, reliving, I imagined, each moment. I allowed him his time. After another minute, he rubbed his eyes and turned toward me, awaiting my response.

I didn't know what to say. I would've had a hard time believing him if I hadn't had my own run-in with one of those men. I'd even had an experience with missing music, but I wasn't ready to tell him about it. First, I wanted to know if he would share more of the Elders' secret information. I held off on my specific inquiries until I had a better approach.

"Are you telling me that no sound came from the choir?" I asked.

"That is right, my brother. No sound."

"That's impossible. How could that be? Was it the men? Did they do it?"

"I don't know. I think so, but I was scared. I didn't know what to think."

"What did you do? Did you follow them?"

"No. You see, until that moment, I don't know about these men. The story come to me little by little. As I meditate, I realize there are many strange things. They start happening as soon as I build the church. Maybe I seen one of them before. I'm not for sure. But I know I never see them in the church before."

"What do you think it meant? What did they want?"

"First, I thought they come because I take the money, but now, I think they want my music. I know it is crazy, but I think that is why they come."

It didn't sound crazy at all and I told him so. I assured him I believed everything he'd told me and that I understood his concerns. But there was something else I wanted to know.

"Why would they want your music?" I asked.

I'd heard similar ideas about this from Michael, but I wanted to see what Ali had to say.

"They want all our music. I think that's why they come."

"What is it about music?"

His answer was surprising.

"I think it is because we know real Music. We know her power. I don't know how much you know, but because they also follow you, you must know something."

He referred to Music as female. It caught my attention again.

"You called Music 'her.' Why?"

"Only female can make you do something without force. Music make you agree with each other. When Music play, no one think about politics, religion, race, or even right and wrong. Even we tune together before we play."

"Wow! Tuning! That's also an agreement, isn't it?" I'd never thought about it like that.

"Yes! The band is better when everyone listen to each other, right?"

"That's right," I answered, excited by the new ideas. "We listen to each other, support each other, and take turns speaking. I don't even know what to play until I listen to what you play."

"Yes, my brother. Think about this; the band is better when all instruments are *different.*"

"Exactly!" I added. "In a band, we celebrate our differences. We don't compete with each other."

"Yes! Yes! When the band play together, we *all* win."

"Including the audience," I added. "That is powerful! And all without force. Imagine if we lived life like that."

"Ah yes, my brother, you know Music very well. That is why they following you, too."

Although we were from different sides of the world, we were definitely related. I was happy we were together. For the first time, I felt like he really was my brother—my brother in Music.

When I first met Ali in the library, he was reading a book about music and religion. He'd come across an interesting passage on scientific tunings. According to the book, sometime after Mozart's era, a group of men had come together and agreed to change the frequency that musical instruments are tuned to. Apparently, before that meeting, the standard tuning was A = 432 hertz (which means the note A vibrated 432 times per second). After the meeting, instruments were tuned to a higher pitch: A = 440 herts, which is the current standard.

Ali didn't know why the frequency had been changed. He had his own ideas and explained some of them to me.

"At my home, we have an old radio. If we turn the dial to the correct frequency, the sound is clear. If the dial is off by just a little, the sound is not so clear."

I understood his point exactly. My attention was diverted by the stereo in the car. It was too clear and too loud. A commercial was on so I turned the volume down a bit. I wanted to hear every word Ali had to say.

"So," he continued, "maybe they make our tuning frequency a little off to make our vibration smaller, less powerful than in Mozart time."

"You think they did it on purpose?" I asked.

"I don't know. Maybe they do."

"But how do we know that we are off and that Mozart was right?"

"Mozart is here for many hundred years. How long do music today last?"

"About three months," I answered.

"Right on, my brother!" We shared a laugh.

On the floor of my car was a magazine for bass players. Ali picked it up, noticing the different articles listed on the front cover: "How to Walk a Jazz Blues," "Chord Shapes for 4-, 5-, and 6-String Bass," and "What's Going On: A Complete Transcription of Jamerson's Historic Bass Part."

Ali flipped through the pages for a few minutes, tilting his head from side to side. I tried to read his facial expressions. He smiled and frowned. I was curious.

"Do you know this magazine?" I asked.

"No. I never seen before."

"What do you think?"

"I realize something. In your land, musician learn *how* to play first. Everything about *how* to play and *what* to play. In my tribe, we learn *why* to play. That come first. We must have good reason for *why* before we learn more. You see, anyone can play 'cause everyone have Music inside, but with the Elders, you must show your calling before they take you further. If they accept you—if *Music* accept you—then you learn true power."

Together, we surmised that Music was being targeted because of her power. Music brings people together. It brought us together. It does not have to be understood, studied, or agreed upon to be enjoyed. And because of that, it is a potentially powerful tool, one someone might be threatened by. We wondered if the men who had altered the pitch after Mozart's era were connected to the men we had encountered earlier that day. These were bizarre thoughts. I wasn't sure what to believe. My experiences were real, but they weren't totally logical. The thought of Music being threatened seemed totally illogical. I tried to add rationality to my thinking.

"Music don't need your belief," Ali said, interrupting my thoughts. "She accept everyone. People come to enjoy, healing, fellowship, or only to experience. Everyone allowed to choose how to be. Not many things make this type of life for you."

"You're right!" I answered.

"But when you truly listen and feel her deeply, she share to you her secrets."

I knew what he was talking about. With Michael, I'd witnessed some of those secrets. I'd seen him musically influence a man to walk across the room and sit down in front of the stage. Another time I saw him locate CDs just by feeling the vibrations from the discs, all while wearing a blindfold. I also stood next to him while he healed an injured man just by singing to him.

Speaking with Ali helped remind me of the magical power of Music. It was true: I couldn't think of anything else that consistently brings people together in agreement without force. Sports comes close, but half the people are against the other half, and someone always has to lose. In the world of Music, everyone wins. Religion is similar, but Music is freer than that.

Ali shifted in his seat, looking up to his left as if recalling a distant memory.

"In my small village, we have no religion. The Elders say belief is individual. We share belief with each other, but I don't have to believe like you. See? Thinking, knowledge, experience, all the same—individual. Religion *should* be individual, too.

"Like this, my brother: you cannot think for me. You cannot hear for me, and you cannot know God for me. So, your thinking, your belief, and your religion are for you only."

"Like Music," I added. "I don't have to choose only one style, do I?"

"Exactly!" He tilted his head and smiled. "Maybe Music is my religion. Maybe Love is my religion, too. We can learn from all. Each one holds a piece. Some people don't like when I talk like this in my church." He turned to me and whispered, "But I don't care."

I liked the idea of helping people find their own beliefs without telling them what to believe. His Elders sounded a lot like my Michael. I hoped to meet them one day. Ali looked at me with a devious smile.

"What is it?" I asked.

"There is a place beyond belief," he answered.

"What is that?"

"In your language, it is called *knowing*!"

"Interesting."

"You see, we only *believe* what we don't truly know—like monsters, ghosts, and things like that."

"I believe in Santa Claus," I joked.

Ali ignored my comment.

"In all religion books I read, no master ever say what they believe. They only say what they know. When you know, you don't believe. To *know* is the key."

◈

"I no longer believed him. I knew he was right."

Although I didn't completely understand everything he'd said, I could feel the validity in his words. Ali leaned back and closed his eyes. A satisfied smile beamed from his face, and mine, too.

In the beginning, I was hesitant, but he had grown on me. I nodded in silence. I'd grown to like him more and more with every word he spoke. I've always been a fan of accents, and his was beautiful and strong.

I felt it was time to tell him more about me. I started by telling him about Jonathan and the man outside his house. That really got his attention. When Ali heard that Jonathan was missing and that his apartment was completely empty, he sat up stiff.

"Did they take him?" he asked.

"I don't know. I don't know what happened to him."

Ali grabbed my arm as he spoke.

"We must be careful, my brother. We must be together. I hope the boy is okay. Do you know other people who saw the men?"

"No. I don't know if Jonathan saw them or not. I thought I was the only one until I met you."

Ali continued, "Essah had a saying. In your language it is something like this: 'Never say what you not going to do because that is your first step to doing it.'"

It was a strange quote and I didn't understand it.

"What does that mean?" I asked.

"Life is tricky. It give you opportunity to do everything you ask for, but it don't always do it how you expect."

"That's the truth."

I understood that part, but only that part. I thought he was changing the subject until he raised his hand and continued.

"When you make a declaration or promise"—he pointed his finger to the sky—"life make it possible for you to prove yourself."

"Okay. Please explain," I requested.

"A smart man called Einstein wrote about relativity. He say that everything is moving relative to everything else. I see it as a principle—a principle of how **opposites**

attract to each other. It is more than theory. Every physical thing on this planet work by this principle. You see, to have something, you must also have something else. To know the speed of something, you must also know the speed of something else. I think that is what Einstein was saying."

I was lost. His accent was thick and his words were interesting, but we were way off topic. It reminded me of listening to Michael. His diatribes were often difficult to follow. He would speak in a wide arc, circling around the topic before zeroing in on his point. Many times, I would not see the point until, like an arrow, it would pierce me. I guess I learned more that way. It was a powerful teaching method. I wondered if Ali had learned the same technique because it sure seemed like he was using it.

"Keep going," I told him, hoping he would quickly get to the point.

"In this time, this existence, we live by opposites. We move ahead by pushing back. We jump up by pushing down. We use dirt to grow beautiful flower. You see? This is what he was talking about. It is much more than theory."

"You're starting to sound a lot like Michael," I told him.

"I like him already. I must meet this friend of yours. *Enshallah!*" He smiled and tapped me on the arm before continuing. "The un-physical . . . no, the no-physical . . . How you say it?"

"Nonphysical?" I asked.

"Yes! The nonphysical work the same way. We must breathe out to breathe in. Darkness have to come before light. The end of sky is the start of space. You get more if you give more. You understand?"

He leaned forward, looking at me. He was saying good things, but none of it seemed relevant.

"Yes," I answered. "Opposites. Like a slingshot. The further you pull back, the further it shoots forward."

His facial expression let me know he didn't know what a slingshot was. Now we were both confused. I continued with a question.

"What does this have to do with the saying you mentioned earlier? 'Never say what you're not gonna do . . .' What does that have to do with anything?"

Ali answered, "You see, your life follows the same way. If you say what you want to do, you will be put in place to do it, to make it true to yourself."

I shook my head, still having a hard time understanding what this had to do with anything. His next comment tied it all together.

"Here is the problem," he continued. "To be good person in good situation is too easy. Life know that. So, Life give you bad situation to be good in. Now, this should make being good easier, but we focus on bad situation too much. We lose focus of our original goal. Like me and my church. I let darkness take over my purpose to be the light."

I was starting to understand. I raised my seat from its reclined position and responded, "Opposites! Like yin and yang."

"Yes, my brother. That's it!" He threw his hands up and nodded repeatedly.

"Bad allows good to exist, and vice versa. I get that," I stated. "But what does it have to do with our situation? What about those men?"

Ali looked out the window, checking our surroundings. I was engaged in the conversation and kept my focus on him. His appearance was calm, so I didn't worry. Eager to understand his point, I asked again.

"What do opposites have to do with us?"

"My teachers say when situation appear tough, it is always the result of something. So, if Essah is correct, it could be the result of something we asked for. Maybe a desire we have, or a statement we make. I learn from my Elders; when I get a problem, look for the opposite. There I may find solution."

"Well, right now, those men are our problem," I said.

"Maybe so," Ali answered. "But maybe what they want is the real problem."

"They want our Music." My tone was animated. "And I'm not giving it to them. Music is sick! No—Music is dying!" I pounded my fist on the steering wheel. "And I made a vow to save her!"

I didn't mean to say it like that. It slipped out on its own and I felt embarrassed. I hadn't spoken about my conversation with Music for a reason. To verbalize it always felt sort of foolish. Plus, I'd done little to live up to my promise. The guilt never left. In the back of my mind, in the depths of my feelings, I could hear Music calling. She needed my help. Although I tried to ignore it, I knew she was the source of my consistent discomfort. But right then, unexpectedly, the words had blurted out of my mouth. I didn't know how Ali would react. He surprised me.

"Yes, my brother. I hear you, I feel you, and my eyes begin to see."

"What do you mean?"

"Life give us opportunity."

"Opportunity for what?"

"To do what we say we want to do."

"And what is that?"

"How can we save Music if there is nothing to save her from?"

The Beat of a Different Drummer

◈

*Sometimes, what you don't hear is more important than
what you do hear.*

I'd actually begun to relax, maybe a little too much. The
sheer horror and angst of being chased had begun to wear
off—at least, for me. Ali continued to glance in all directions
as we sat on the hood of the car. I'd told him that I needed
fresh air, but it was just an excuse. My dissipating adrenaline had caused me to feel a bit drowsy. I hoped the cool
fresh air would keep me from nodding off.

Time eluded us. We shared stories for more than an
hour. Cars came and left, but we hadn't seen anything out
of the ordinary. Just in case, we'd left the engine running
and the radio on for added security.

In the middle of a sentence, Ali's expression changed.
He stopped talking and his body stiffened. I became quiet.
On high alert, he hopped to his feet and made his way into

the passenger's seat. He immediately began whispering very loudly through the window.

"The radio!"

"What about it?" I asked.

"Did you turn it off?"

"I don't think so."

The static sounded louder than the music, as if the station was fading out. I was curious but determined not to freak out every time I *didn't* hear Music.

"Let's go!" Ali ordered.

"I need to use the toilet. Can I run inside first?"

"No! We must go!" he whispered a little louder.

"Ali!" I replied in a stern tone. I looked around to see if anyone was listening and then calmed my voice. "I have to go to the bathroom. I'll be right back."

"Okay. Be careless," he said.

I chuckled.

"I think you meant to say, 'be care-*ful*.'"

He didn't smile. "Yes, my brother. Full of care. That is what I mean."

I walked away from the car, being sure to stay alert. The sound of Ali locking the doors caused me to glance back. The look on his face was one of concern. Maybe he was being smart, but I shrugged it off, trying to convince myself everything was fine. That thought changed when I entered the store.

As soon as I walked through the door, I could feel it. More accurately, I could feel *nothing*. The place felt emotionless. People moved around as normal, but no one spoke or interacted with each other. There was no music playing and even the cash registers refused to speak. It was as if I was watching a musically silent movie. I tried to tell myself all was well, but my stubborn intuition told me otherwise.

In the distance, a young Asian girl exited the women's room. I didn't know why she caught my attention. She appeared to be in her teens and traveling alone. It was obvious she'd been traveling for a long while. The backpack she wore, as well as the few items she carried, seemed to be weighing her down. I felt driven to help.

"Hello."

I spoke in a cheerful voice as if speaking to a child. Her expression was clear. She wasn't a child and didn't appreciate my tone. She glanced at me without turning her head and kept walking without offering a verbal response.

"Hello," I repeated. "Do you need help?"

Again, she didn't respond. I was curious. I turned away, but my attention stayed with her. My mind was so preoccupied that I almost didn't notice the dark-suited man hurry into the stall as I entered the men's room. That shouldn't have been unusual, but something didn't feel right. I could see his black shoes in the stall as I walked closer. *Is he wearing headphones?* I tried to convince myself I was being overly cautious. I even forced a soft chuckle. I chose a urinal closest to the exit just in case.

As I left the bathroom, I noticed an employee with a ladder.

"Everything cool?" I asked.

"Yeah. Should be simple. I'm just checking the speakers. The music shut off for some reason."

I hurried outside not waiting to hear more.

Ali had pulled the car into the nearest parking space and was sitting in the driver's seat. I ran to the passenger's side.

"Drive!" I said in a snapping tone.

"Everything is fine, my brother. I haven't seen anyone," he replied.

This time it was my turn.

"Drive! Now!" I commanded.

Without saying another word, Ali drove toward the exit. As we neared the highway, I raised my hand, alerting him to stop. The young Asian girl was sitting alone on the edge of the entrance ramp. She held a small piece of cardboard with *Nashville* handwritten on the front.

"Is that a djembe?" Ali asked.

She appeared to be carrying an African drum.

"Yes. I think it is," I replied. "And it looks like she's going to Nashville, too."

"The City of Music," he said with surprise. "This must mean something. We must take her."

"I agree."

We pulled over to the side of the road and watched as the girl grabbed her things and ran toward us. I wasn't accustomed to picking up hitchhikers, especially someone who looked so young, but I knew there was a reason behind it all.

Ali and I introduced ourselves as she quickly loaded her things into the back seat of the car. We tried to help, but she wouldn't allow it. When I tried to put her drum in the trunk, she grabbed it from me and brought it with her into the back seat. We were still standing outside as she entered the vehicle, closing the door behind her. She hadn't said a word, still ignoring me. I guessed by her appearance that she was of Japanese descent, and although at first I estimated her age to be in the midteens, upon closer inspection I realized she was probably in her early twenties.

She was a small woman and her blue jeans hugged her petite frame, causing her to appear even tinier. A black denim jacket, too light for the present weather, covered her upper body. Black high-top sneakers adorned her feet. When Ali offered her his jacket, she didn't respond. She was not the talkative type and had barely raised her head when we introduced ourselves. I felt she would have been at least an inch taller if she'd stood up straight. I elected not to tell her that. I hoped we weren't making a mistake.

She began fidgeting with her drum as soon as she entered the car.

"What's wrong with it?" I asked as I buckled myself into the driver's seat.

She didn't answer. I apologized for bothering her and assured her that we only wanted to help.

"You're safe with us," I said, looking back at her. "You're lucky. We're going to Nashville, too. We can take you all the way and you can get your drum fixed when we get there. I know the perfect place."

"Drum not broken before, only broken now," she replied with a blank stare.

"Can I help?" Ali asked.

"No!" she answered stubbornly.

"I come from Africa. I know this drum. Let me see."

After a thoughtful moment, she reluctantly passed the large drum over the seat to Ali, who looked at it from all sides. He played a rhythm that caused her to lean forward.

"Sound is good," Ali remarked.

"Ai? Very strange," she replied.

Ali handed the drum back to her and she instantly began playing complex rhythms. Ali looked at me and back at her.

We were surprised. Her style was unique. She definitely had **the beat of a different drummer**. Her rhythms were amazing and like her accent, they were obviously from another continent. She continued playing without saying a word. Once she stopped, she became animated and very talkative.

"Too strange. Now, sound is good. It never break like this before, but earlier, sound go away. At store, I'm playing to make money for trip—drum stop working—only small sound coming out. I don't know why."

Leaning over the back of his seat, my inquisitive friend began questioning her.

"What happened? Tell me exactly. When did it work and when did it stop? Tell me everything!"

"I don't know. I playing maybe one hour, make no money. I get excited when man come. He wear a nice suit. I hope for a lot of money. So, I play louder and start singing. My song is good, but he listening to his own music; he not listening to me. I get mad. Drum stop working and no money. Crazy man!"

I thought about the store employee at the top of the ladder. He said that the speakers had also quit working. The pieces fit.

"You said the man was listening to his own music?" I asked.

"Ai, but he no listen to me and he no give me money. Stupid jerk." She wasn't laughing.

"Did he have headphones on?" Ali asked.

"I think so. Black ones. My eyes no good and I don't like wear my glasses. But he no need to wear them things when I playing. Very strange man. He have no footsteps."

"What does that mean?" Ali asked.

◈

*"Sometimes, what you don't hear is more important than
what you do hear."*

That was an interesting way to say it.

"Do you mean his feet didn't make any sound?" I asked.

"Ai. Everybody feet make rhythm, but his feet make no
sound when he walk."

Ali looked at me. His facial expression was enough. I
pushed the gas pedal a little harder.

She was happy to be riding with us and gradually began
to relax. Eventually, with a little prompting, she told us that
her name was Seiko and that she had recently arrived from
Japan. She actually smiled when we reminded her that we
were taking her all the way to Nashville.

A short while later, quiet and calm returned to our
vehicle, but the chatter of my thoughts continued. The
monotony of driving for hours caused my mind to wander.
I searched for answers, but they were largely outnumbered
by questions. I knew where we were headed, but I still
didn't know why.

I was just thinking about how diverse my passengers
were when a large globe sitting high atop the town of Knox-
ville came into view. Named the Sunsphere, the golden glass
monument is seventy-five feet in diameter and sits upon a
thick, 266-foot-high steel structure. Erected as part of the
1982 World's Fair, it is a recognizable icon of the city.

The globe was a welcome reminder that the three of us
had come from different parts of the world and had somehow been brought together with the unified goal of getting

to Nashville. What we would do once we arrived was still unknown. I watched in my rearview mirror as the Sunsphere faded into the distance. A reflection of the setting sun shimmered off the grand sphere, which I took as an omen that we were on the right path.

Ali appeared to be sleeping, so I turned my attention to Seiko, who was still awake. I was certain we'd been led to her or she to us. From what she'd said, it appeared she'd also had a run-in with one of the men. Were they also after her? If so, why? If Ali was right, it must have something to do with her knowledge of Music. I needed to know.

I kept glancing at her in my mirror. Her attention remained on the drum. I'd learned you could get someone to talk by keeping silent. I kept my mouth shut and continued to stare. I didn't want to appear mean, but I did want her to know that we were in charge—that *I* was in charge. After a moment, she looked up and broke the silence.

"What?"

She spoke with a tone of sarcasm. I was determined not to allow her tough-girl persona to work on me. I held my ground and didn't say a word.

"What you want?" she asked again.

My silent plan was working. I stared at her in my mirror, trying not to smile.

Seiko, not giving an inch, lowered her head and continued playing her drum. Her rhythms were very good, but I tried not to react. With a smirk, she looked up at me out of the corner of her eye and down again. Her quick glance assured me she was not interested in playing along with my tactics. I'd seen a detective use the silent technique on television. It worked for him, but it was no longer working for me. Ali, taking the direct approach, taught me a lesson, once again.

"My brother, why don't you say what you want?"

"I thought you were sleeping."

"Her rhythm too good for sleeping."

Ali turned and asked a question.

"Seiko, why you want to go to Nashville?"

She placed the drum on the seat next to her and raised her head.

"I don't know. I not sure."

"You came all the way from Japan and you don't know why?" I asked.

"Ah, now you talk to me?" she replied with a frown.

"I'm sorry. We just need to know as much as we can."

"You want answer; you ask question. Very simple!" she snapped.

Ali looked at me and smiled.

"And keep your eye on the road," Seiko added.

Following Ali's example, I asked question after question, hoping her answers would give Ali and me insight into our own situations. It didn't take long for me to realize that she was as confused as we were. She was on a search for something, too. She didn't know what it was exactly, but for some reason, her intuition was leading her to Nashville.

Seiko had saved only enough money for the flight. The rest of her travel had been accomplished by hitchhiking and sneaking onto public transportation. Having journeyed for over a week, and not knowing the geography, she'd finally made it to eastern Tennessee. It was a dangerous way to travel, she admitted, but growing up with two older brothers had garnered her a few necessary survival techniques.

Ever since she was a child, she'd had an affinity for rhythms. Although at first she had no idea what they were, they kept finding her.

"I could feel them," she told us. "When I was baby, I don't have name for it, but everything I hear make a pattern. I know voices by the pattern. I know who is walking by the pattern. Even the wind make a pattern. It always speaking to me. My eyes not too good. I much better when I listen."

Because of her weak eyesight, rhythms had become her way of interpreting the world. It was when she discovered the drums that she began to understand what she'd been feeling. Now, her understanding was at a high level.

She looked at Ali. "You talk to me in rhythm of four. He talk to me in five."

"I don't know what you're talking about," Ali replied.

I laughed. "She's right. You spoke exactly in 4/4 time."

"And you talk now in five." She laughed, pointing at me.

I replayed my comment in my mind only to realize she was correct. I made a point not to do it again. It didn't work.

"Seiko," I asked, "do you hear everything as rhythm?"

"Everything *is* rhythm," she answered. "Listen. Tell me. What is this?"

She played a pattern on her drum. Ali and I looked at each other, confused. She played it again. Still no answer from us. She began playing the rhythm repeatedly.

"6/4 time," Ali said.

"No rhythm," she replied.

"It has nothing to do with rhythm?" I asked.

"Right!" Seiko answered. I could hear the amusement in her voice. She was having fun with us.

"Listen close." She began playing and speaking in unison.

"Quarter, quarter, eighth, quarter, quarter, quarter, eighth. Quarter-quarter-eighth-quarter-quarter-quarter-eighth."

"That sounds like 6/4 to me," I said.

"No rhythm, I said!" she shouted. "Think like notes."

I was baffled and turned my attention back to the road. After a minute, Ali laughed and hit me on the leg.

"I got it," he said.

"What is it?" I asked.

"A major scale."

"Huh? What do you mean, 'a major scale'?"

"See. You talk in five," Seiko said, pointing and laughing.

"Stop it, Seiko. What are you talking about?"

"Five again," she snickered.

"Listen, my brother. She is brilliant."

"Four!" she remarked, pointing at Ali.

"Seiko!!" we shouted in unison.

She was lying sideways on the seat, laughing and holding her stomach.

"Ali, please help me out," I begged, making sure to count my syllables.

Ali laughed and offered enlightenment.

"Listen, my brother. If a quarter note equal a whole step, an eighth note equal a half step. So, her pattern equal a major scale."

"No way! Seiko, play it again."

She held up five fingers and continued laughing. I silently replayed my last sentence. I had to admit, she was sharp. Seiko and her taunting laugh initially annoyed me, but now I could feel myself gradually starting to adore her. Yes, she marched to her own beat, but I was beginning to groove with it. I laughed along with her. She replayed the pattern on her drum, and after a few repetitions, I finally understood.

"Oh! I get it. Your rhythmic pattern is two quarter notes and an eighth note, then three quarter notes and an eighth note. The pattern for a major scale is two whole steps and a half step, then three whole steps and a half step. That's really cool."

I was proud of myself. Seiko wasn't impressed. She pointed at me and then at Ali.

"You dumb. He smart."

I could hear her place her hand over her mouth, suppressing her laughter. A bit frustrated, I kept my eyes on the road.

Seiko further explained that using the quarter note/whole step relationship would allow any melody to be turned into a rhythm and vice versa. It was a revelation to me. Ali was right. She was brilliant.

According to Seiko, her advancements in understanding came from a teacher she referred to as Kiladi. Somehow, this man was the reason for her attraction to Nashville. And like Ali, she wasn't sure what it meant. All she knew was that her acute rhythmic awareness was leading her there.

To compensate for her impaired vision, she learned to heighten her other senses to make up for the small disability. She knew that all things vibrated, but according to her teacher, if she could learn to accurately decipher the vibrations, she would be able to see with her ears better than most could see with their eyes.

Like Ali and me, Seiko was a musician, and because of that, she was of particular interest to the strange men, just as we had been. They seemed to be attracted to our type. I asked her if she had ever seen a man like the one at the truck stop before. I also wanted her to relate any other strange occurrences she felt we should know about. Since we'd just met, I didn't know how forthright she would be. She surprised us. Once we heard her story, we knew we were destined to be together.

Music had brought us a sister.

Herstory

✛

Coincidences are Life's way of whispering.
Accidents are Life's way of shouting.

Seiko is awakened by anticipation. She opens the window to check the weather. Although the sun is bright and the sky is clear, there's an unfamiliar chill that lets her know with full certainty it is not going to be a good day.

They had purchased their tickets early, excitingly awaiting Japan's largest music festival. Along with her boyfriend and another couple, she looked forward to spending time with her friends enjoying their favorite bands. The day had finally come.

Seiko, the youngest of three children, was an independent woman. Unlike her mother, she refused to play a submissive role to the opposite sex. She, in turn, made a habit of walking three steps ahead of her boyfriend instead of the customary reverse. Unwilling to conform to many of her country's customs, Seiko felt out of place.

On numerous occasions, she was sent home from school for not wearing the mandatory uniform. It wasn't that she didn't like the white blouse and dark skirt; Seiko knew that all people were unique and felt the need to repeatedly remind her seniors of that fact. The thick glasses she'd worn since childhood set her apart and made her unpopular with her classmates. She felt alone and often dreamed of an escape. Support at home would have helped, but that was not the case.

As a young child, she developed an interest in drumming. Having no desire to learn the Taiko style, which is traditional to Japan, she longed to play the rhythms found in the rock and roll music she preferred listening to.

Against her father's wishes, she visited music stores on her way home from school. There, she could slip into another world as she pounded away on the electronic drums. The vibrations helped shake loose a beautiful part of her soul that survival kept buried away. It was while drumming that she felt most like her true self.

Her father was a high-powered businessman who wished for his kids to follow in his footsteps. In this way, the family business would stay intact. This, to him, was security. Seiko didn't feel responsible for her father's security and had no interest in joining the family business. She would not follow a dream that was not hers. Not pretending to show even the slightest interest in her father's desires, she knew she would never hold the same place in his heart as her two older brothers.

This resulted in arguments. Her brothers sided with their dad, causing Seiko to feel distant from them, too. Her father, feeling like his only daughter had forsaken him, gave her an ultimatum that resulted in her leaving home. Her mother secretly mourned her daughter's departure but remained silent. In her final year of high school, Seiko found herself living on the street.

Soon after, she befriended an older gentleman who helped guide and protect her. She called him Kiladi. To Seiko, he was the supportive father she'd never had. Her new friend had an earnest desire to help all the wandering children but took a special interest in her. Kiladi recognized Seiko's gifts and happily aided her in perfecting them.

Unlike her real father, who was ashamed of her for playing such a masculine instrument, Kiladi nourished Seiko's desire, helping to unearth talents she never knew she had. Through him, she learned to focus her skills in ways well beyond her imagination. To Seiko, this was what school was supposed to be.

The city became Seiko's learning ground. Introduced to a new world of vibrations, she realized that the city was alive, complete with a soul and a heartbeat. With her teacher at her side, Seiko learned to hear and decipher the patterns of the streets. The more she listened, the more the city spoke to her.

Seiko was a quick learner and full of questions. Kiladi loved her for that. Although she was young (and maybe because of it), her mind was open and receptive to all he had to share. Many of the kids her age showed little respect for their elders, but Seiko recognized the treasures hidden inside her mentor. Sensing that their time together would be short, she aspired to learn as much as she could while she could.

One day, with Kiladi at her side, Seiko foiled a purse-snatching attempt by accurately interpreting a broken rhythm. Turning in the direction of the sound, she noticed a man moving down the street in an irregular pattern for that time of day. He appeared apprehensive, as if searching for something, and his stride was unnatural for his size. His body language indicated a man with deceitful intent.

Seiko spotted the assailant's target a few meters ahead of him: a tourist walking casually with a purse slung over her back. Speaking loudly enough to draw attention, Seiko told the man that the purse he was about to take was not his color and that he should let the nice woman keep it. The man, obviously startled and embarrassed, looked around for the reprimanding voice. Seiko crouched down low. Not finding her, the man reversed his steps and hurried away. Kiladi was proud of his young student. He picked her up and gave her a squeeze.

Seiko loved her teacher like she had never loved anyone. She felt safe and free. With Kiladi, there was a father-daughter connection she longed for at home but knew she would never acquire. She also felt that he could teach her anything and that she would one day understand the rhythms of the world if he would just keep teaching her.

So, when Kiladi told her that he would soon be taking a faraway trip and that she would not be allowed to join him, Seiko was heartbroken. Kiladi wouldn't even tell her where he was going. The only thing he said was that he was going to a city of music, and although she kept asking, she would not be allowed to travel with him. She was told to follow the rhythms of her heart, and that if they led her to him, he would be waiting. Soon after, Seiko found herself alone on the streets once again.

Late one evening outside a nightclub in Roppongi, a popular district in the central part of Tokyo, a rude stranger accosted Seiko. She broke free of his grip and escaped through a crowded street. Rounding a corner while looking behind her, she bumped into a man, knocking him to the ground. Mortified, she helped him to his feet and apologized profusely. The man was polite and charming. He was also a few years her senior and handsome. Responding to Seiko's kindness and obvious distress, he offered her a place to stay. Homeless and having nowhere else to turn, Seiko agreed.

Seiko thought long and hard about what to do with her life. Going back home was not an option. Living in a small apartment with her new "boyfriend," who she had no feelings for, was not ideal either, but she was happy to be free of the constant risks and struggles that came with living on the streets. Still, she yearned for guidance, searching the streets day after day for her teacher. She hoped to find him at the music festival.

On the day of the concert, she arrives with her boyfriend just as the front gates are opened. The promise of rock and roll, drum circles, and good food raises her spirits. She walks ahead, lost in contemplation. The noises from the crowd are not enough to mask the unsettling thoughts infiltrating her mind.

Although she feels safe with him, her undisclosed plan is to continue living with her boyfriend only long enough to attend the festival. Was it wrong to manipulate him into buying the tickets? Should she confess to him or just disappear like she'd done at home?

Her churning stomach is fueled by a festering guilt. She

knows she has been deceitful, keeping him in the dark, and that she has simply been using him.

Her preoccupation makes her oblivious to the twisted rhythms formulating around her. The winds change direction. Seiko doesn't listen. The birds fly away. Seiko doesn't see. The clouds forming in the distance also go unnoticed. The changing patterns should have alerted her, but it is only when her teacher's words appear in her mind that she becomes alert.

⊕

*"Coincidences are Life's way of whispering.
Accidents are Life's way of shouting."*

Although clouds circle above her head, the lack of movement in the air is suspicious. The trees are silent. Seiko thinks back to the morning train ride and realizes that no musical sounds were present. No longer believing in coincidences, she wonders what it means. She examines her surroundings. Her teacher's words are ringing true. Life is beginning to shout.

The sudden roar of the crowd brings her attention to the stage. As the announcer introduces the first band, the sound of static in his microphone raises her suspicion. In the distance, a boom of thunder rumbles through the air. There is no rain. Something is wrong.

The crowd cheers in anticipation. The announcer motions to the band. Seiko remains still, her nerves on edge. The only other people standing motionless are a few well-dressed men scattered throughout the audience. The man closest to her removes a small set of headphones from his pocket and places them over his ears. Seiko is confused. No one else seems to notice.

Seiko grabs her boyfriend's arm for security. Oblivious, he turns and smiles. Just as the band counts off their first song, a bolt of lightning strikes the scaffolding of the stage. The singer tumbles backward as the microphone is jolted from his hands. A rack of speakers falls from the rafters, bouncing into the audience. The crowd scatters.

The warning signs were clear, but Seiko had ignored them all. She covers her face and drops to her knees. She thought it was just a story, but as Kiladi had foretold, there would be no Music that day. Seiko knew it was time for her to act. *I must do something!* she thought. The next morning, she was on a flight to Chicago.

———

We listened intently to **her story**. It had similarities to our own as well as important differences. We compared our experiences and agreed that we'd met not by coincidence, but by divine intention. Somehow and for some reason, we'd been brought together, chosen for a special task—a task I wasn't sure we were ready to tackle.

Ali and I had only seen one or two of the men, but according to Seiko's story, there were many more than that. It was now clear that they were spread out around the world and their abilities were stronger than we'd realized. If their plan really was to end the life of Music, they seemed to be succeeding.

We didn't know why or how the men were getting things accomplished, but we were convinced the three of us had come together with the joint purpose of stopping them. We had no idea what we were going to do, but we knew we would have to act together.

Despite my earlier reservations, the coincidences that brought us together were too important to ignore. My parents might not have liked the idea of me picking up strangers, but they'd also raised me to trust my instincts, which were speaking to me at an all-time high. It was playing out like a science fiction movie, and the three of us were the leading actors.

Our lives had parallels. We'd each been mentored by an eccentric teacher. We'd had encounters with strange men. We individually recognized there was a problem with Music and set out to do something about it. We had no idea what we were getting ourselves into but were determined to see it through. We needed answers. We also needed a plan, and we needed one quickly.

Another similarity was that, in some way, each of us was beginning to lose our way. We'd become discouraged with our lives and had done things we were not proud of. We wondered if the strange men also had something to do with that. Maybe they'd been a part of our lives longer than we'd realized.

Seiko was a welcome addition to our small party and slowly warmed up to us. Although she looked like a child, her wisdom spoke of someone much older. With her diminished eyesight, she'd augmented her other senses to an extremely high level. She could sense things in a way that seemed impossible. When asked if she had extrasensory abilities, she answered with an emphatic "Yes!" She claimed we all did. According to her, if we used the basic five senses to their highest potential, we could do things previously believed impossible. Of course, I had to ask her about that.

Seiko explained that humans have many senses and that the fundamental five are highly underutilized. We can hear, taste, feel, smell, and see much better than we realize, but we have meekly accepted a limited version of our full abilities. Since she was in a talkative mood, I asked if she would explain further about the other senses, as well as how we could improve upon the five common ones.

She began by explaining what she referred to as "very simple stuff." She showed us how to place our hands behind our ears to make them larger. Like animals who can individually reposition their ears to triangulate and pinpoint certain sounds, we can use our hands to do the same. Because I was driving, I used one hand only and was surprised at how much my hearing improved. Not only did the volume increase, but the frequency also changed. I raised my hand up and down, noticing how everything sounded brighter when my hand was behind my ear, as if someone had turned up the high-mid range on an equalizer. I made a mental note to experiment more.

We learned that a dog's long nasal passage aids in their sense of smell and that dogs take short rapid sniffs rather than long inhales. According to her, we could increase our sense of smell by doing the same. Smell had always been a weak sense of mine. I looked forward to experimenting with that technique also.

Seiko's thought is that it's possible for humans, like dogs, to heighten this sense to the degree that we can actually smell disease and possibly emotional states. That's pushing the possible limits, in my opinion, but Seiko claimed that she knew of a Chinese acupuncturist who could do just that.

I remember reading about an amazing study done on dogs and their ability to sense and detect uncommon things. Apparently, dogs are already being used to detect seizures in humans. I'm still shocked and surprised by that! But a human with these abilities seemed implausible. Seiko was convinced we could always improve our brains and therefore our senses. She'd already impressed me with her abilities. I had no good reason to doubt her.

"What about the vision?" I asked. "Is there a way to improve our eyes?"

Seiko was prepared, as if she knew my question was coming.

For most of our lives, we have been told to *focus,* but Seiko said we could gather more information if we learned to use our whole eye (peripheral vision) and not just the center. Unfocusing the eyes is the key. "Focus the mind but not the eye," Seiko told us. She said it was imperative to use this technique at night since light is mostly received by the receptors on the outside of the pupil. I'd realized this while stargazing. Faint stars are always easier to see when I don't look directly at them. Now I knew why.

Seiko believed that using our peripheral vision or wide-angle vision (as I call it) would trigger our spirit or our invisible self (as she called it). She claimed that her invisible self allowed her to feel trouble before it occurred and that this was the number one thing that kept her safe while living on the streets.

To Seiko, recognizing only five senses demonstrates only a basic level of understanding. Her expanded version includes the sense of emotion and feeling, imagination and creativity, as well as belief and knowing. She also said that most people were already aware of their sense of time, direction, balance, and fear but didn't think of them as real senses. She explained that we are born with these senses and that our lives would not exist, as we know it, without them.

We devoted our full attention to Seiko. Her information was exhilarating. I'd never thought about the senses in her way. Whether I believed her or not, I knew for sure that something other than our five senses had brought us together.

A week had passed since Seiko began her journey in search of her teacher. Although she'd told herself she was looking for Kiladi, she knew her search was more than that. Playing her djembe along the way, she'd earned only enough money to eat. She was happy to have met us. She felt safe for the first time since she'd entered the country.

Ali had also recently arrived in the United States. Through a series of unforeseen circumstances, he'd boarded a plane, which landed at Patrick Henry Airport in Newport News, Virginia. Not knowing where he was, and having exhausted his money, he'd walked from the airport in search of a sign. Too tired to continue, he took refuge in a small library, which is where we found each other.

Me? I'd run home to Mom and Dad. I felt a little foolish about that but realized I may not have met my new friends if I hadn't made the trip. I definitely wouldn't have met Jonathan. Maybe he would have been better off if we hadn't met. I hoped he was okay. I was convinced the strange men had *something* to do with his disappearance, but maybe I had *everything* to do with it.

We entered Davidson County and headed for the Nashville airport, where we returned the car. Our plan was to go to my house and get some well-needed rest. The next morning, we would decide what our next steps should be. We were happy when a taxi pulled up as soon as we stepped outside. The trunk opened on its own as the cab came to a halt. The driver kept his seat while we loaded our luggage.

Seiko entered the rear seat and I followed, closing the door behind us. Ali entered the rear from the other side. As my door slammed, it locked automatically. Seiko grabbed my arm. I confirmed with my expression that I could feel it, too.

Something was about to go terribly wrong.

Toward the Light

◈

If I was still alive, I wasn't sure how happy I was about it.

For a moment, the silence was deafening. It played tricks on my mind. Time seemed to slow down as I surveyed my surroundings. We sat in the back of the taxi for probably only a few seconds, but it seemed much longer.

Always thinking, Ali asked the driver if he could retrieve something from the trunk. The driver raised his head but didn't respond. Ali tapped him on the shoulder. The driver turned around with a cold stare. Our fears were confirmed.

"Him!" Seiko screamed.

"Headphones!" I whispered urgently.

Seiko screamed something else in Japanese and began pushing me to get out. I tugged on my door handle and was horrified that I couldn't unlock it. At the same time, Ali opened his door and jumped out of the car, dragging Seiko along with him. I tried to shuffle over to his side, but my seat belt held me in place. I could see the terror on their faces as I struggled to get free.

The driver began to pull away with me in the back seat. I managed to unbuckle my belt and scurry over to Ali's side. I quickly sprang out of the moving vehicle, tumbling onto the asphalt. I heard the taxi screech to a halt, but I didn't look back. Adrenaline masked my pain as I rose to my feet and ran toward my friends. Passing them, I motioned for them to follow.

"My drum!" Seiko shouted.

She turned to go back but Ali grabbed her. I ran up the escalator and into the baggage claim area. I felt we would be safer inside where there were more people. A small group was waiting for their luggage. I merged into the crowd and waited for my friends.

Ali arrived first with Seiko straggling behind. Her face was somber and she wasn't carrying her drum. I looked at Ali. He shook his head.

"Forget about it, Seiko," I told her. "Your drum is gone and so are my things. We have to get somewhere safe. Ali, my door was locked. How did you get out of the taxi?"

"I feel something right away, so I never close it," he responded.

He was the smart one and I was thankful to have him with us. I wished I had his awareness. Instead, I had a terrible habit of always questioning my feelings. That was a mistake. Ali walked ahead; I followed. He moved slowly through the airport, looking at the signs on the walls.

"My brother, this is the City of Music?" he asked.

"Yes. We call it Music City," I answered.

"I see pictures of some musicians but not all. Where are the rest?" he asked.

I knew what he was referring to.

"Ali," I responded, "now is not the time for that. We have to figure out where to go."

"Yeah! Rock drummers, where are they? How come no pictures?" Seiko asked, either unaware or unconcerned that we were whispering.

"Shhh, Seiko!" I snapped, raising a finger to my lips. "Nashville is filled with all types of musicians. You just won't find all of them on the walls at the airport. Anyway, we have bigger problems to deal with right now. We have to get to my house."

Ali gave me a serious look. "Listen, my brother. In my country, we hear about the City of Music, but if it doesn't represent all music, why they call it that?"

"Ali!" I cautioned, but he wasn't finished.

"It is like: Music City with a small 'm.'"

"I hear you, Ali, but let's deal with it later. We have to go."

He may have been right, but I didn't think it was relevant to our current situation until Seiko spoke up.

"Maybe the headphones men have affected the whole city?"

We looked at each other. No one offered an answer.

The airport was unusually quiet. There were a few people present, but the sounds of country music that usually played throughout the airport were absent. The only semblance of music was the rhythmic patterns of the moving baggage carousels. I knew we had to get out of there.

Making sure we weren't followed, I led my friends outside where we found a bus heading to the economy parking lot. This lot is located at the back of the airport farthest away from the terminal. From there, we could walk to the house of one of my friends who I hoped would drive us where we needed to go. We boarded the bus, scrutinizing the driver's eyes and ears. All appeared safe.

I was exhausted and sank into the seat, fighting to keep my eyes from closing. As my body relaxed, the pain from jumping out of the taxi gradually began to emerge. We'd also been driving all day and I could feel the result of each cumulative hour. Running scared had robbed me of precious energy. I knew that my friends were feeling the same.

Ali had been walking most of the morning when I found him, but at least he had slept in the car. Seiko had barely slept at all. She'd spent the beginning of her day hitchhiking and playing for tips, while the majority of our trip was spent telling us her story and tending to her drum. I hadn't slept much either, having awoken early as the result of my bizarre dream about birds.

Although the bus ride was short, it was no surprise that I fell asleep. Ali shook me awake at the first stop. I awakened Seiko and told them both it was time to go.

We departed the bus and walked out of the parking lot at the nearest exit. From there, we followed a small road until it connected with Donelson Pike, the main road leading out the back of the airport. We walked briskly, looking in all directions for signs of anything unusual.

As we made a left onto Murfreesboro Road, the feeling returned. We stopped in unison. We appeared to be alone, but something was amiss. With my body and mind fatigued, I fought hard to remain attentive. This was the last road before reaching my friend's house and I was determined to make it there.

Murfreesboro Road, a multilane thoroughfare with a turn lane in the middle, was totally vacant. It was extremely unusual for that street to be deserted any time before midnight. The streetlights were off, causing the area to appear darker than normal. We huddled together and proceeded with caution.

"Look!" Ali whispered.

A man was walking toward us from across the street. He seemed to have appeared out of nowhere.

"That's him," Seiko whispered.

"How do you know? It's dark. I can barely see," I said.

"No footsteps," she answered.

I listened. She was right.

"We must go!" said Ali.

Ali waved his hand and we reversed our course. The man sped up. Wasting no time, Ali grabbed Seiko by the arm as we started to run. We ran back to the corner and crossed the street without hesitation. I looked behind us, but the man was gone. I alerted the others. No one said a word.

We cautiously walked up the quiet street in the opposite direction of our destination. Ali took the lead with Seiko close behind. Suddenly, we were startled by a loud noise. It was a stark contrast to the quiet that previously surrounded us. I instinctively grabbed Seiko by the hand.

The blinking light and sound of a crossing signal came as a shock as it cut through the silence. It was the first musical note we'd heard since arriving in Nashville. I welcomed the sound. I dropped Seiko's hand and walked **toward the light** as if it were a beacon in the night—a savior of some sort.

Recalling Seiko's technique, I unfocused my eyes and used my peripheral vision. My whole body became more receptive. The sound caused a tingling sensation in my scalp as well as on the bottoms of my feet. I don't know why, but it was as if the crossing signal had become my own sign of hope. Fear receded as I stood, captivated by the sound. I vaguely remember hearing Ali's voice. I didn't respond.

I closed my eyes and stood erect—my arms at my side with open palms facing the light. Like reuniting with an old friend, the signal and I welcomed each other. Although it was mechanical, the sound felt alive.

Gradually, a feeling began to emerge in the back of my mind—a slight tug as if someone was beckoning me.

"Listen . . ."

I sensed it more than I heard it. My friends stood a few paces behind me and remained silent. I didn't know if they could feel it or not. I didn't ask. I struggled to maintain the connection.

"Listen to . . ."

This time it was clearer.

"What?" I said out loud.

"Listen to me."

The voice was faint, but I could clearly tell it was female.

"Who are you?" I asked.

"If you must ask, you are in grave danger."

"Music!" I screamed.

It had been years since I'd spoken with her. Her voice was sweet but weaker than I remembered. She'd done so much for me, but had I done enough in return? I knew the answer and didn't like it. I felt a mix of elation and dishonor.

"I'm sorry. I didn't recognize your voice," I responded.

"You must . . ." The voice faded away.

"Wait! I must what?" I asked.

There was no answer. I was losing it—losing control—

losing connection. This time it was Michael's voice that spoke to me.

"Try easy, my friend. Try easy."

Everyone in my past had always told me to try harder. Michael's advice had been counterintuitive but worked when I was with him. I took a deep breath, held it for a few seconds, and let it out slowly. Her voice returned.

"You must feel me . . ."

I inhaled slowly.

"You must feel me at all times and in all things, even in the beeping of a crossing signal. That is important! If you don't . . ."

Her voice faded into silence as my attention was diverted by Ali.

"Victor, we must go. They are coming!"

I opened my eyes to find Ali pulling Seiko by the hand. I didn't know why they were running.

"Ali, wait! She wasn't finished, but I think I understand."

Music was telling me something important. I didn't want to abandon her again. I closed my eyes in an attempt to relax, but my breath was too unsteady. My eyes reopened on their own. The beeping sound was gone, and the flashing light had stopped. She was gone. I tried to feel her. I felt a cold silence instead. I clenched my fist and tried harder to concentrate. It didn't work. Then, I heard a scream.

Ali ran wildly, pulling Seiko along. She was desperately trying to maintain her footing. As I stood there watching, a man in a dark suit came into view, seemingly from nowhere. The darkness of the night in combination with my fatigue made it difficult to focus. I shook my head and wiped my eyes. The man was still there. I was scared.

"Help! Somebody, help!" I screamed.

I ran toward my friends but was cut off by a dark van speeding around the corner in front of me. I jumped backward. The van barely missed me as it sped straight toward my friends.

Ali darted across the street, losing his grip on Seiko, who stumbled to the ground. He turned to help, but the van drove onto the curb, creating a gap between them. I heard a door open on the far side of the van. When the van pulled away, Seiko was gone.

"Ali! Seiko!" I yelled.

Ali ran toward me but stopped suddenly. He stared in my direction as if looking past me.

"Victor!" he shouted.

I turned just in time to see a masked man reaching toward me. He grabbed my wrist, but I instinctively dove to my left and rolled away. I regained my footing and ran across the street as fast as I could. Unfortunately, I was getting farther away from Ali. My body trembled. I tried to scream but was too frightened. It felt like a nightmare, although I was completely awake.

Scared for my life, I left Ali behind and ran. At the next corner, I turned back. A feeling of horror took over my body as I watched a dreadful scene play out.

A man wearing dark clothing emerged from the bushes. Ali, usually aware, appeared oblivious to the man approaching from behind. I screamed to get Ali's attention but was too late. He was quickly subdued before he could react. I was petrified as his body fell limp. The man lowered him to the ground and laid him on his back.

Before I could move, the black van returned. I watched in shock as Ali's limp body was placed inside. The van sped away as the door slid closed. My heart sank. I'd lost both of my friends in a matter of seconds and had done nothing to try to save them.

I was alone. There were no cars or people—no lights or sounds. Even the wind had abandoned me. I was mentally frozen, not knowing what to do or where to go.

Earlier that morning, I'd found Jonathan missing from his house. I'd acquired two new friends who, now, were also missing. I was scared, and like a child, I wanted my parents. I closed my eyes and silently asked for help. To my surprise, in the midst of stillness, I heard a sound.

The crossing light was flashing again. I stepped off the curb and ran toward it, hoping to find Music waiting for me. As I approached, the light continued but the sound stopped. I questioned whether I had imagined it. I stood in the middle of the street, searching for the sound—any sound.

I took a deep breath and was able to reduce my tension. As soon as I did, I heard a faint tone. *Music!* I looked around, unable to discern the sound's origin. I ran to the next corner. It was not there. I turned in circles, hoping to pinpoint its direction. No success. As my frustration grew, the tone began to fade.

Music always seemed to make me calm. Even fear would subside when she was around. I wondered if the opposite was also true. Were my extreme fear and frustration pushing her away—keeping me from hearing her? I needed to control my feelings. Music once told me that she needed to be felt at all times. She also alluded to the fact that I would be in danger if I couldn't always feel her.

I needed to figure it out. I'd felt her earlier, but I was having trouble regaining the feeling. Fear and frustration had taken her place. I was in a near panic. My friends had been captured, and now, someone was after me. I was alone and Music seemed to be my only hope.

I looked around. The streets were bare. Not knowing where to go or what to do, I sat down on the street corner and leaned back against a pole. It was a toss-up between getting up or giving up. The crossing signal, my beacon of hope, sat dark and silent just above my head, seemingly mocking my very presence. *A musician, but you can't hear a crossing signal?* The thought was loud and clear.

The words reverberated in my head, making me furious. I stood up, found a rock, and threw it at the light, shattering the bulb. Fear had turned to anger. I questioned Music. She had abandoned me when I needed her most. I cried out in agony, yelling at the top of my lungs. I was helpless, confused, scared, desperate, and exhausted. I was in an emotional battle that I was losing.

Tears filled my eyes as the feeling of hopelessness escalated. My strength, as well as my mind, were giving out. My body lowered itself back onto the pavement. Curled in a ball, I lay there, barely able to move.

Unexpectedly, I felt an unpleasant feeling slither into my body. It was the same feeling I'd felt when I saw the man with headphones staring at me. I wiped my eyes and looked around. I appeared to be alone but knew someone else was there. The man with no footsteps was close.

With my last bit of energy, I uttered these words: "I'm sorry. Please forgive me." I didn't know why I spoke them or to whom I was speaking, but I was honest.

Then, I heard it again. I turned my head and listened. A different crossing signal had begun flashing on the other side of the street. The beeping sound spoke to me. A trace of energy returned. I had to reach it before it stopped.

I made a feeble but successful attempt to stand. The light from the crossing signal danced as vertigo played tricks on my eyes. I stumbled off the curb and fell into the street. I was again jolted alert by the sound of tires screeching on the pavement. From my left, a black van sped in my direction. Fear returned in full force. I ran toward the signal, hoping it would keep me safe.

A man suddenly appeared in front of me. He stood directly under the light. I couldn't believe what was happening. I tried to stop, but my legs didn't cooperate. I stumbled to the ground, scraping the palms of both hands. I glanced up. The light was still flashing but no sound was present.

The man stepped off the curb and walked slowly toward me. He was wearing headphones. My ears felt as if they were receding deeper and deeper into a vacuum. Fear turned to panic. I tried to scream but was capable of only a muffled tone. It was as if all audible vibrations were being canceled out.

There was nowhere to turn. All hope left my body. I sat motionless on the ground, making no attempt to move as the man looked down from above. His face was in full shadow but the red reflections from his rapidly blinking headphones caused him to look even more menacing. Kneeling down, he removed something from his breast pocket. There were more blinking lights. In slow motion he extended his arms, preparing to place another pair of headphones over my ears.

I felt like I was being hypnotized. I blinked rapidly in an attempt to break loose from his control. My eyelids felt heavier and heavier with each attempt, but in a way that kept them open rather than closed. Unable to avert my focus, I was lured deeper into his horrid spell.

Music told me that I needed to feel her at all times, but I was too scared to feel anything other than fear. As a final effort, I tried to sing. No sound. I tried to hum. There were faint vibrations, but I heard no sounds. My ears had become numb. I was losing the battle. In my mind, I pleaded for help.

Imagined or not, I wasn't sure, but a melody formed in the back of my mind. I could sense it. With all of my remaining effort, I was able to increase the intensity. It was a happy song, unfamiliar but beautiful. I sank into the melody, allowing its vibrations to spread throughout my body. It was working. The man recoiled his arms, which lessened his spell.

Gradually, I regained sense in my body. The hypnotic hold on my eyes was lifted, allowing me to close them, which completely severed the unseen power that had held me unable to move. As the vacuum in my head began to subside, sounds flooded my ears. I felt light-headed, as if I'd rapidly descended in altitude.

I finally opened my eyes to find the man backing away, abandoning his inaudible attack on me. The blinking lights on his headphones slowed. His gaze appeared to be focused on something else. I was happy to be free.

Suddenly, I was startled by the sound of footsteps quickly approaching from behind. I rolled over just in time to see another dark figure emerging from the shadows. A black mask covered his eyes. This time, I was quickly grabbed and subdued. I tried to fight, but the masked man prevented me from moving. The man with headphones stood motionless a short distance away. They must have been working together. I fought to free myself, but my arms were quickly pinned beneath me. My legs, tired and injured, were of little use.

One of my assailants wore headphones, the other a mask. One moved slowly, the other amazingly fast. The man with headphones had vanished and the masked man was about to put me in a dark van. Why were they putting me through this, and where were my friends?

I've always been an athletic person with more than average physical strength. With all my might, I yelled and exploded with a burst of energy, using every ounce of force to muscle my way to freedom. It didn't work. I was easily held in place.

I heard what sounded like muted laughter from the masked man. There was nothing funny about the situation. I gave a final attempt to free myself, but he pulled out a dark knit cap and placed it over my head. I froze. Now, trapped and unable to see, I became claustrophobic. As my last and only hope, I attempted to reason with him.

"Take what you want. I don't have anything, but take it anyway. Just, please, please, let me go."

"Don't talk! Relax!" he replied.

His voice surprised me. It was much gentler than expected, but it didn't calm my nerves. I raised my voice.

"What do you mean, relax? How am I supposed to . . ."

That was the last thing I remember before I blacked out.

～～～～～

I came to as the van stopped. I had no idea where I was or how much time had elapsed. My eyes were still covered and I could feel the pain in my arms and legs, but I couldn't move them. I heard the van door open and felt myself being carried outside. I remained quiet, listening intently.

Being upside down and blindfolded made it difficult to gather information. I didn't know what was happening, what had happened, or what was going to happen next. This was a new experience and I didn't like it. I'd never been kidnapped before. Out of curiosity, I pinched myself.

✛

"If I was still alive, I wasn't sure how happy I was about it."

Homecoming

✥

In letting go, I found myself.

Fear was a complete understatement. I found out that after a certain amount of time, fear eventually turns to numbness. I could barely feel my body, and my equilibrium was completely off. I kept fading in and out of consciousness, which made it difficult to piece together a timeline or recall anything that could be a clue to my whereabouts. I didn't remember hearing any other vehicles, so I figured it was still late at night, but in actuality, it could have been any time of day.

I vaguely remember being lifted out of the van. The walk from the vehicle was quite short, and it sounded like I'd been carried across grass. Something felt familiar as we entered the building, or more accurately, sounded familiar. It had to do with the way sounds reverberated through the air. I could clearly hear footsteps as we entered, but then I was taken to a separate area that must have been smaller and carpeted. The sound was quite different. It was unlikely, but it seemed like I'd been there before. Nevertheless, I didn't want to be there right then.

I was left lying alone on a mattress. I remained motionless and reminded myself to listen and be silent, paying close attention to anything that might aid in my escape. I could hear people shuffling around, but I couldn't see anything. I couldn't discern the voices, but it sounded like there were at least three others in the building.

The knit cap covering my eyes had slipped down over my nose, forcing me to breathe through my mouth. The sounds of my labored breathing began to mask all the other noises. I tried to roll over in a way that would enable me to better hear, but I hadn't regained control of my arms and legs. At first, I thought my limbs were asleep, but that familiar tingling sensation was nonexistent. I could feel my limbs, even the scrapes and bruises; I just couldn't move them.

Then I got a musical idea. With the left side of my face pressed against the mattress, I hummed a note, causing the springs inside the mattress to vibrate. Surprisingly, the vibrating springs produced a G, the same note the mattress at my house produced. I was sure of it. I'd done it many times late at night while trying to fall asleep. This was too much of a coincidence.

Repositioning my body was difficult, but I was able to lift my head just enough to add to my frustration. With all my strength, I twisted my neck back and forth, rubbing my forehead against the mattress. It worked. Lengthening and contracting my neck, I was able to lift the knit cap slightly, allowing me to peek out from underneath. Although the room was dark, ambient light seeped in through the open door. What I saw shocked me.

The bed covering looked identical to a quilt my mom had made, which was exactly what I currently had on my own bed. *Wait a minute!* Full of excitement and dread, I found the energy to turn my head. In the darkness, I was able to determine that I *was* lying in my bed. I was stunned! Why was I in my house? More importantly, why were *they* in my house?

I was more puzzled than pleased. I thought hard but could come up with no reason for me to be where I was. Why would someone kidnap me, blindfold me, and bring me home? Although my house had been my original destination, this was not the **homecoming** I'd expected.

What did the headphones men want with me? Had I been followed all the way from Virginia? How did they know where I lived? What did they plan to do? If I was lucky, they would only ask questions. If I was unlucky, they would harm or even kill me. I didn't feel lucky right then.

I lay in my bed confused and scared, thinking about my next move. I felt the urgency to act, but I had no idea what to do. Sneaking out of the window might work, but right then, my body wouldn't cooperate. Yelling for help was an option, but I decided against it. Not letting them know I was awake seemed like the best choice at that moment.

I was anxious. My chest expanded and contracted with tightness. Although I was sweating, my mouth felt desiccated. I fought for air. Every physical effort caused my breathing to become more labored, as if someone were sucking the air out of the room. I needed to compose myself and slow my breathing. Nothing worked. Fear continued to rule. Guilt ran a close second.

I'd watched my friends get captured, and now I'd suffered the same fate. I had no knowledge of Ali and Seiko's whereabouts or condition. The fact that I hadn't helped them was beyond burdensome. What could I have done? If I hadn't picked them up back in Virginia, they'd both be okay. Regardless, I was responsible.

Horrid scenarios played out in my mind. Thoughts of my friends being questioned, tortured, or worse swarmed me. I'd been worried about Jonathan all day and still had no idea of his fate. And now, since the strange men were at my house, I also feared for my neighbors.

My parents. What about them? I'd left their house without telling them anything. I should've told them what was going on, or at least told them to be careful. While there, I'd only been concerned with my own safety. They'd raised me to be more considerate than that. For all I knew, they were also in danger. The thought of being the cause of my parents' harm was sickening. I was responsible for everything that was happening. I was flooded with guilt and shame.

Tears poured from my eyes, soaking into the knit cap. Being unable to wipe my eyes added to my discomfort. I lay there trembling uncontrollably as I gasped for air. I knew that my sounds of sniffling and snorting were drifting into the other rooms, but I no longer cared. All concerns of remaining silent were gone. My trembling muscles signaled the increasing control of my arms and legs, but all thoughts of escape had also been put aside. The men might kill me if they realized I was conscious. Maybe that would be a good thing. I mentally prepared to accept my punishment. Whatever happened to me would be justice for what I had *not* done for my friends.

I also hadn't upheld my promise to Music. My attempt to save her had failed, not because I'd tried but because I hadn't. When she needed me most, I wasn't there. She'd reached out to me. She even tried to warn me, and I'd done nothing. I wondered how she felt about me now.

I'd always been told that my life was in my hands. At that moment, it wasn't true. Yes, I still had my life, but there was nothing left to do with it. This was the end. All emotion seemed to fade away as I simply gave up, or gave in, if there is a difference. Relinquishing all ties to my existence, I exhaled and sank deep into the mattress. Gazing off into nowhere, I apologized once again.

"I'm sorry! Please forgive me!"

⊕

"In letting go, I found myself."

I closed my eyes for the last time, I presumed. And as I did, a vision of Michael's face appeared in my mind. It came as a surprise and, for some reason, released me from the grip of despair. It was only a quick flash, but in that instant, I could discern his entire expression.

"What are you choosing?"

My mind was playing tricks on me, but it *was* in Michael's character to ask stimulating questions. And in absolute Michael fashion, it caused me to rethink. *What am I choosing?*

"I don't have any choices," I whispered aloud.

"You always have choices . . . or not."

Wait a minute! Who said that? There was only one person who spoke like that. *My mind must be playing tricks on me.* But it sounded so real.

Mustering up all my courage, I managed to maneuver my head and wipe my eyes on the bed. In the process, I was able to completely remove the knit cap. With my full vision restored, I turned my head and looked around the room. My broken unicycle was leaning against the wall. *Strange!*

My bedroom door was slightly ajar. Light from the other room caused shadows to dance across the floor. I listened closely. Although I could hear the murmurs of voices, I still couldn't discern whose they were.

The sound of footsteps grew louder, causing my nervousness to return. Someone was standing just outside my door. I tried to remain calm but was unsuccessful. I held my breath, uncertain of what was to come. Other than the sound of my racing heart, all was silent.

Thirty seconds passed. Nothing happened. I opened my eyes and lifted my head. The ease of my movement shocked me. I opened and closed my hands. I moved my arms. My body seemed to be working, so I instinctively sat up. The door to my room was completely open now. I decided to ease my way toward it. As soon as I leaned forward, a hand grabbed me from behind. I froze in terror. I'd thought I was alone. A feeling of electricity coursed through my body, causing my muscles to contract.

I turned my head slowly and saw the masked man standing behind me. His powerful grip held me in place. I was too frightened to scream. My chest heaved and my body shook uncontrollably. I tried to turn and back away. He leaned forward, pulling me closer, his menacing eyes peering through the mask.

"Should I finish him?" I heard him ask.

I didn't know who he was talking to and I didn't care to find out. I forced a scream and tried, again, to break free. He tightened his grip. The power in his hand sent a clear message. I obeyed. I sat still, eyes closed, afraid to breathe, and prepared for the worst.

"Leave him alone. He's been through enough already."

His voice came from the other side of the room.

Impossible!

Why was he here?

First Lesson

☖

Teaching completes the circle of knowledge.

It's amazing what you see when you can't see. A familiar silhouette stood in the doorway. It was still dark in my room, so I could have been mistaken. I couldn't see details but his aura was clear. There was an actual glow and I could feel it. I could feel him. This same feeling had caused me to open my eyes one afternoon a few years earlier.

My mind raced back to the day he first appeared. I was lying on my couch with a bass guitar in my lap when a man donning a blue NASA-style jumpsuit and a black motorcycle helmet seemed to materialize in front of me. I didn't know who he was or why, or from where, he'd come. How he'd gotten into my house is still a mystery. I hadn't given him a key.

Once again he was here in my house and, once again, *how* and *why* were still questions. Once my eyes adjusted, I was surprised to see him dressed normally, in black slacks and a button-down white shirt. This assured me that he was here on a serious mission. I wanted to know what it was. I could feel his spirit. I could also feel the spirit of Music. They were always together—a dynamic duo. Where did I fit in? Questions flooded my mind, but they would have to wait. I was too excited to see him. One thing I knew for sure: the lesson was about to continue.

"Michael!" I screamed with delight.

Happiness and excitement wrestled with confusion and curiosity. Had Michael also been captured? What about the masked man who still had an unbelievable grip on my arm? Whose side was he on? For a moment, I didn't care. Michael was here and I wanted to see him. I tried to get up, but the masked man didn't allow it.

"Sifu. That's enough!" Michael said firmly.

"Dang! We were just starting to have fun," the masked man said as he slowly released his grip.

I rose to my feet, but my legs gave way. I fell to the floor.

"Easy now," Michael responded. He kneeled down next to me. "Take your time. You're still weak. Sifu, help him out."

The masked man reached toward me. I retracted in fear, uncertain of his motives.

"And please remove the mask," Michael said with a chuckle.

"Oh, come on. I think he likes it," the masked man replied.

Although he removed his mask, I was still afraid. Michael assured me that Sifu was okay. I trusted Michael completely but the masked man, not so much.

Sifu rolled me onto my stomach and proceeded to adjust my neck, back, and hips. My bones popped repeatedly as he pressed, twisted, and pulled. His touch was surprisingly gentle, but it still took every ounce of nerve for me to allow him to do it. Thinking back, I know there was nothing I could've done to stop him. Fortunately, he healed my body instead of injuring it.

Near the end of his procedure, he rubbed a brown liquid on different parts of my body. He said it was a mixture of herbs, tree bark, and other things I don't remember. He referred to it by its Chinese name that I also don't remember. I don't know what he did, and I really don't care. What I do know is that when he was finished, I could easily move my legs. I wasn't 100 percent, and my bruises still hurt, but I was much better than before. I thanked him and then proceeded to find out what I really wanted to know.

"Michael. What's going on?"

He helped me to my feet and whispered in my ear, "I will tell you, but first, come in here."

I followed him into the living room. My legs were still weak, so Sifu held me by the arm. It took a moment for my eyes to adjust to the light, but when they did, I couldn't believe what I saw. I stood there with my mouth gaping wide, unable to speak. It was as if there was a surprise party going on and I was the last to attend.

Ali, Seiko, and Uncle Clyde were in my house. As happy as I was to see them, I was even more confused. A mix of emotions caused me to stand silent with wide eyes. I looked back and forth at everyone. They sat silently, smiling back at me. Michael stood to my right just inside the doorway, allowing me time to take it all in. I knew that he could tell exactly what was going through my mind.

Uncle Clyde was an older, wise man whom Michael introduced me to years earlier. Together, they taught me more about Music and Life than anyone else ever had. I was shocked to see him sitting with his arm around Seiko. They acted as if they were best friends.

"Howdy do, son," Uncle Clyde greeted in his distinctive tone.

He offered a friendly nod. I didn't know what to say. I stared at him and Seiko.

"Kiladi!" Seiko said, pointing at Uncle Clyde.

She leaned over and kissed him on the cheek. He smiled and gave her a squeeze. I couldn't believe what I was witnessing. It was beautiful but baffling. I thought Uncle Clyde had died years earlier, but now it seemed that he'd been in Tokyo teaching a young girl how to play drums. I was as happy to see them as I was stunned.

When I was first introduced to Uncle Clyde, he was living under a bridge in downtown Nashville. He told me that he chose to live that way. I didn't understand it at the time, but once he explained, I found his reasoning both enlightening and sensible. He chose to live as a homeless person because it was the best way for him to be left alone. According to him, being homeless allowed him to do his work undetected and unnoticed, which is how he preferred it. I understood his logic, but in my opinion, he should have been playing and teaching music. He sure taught me a lot, and he was still the best harmonica player I'd ever heard.

Uncle Clyde was a spry older man, although I never found out his actual age. The one time I asked, he responded with an unusual answer.

"As much as I'd like to be older, I's only as old as I's allowed to be. I's doing my best though." I never asked again.

Seiko and Ali sat on opposite sides of Uncle Clyde. I was elated to see them. I assumed that the black van had brought them here, too. I wondered if they'd also been blindfolded. They looked happy—much different than the last time I'd seen them. I glanced back and forth, not knowing who or what to ask first.

Unexpectedly, the familiar sounds of bells and chimes rang from the kitchen. It had been years since I'd heard them. I knew what it was immediately. More accurately, I knew *who* it was.

"Isis!" I screamed, her name blurting out on its own. I inhaled and looked to my right, holding my breath with excitement.

A very short woman waltzed out of the kitchen wearing a flowing blue dress. Although I couldn't see them, I could tell that she had small bells and chimes strapped around her ankles. The cheerful sounds brought a smile to my face. I looked closely and yes: her very visible mole was still in place just under her bottom lip. I laughed out loud at the memory of watching it bounce up and down as she spoke.

"I'm very happy to see you, my child."

Her voice gave me chills. I hadn't heard her Eastern European accent since she accosted me in a bookstore years earlier. It was a short encounter but one I will never forget. Seeing her in my house caused memories to come rushing back, and I welcomed every one. Like the day we first met, I was speechless. I couldn't remember ever being so happy to see a group of people in my life.

Isis strolled toward me with her arms open wide. My eyes welled up with tears. I wanted to run to her, but I was in shock. I looked around the room. Isis, Uncle Clyde, and Michael, my three wonderful teachers, were all in my house. This was a first. My two new friends were also there, and one of them was a student of Uncle Clyde's. That was a strange coincidence. I stood there hugging Isis when another curious thought entered my mind. Putting two and two together, I looked at Isis and then at Ali. He nodded his head and smiled, confirming my notion.

"Yes, my brother. Essah!"

"It's a small world," I replied, shaking my head.

Isis picked up a glass and handed it to me.

"Here, my child, zis is for you."

Her accent was as strong as ever, and she remembered my favorite beverage. I took the glass and gave her another squeeze. I'd forgotten how short she was. Her head barely reached my chest. Isis made me feel tall. I loved her for that.

I'd only met her once, but she'd had a profound effect on me. We met in a bookstore where she was working, or maybe not working. I never figured it out. She knew I was a musician as soon as I arrived. The only thing she talked about was space and the number zero. At the time, I had no idea who she was or why she was making me listen to her.

As crazy as it was, the few minutes I spent with her changed me forever. When I asked her if she knew Michael, she responded with a crazy nonanswer. I should have figured it out when Michael also skirted the question. Seeing them together for the first time, I was satisfied to finally know the truth.

I tried again to walk, but my left leg gave way. Ali stood up, took the glass of juice from me, and set it on the table. With him on one side and Michael on the other, they helped me into my seat. I tilted my head and looked at Ali. Reading my expression, he gave me a big hug and whispered in my ear.

"They will explain. No worry, my brother." Then his expression changed. "Well, maybe a little worry."

He wasn't smiling. That didn't comfort me at all.

"I don't understand," I said. "I'm happy to see all of you, very happy, but I don't get it. I'm so confused."

"Drink, my child, drink," Isis said as she returned my glass. "Don't worry. We will answer everything to you. Zer is no hurry. First, let us have a look at your knee."

"No hurry?" Michael questioned. "I hope you're right, Isis, but I'm not so sure. *We* may need to make the next move."

Uncle Clyde chimed in. "Settle down, Michael. Let the boy relax fo' a minute. We're safe here. Isis is right. Let's take care of that leg first."

Michael walked into the bedroom. Isis walked into the kitchen. Seiko asked a random question.

"Victor, what's your favorite animal?"

"What? What do you mean?" I asked as I reclined in the chair.

"Just name an animal," Ali replied. "Any animal you like."

I didn't know what that had to do with anything, but I played along. I carefully thought about my answer. My favorite animal is a dragon, but that's fictitious. I could pick a dog since that was my childhood pet, but that would be too normal. Not knowing what it was all about, I decided to name something random—the first animal to pop into my mind. I closed my eyes. *This will be a stretch,* I thought. Little did I know how accurate I would be.

"A giraffe," I answered. "How about that?"

Both Ali and Seiko burst with laughter. Seiko actually fell onto the floor, holding her stomach.

Uncle Clyde nodded his head with a sly smile.

"What's going on? What's so funny?" I asked.

"Did it work?" Isis asked, walking in from the kitchen.

"Like a charm," Uncle Clyde responded.

"What?" I asked. "Did what work?"

"I don't believe it," Ali exclaimed.

"Me too," Seiko said, while picking herself off the floor. "It so easy. Music really powerful!"

"Come on, guys. Tell me what's going on." I was curious and wanted to be let in on the secret.

"Essah taught us a trick," Ali told me.

"Oh no," Isis stated, looking at me. "This is no trick. Only serious. Listen closely, my child."

What she told me was amazing. It was similar to a technique Michael had shown me years ago, but Isis enhanced it. It is a powerful tool and a potentially dangerous one. The ability to place a thought in someone's mind can easily be abused by a person with bad intentions. Because of that, I'm reluctant to share the technique here, but I will trust you to treat it wisely, knowing this tool can also be used for good. Here's the simple version of what Seiko and Ali did to me.

While I was asleep, Isis taught them how to infuse Music with energy—it could be a thought, a feeling, or an image. Seiko and Ali decided on a random word they would try to get me to say. Together, they chose the word *giraffe*. While playing softly in the key of G (for *giraffe*), they pictured the image clearly in their minds and then placed that image inside the music. Next, they imagined it traveling into my bedroom and landing on top of me. That was it. Other than the music, the whole process had been carried out in their minds. Since music is a vibration that penetrates the listener, lacing it with an emotion makes it that much more potent. Even though I tried to trick them with my answer, I'd played right into their plan.

I remembered hearing music while I was lying on the bed, but I'd thought it was part of a dream. Maybe that's what gave me the idea to hum into my mattress.

I looked at my friends and shook my head. Seiko was still laughing. Isis was looking at me. Her face was stern. I knew what it meant. This was not a game to be played around with. I nodded in affirmation.

Michael returned and knelt in front of me. He was holding an attractive box. From inside, he produced a large pair of headphones. Instinctively, I recoiled in fear. He assured me that they were safe. "These are special phones from Gus," he told me.

I didn't know who Gus was or what made them special, but after what I'd been through, I didn't ever want to wear headphones again.

"Don't worry," Michael said, "these are for your knee."

That didn't make any sense, but I was relieved not to have to wear them on my ears.

Michael raised my left leg and placed it on a cushion. Isis brought a pair of scissors from the kitchen and used them to make a long cut up the side of my pant leg where, unbeknownst to me, I had a large abrasion on the outside of my left knee. It had been throbbing the whole time, but I hadn't realized the severity of the wound. I also wondered how they could have known about it.

Michael plugged the headphones into a small audio player and pushed a button. He then placed the headphones over both sides of my knee. I froze with a look of shock. All I heard was silence, but what I felt was loud enough to arouse my curiosity.

"What is that?" I asked.

"Your special song," Michael answered.

"What? 'Amazing Grace'?"

"Exactly!" he replied.

"You mean, you're playing it for my knee?" My expression must have shown bewilderment. I picked up the headphones and listened through one ear just to be sure.

"Sit back and relax and allow it to work." Michael chuckled as he repositioned the Music around my knee.

I felt a little silly. I was sitting there with a pair of headphones fastened to my knee. Isis gently rubbed the top of my scalp while Michael adjusted the cushion. Maybe it was working. It was definitely doing something. At first, the pressure from the headphones caused a bit of pain, but soon after, all I could feel was a pleasing energy flowing through my leg.

Michael reminded us that Music is energy and that she can be used for many things. Like medicine, we don't have to focus on it or believe in it to reap the benefits. But when we consciously and purposefully engage our feelings with Music, her power (and ours) grows. Currently, because Music is ill, we need to increase our efforts. Michael told us that feeling and listening at all times is a good way to help her.

According to Michael, certain songs resonate differently with different people. If we can find the right songs and match them with the right people, miracles will happen. He remembered my connection with this song. That's why he felt it would be a good choice. He told me that allowing Music to work on my knee would help her as well as me.

Using live musicians was Michael's first choice, but because we needed to have a group discussion, these particular headphones were the next best option. Apparently, they transmitted more frequencies than others. They would continue to work while we talked. Before then, I would have thought placing them on my knee was a crazy idea. Actually, it *was* a crazy idea! I'd learned a lot from Michael and his tactics, and although this one seemed to be working, I still put it at the top of my "crazy" list.

"Okay. Let's catch him up on everything," Michael told the group.

"Please do," I replied, "and don't leave anything out."

Michael took a seat in the chair directly across from me. It was the chair I used to refer to as Michael's Chair. That was where he'd done a lot of teaching during our time together. It was ironic: he and I were sitting in the exact same places we sat on the first day we met.

Everyone took a seat except Sifu, who remained standing in the bedroom doorway. There was one empty stool in the corner of the room. I offered it to him. He shook his head. Michael told me that Sifu always preferred to stand.

"Who is he?" I asked, trying to whisper.

I don't know why I was asking Michael when Sifu was standing right there. I guess I was still a bit suspicious of him. He was the only one in the room I didn't know. I'd also seen him emerge from the bushes and grab my friends. I wanted to know what that was about.

"I'm your Sifu," he answered from his position in the doorway.

"My who?"

"Your Sifu," Michael responded. "Your teacher. He will help prepare us for what we have to do."

"What *we* have to do?" I didn't like the way that sounded.

Michael explained, "Yes. Years ago, you learned that Music was sick. Since our time apart, the situation has rapidly worsened, and someone is trying to speed up the process."

"They doin' a darn good job, too," Uncle Clyde added.

Michael replied, "That's true. They do appear to be succeeding. She is already disappearing in places."

"Yeah, Michael, I met a kid named Jonathan just a few days ago. He was a good bass player. I had just started giving him lessons, but he disappeared—totally gone. His apartment was empty. I don't know what happened to him. I made a copy of the measures you gave me. I was gonna share them with him, but one of the measures was gone. I mean, it just disappeared off the paper."

Seiko laughed, which seemed out of place. I didn't think it was a laughing matter. Just then, Sifu spoke.

"Someone's at the door. I'll get it."

"Sound like Jonathan. I hope he found it," Seiko said.

I didn't understand. I don't have a doorbell at my house and I hadn't heard anyone knock. And which Jonathan was Seiko referring to? As soon as I turned to look, there was a knock at the door. I looked back at Michael. He smiled. Sifu unlocked the door and a familiar face walked in.

"Jonathan!" I yelled. My mind was swirling.

"My drum! You found it!" Seiko screamed.

He was carrying her djembe. I didn't know how he had

acquired it and I didn't really care. I was so happy to see him. Seiko leapt from her seat and met Jonathan at the door.

"Thank you, Jonathan. I so happy you get it for me."

"You're welcome, Seiko," he replied.

They also acted as if they knew each other. Again, I looked at Michael.

"You were asleep longer than you think," Michael told me. "We had to get started without you. When we heard that Seiko's drum had been left in the taxi, Jonathan went to retrieve it."

"How did he know where it was?"

"Jonathan is gifted" was all he said.

Michael walked over and began speaking with Jonathan. Seiko took her seat and immediately began banging on her drum, which kept me from hearing what Michael and Jonathan were saying. After their brief conversation, they sat down with us. Without acknowledging me, Jonathan took the seat to my left. I raised my hand as if I were in school.

"Yes, Little Victor. You have a question?" Michael asked with a smile.

"Jonathan." I pointed to my left. "Please explain."

"Hi, Victor. It's good to see you, too," Jonathan responded. He looked me in the eyes and extended his arm. I shook his hand and turned back to Michael. I wanted answers. I wasn't angry, but I *was* disappointed. I felt deceived. I didn't know what had happened to Jonathan. I thought he might have been captured, hurt, or worse.

"Teaching," Michael answered. "You needed to teach."

◆

"Teaching completes the circle of knowledge."

"What does that mean?" I asked.

"We hoped you would have start sooner," Isis responded.

"Yeah, but you was lazy," Uncle Clyde added.

I wasn't sure if he was joking or not.

"I almost started—" I wanted to explain, but Uncle Clyde cut me off.

"Yeah, I know you *almost* did, but you didn't, son."

"Zat's why we had to send ze boy."

"Really? Are you telling me you guys sent Jonathan for me to teach?"

"Yes, my child. We needed you to complete ze circle, you see?"

Michael added, "You kept missing your opportunity and there was no more time. Virginia was our last hope."

"No way!" I exclaimed. "We met by chance. I found him by accident. I almost didn't even open the door."

"But you *did* open the door, right?" Uncle Clyde asked.

"Of course I did."

"And you think you did it all by yo'self. Is that right?"

"Well, I thought I did."

Uncle Clyde leaned forward as he spoke. "Learnin' from us was jus' the beginning. Yeah, if you runnin' in a race, it might be best to start in a crouched position, but you ain't supposed to stay down there. You needed to stand up and learn to teach, son."

"Zere was not much time, so we push you a wee bit."

"Even when it appears as such," Michael added, "nothing happens by chance."

I lowered my head and shook it from side to side. Ali and Seiko sat quietly. I motioned toward them.

"So, did you send them also?"

"No," Michael answered. "Music orchestrated that. Yes,

we played our part by combining our intentions, but Music did the rest. She made it happen."

"That doesn't make sense," I said.

"I know" was Michael's simple reply.

It sounded crazy, but I had learned to accept crazy as normal when I was with him. Although he was conducting himself more seriously than I remembered and was not wearing a bizarre outfit, the unusual circumstances remained.

I'd learned a lot about Music. I'd even spoken with her, but I couldn't understand how she could bring strangers together from around the world. Somehow we had all managed to end up at my house. Did Music really orchestrate that? Was it possible? Uncle Clyde, seemingly reading my thoughts, offered an answer.

"You see, the air you breathin' right now is the same air they breathin' in Japan, Africa, Russia, or anywhere else in the world. There ain't but one air. There ain't but one water. All the water in the world is connected. Music is the same. There ain't but one. And once you connect with her, now I mean *really* connect with her, you got to feel her, you see; and once you do, you have the chance to connect to everybody else who feels her in the same way. Most people do it at some time or another. They just don't realize what they doing. They wonder where all their ideas come from. They don't know that they comin' from all over the world. That's what happened to you kids." He pointed to Seiko, Ali, and me. "Y'all just tuned into the same frequency. That's all. Michael, Isis, and me, we connect whenever we wants to. Lil' Johnny here, he's getting pretty good at it, too."

"Aiii?" Seiko exclaimed. "We talk with Music?"

"I knew it!" Ali said. "Music give us connection! That is how I know your name before." He pointed at me.

"Right!" I responded. "That was amazing! It didn't make sense, but it did make sense. I'd done the same thing with Jonathan. I just didn't understand how I'd done it." I looked at Jonathan. He flashed a gentle smile.

"Yes," Isis added. "We can connect to each other, ze animals, our great Mother Nature, and all kinds of objects if we care to. Everything is a vibration, but ze most powerful vibration is love. Ze more we love, ze easier it is. Music helps us connect with each other because we love each other and we love Music."

"But what if we don't love each other?" I asked.

She offered a curious look. "Why would you choose to do zat, my child?"

"We can make sense of it later," Michael interjected. "Right now, we need to move. Jonathan, do you have the manuscript I wrote?"

Jonathan grabbed a piece of paper off the table and handed it to Michael. It was a piece of music staff paper with something written on it. Michael looked at the paper and then handed it to me. I was surprised. It was the same fourteen measures he had written for me years ago, but like my copy, one of the measures was missing. I looked at Jonathan. He shrugged his shoulders.

"I was actually working on them just before you arrived at the apartment. I wanted to be prepared."

"What do you mean? You knew I was going to show them to you?"

"No. Michael knew. He just wanted me to get a head start. All the measures were there in the beginning. A few days later, when one disappeared, Michael told me to leave."

"Were you in danger?" I asked.

"No," he responded. "You were."

"More importantly," Michael interjected, "Music is in grave danger, which puts the world in grave danger. If we do not succeed . . ."

I waited, but he didn't finish his sentence. Jonathan said that I was in danger—in danger of what? I was about to ask but Ali spoke first.

"What we do now? Can we stop it from happening?" he asked.

"Well . . ." Michael glanced at Uncle Clyde and then at Isis. "I hope we can. We will do our best. That is why we are all here. Together, we make a strong team, but first we have to prepare, and then we have to act. We will see what happens."

"But wait! I was in danger?" I asked.

"Not as much as you in now," Uncle Clyde answered.

Again, I couldn't tell if he was joking. He wasn't smiling. An image of the strange man I'd seen at the bottom of Jonathan's staircase flashed through my mind. That didn't calm my nerves.

"No worry, my child." Isis placed her hand on my shoulder. "Zer is never a need for worry. We are here together. All is okay."

I wasn't sure about that, but her comment did bring a bit of relief. I took a deep breath and tried to calm myself.

"How do we prepare?" I asked.

Michael, who always seemed to be in control, offered an answer.

"Isis, Clyde, and I will keep working on the plan. Jonathan, good job today. Rest for now. You can go back out tomorrow. Seiko, Ali, and Victor, you will begin working with Sifu first thing in the morning."

"What do you mean?" I raised my head and gestured toward the bedroom doorway. "I didn't know he was a musician." I looked at Sifu. "What instrument do you play?"

Sifu didn't respond. He leaned back against the wall and folded his arms. His smile was unreadable.

"Sifu," Michael explained, "he does kung fu."

"Really?" I asked. "Like Bruce Lee stuff?" I was surprised and excited.

"Exactly!" Michael answered.

"Did you like my Kato mask? Nice touch, eh?" Sifu held the mask in the air.

"He will show you a few things that will hopefully help us in the times ahead," Michael added.

"What? You mean, like, we're gonna have to fight?" I asked.

"The way you responded out there, let's hope not," Sifu teased.

"Hold on now, Sifu. He sho' nuf got away from you one time. Don't act like that didn't happen," Uncle Clyde added with a chuckle.

"That's just 'cause the Hornet never showed up. I had to do all the work myself," Sifu retorted with a wink.

Sifu was intimidating but comical. I found out that he was sent by Michael to rescue my friends and me. He'd worn the mask just for fun. Like me, he was a fan of *The Green Hornet,* a 1960s television show costarring the legendary Bruce Lee as Kato. Sifu even referred to his van as the Black Beauty, the same name that was used for the vehicle in the show. Because Kato wore a mask, Sifu did the same. According to Sifu, his kung fu teacher was a classmate of Bruce Lee. I'm sure Sifu used wisecracks to deflect the fact that he could easily rip someone apart. His position in the doorway offered him a perfect view of the whole room. He remained there with his arms folded, ready for action— Kato mask in hand.

"So, he was the one who grabbed Ali and Seiko?" I asked.

"Yes. He saved you also. Let me explain," Michael answered.

Michael referred to the strange men as Phasers. Somehow, they could render Music inaudible by reversing its phase. Like noise-canceling headphones that cancel unwanted noise for the listener, the Phasers were using their headphones to cancel out all music in the surrounding area. Michael knew that their blinking headphones were involved, although he wasn't sure how.

I was familiar with the musical term *out of phase*, which refers to an audio signal being reversed. It had something to do with a waveform going up when it's supposed to go down, or something like that. That's all I knew. I'd never totally understood it.

I did remember hearing musicians refer to a sound being out of phase. I never totally understood what it meant, but every time the sound engineer flipped a switch, reversing the phase, the sound came back much fuller. Somehow, the Phasers could cause sounds to go out of phase, and apparently, they could do it from a distance. I couldn't understand how that was possible. Michael wasn't sure about it either but surmised that as Music's health declined, the Phasers' power increased.

According to Michael, we are most susceptible to Phasers when we are not living our highest ideals. Low self-esteem, dishonesty, selfish ego, and similar attributes bring our vibrations down. It is as if we put ourselves out of phase, which makes the Phasers' job much easier. When we are individually out of phase, it diminishes our connection to Music. In turn, we connect with each other less.

Michael said that we were all connected by Music. I could understand that up to a point, but I still didn't understand how that led Michael or the Phasers to us. Michael felt we were rapidly reaching the point of no return and that it would take as many of us as possible to keep it from reaching that low point. So far, eight of us were all we had. That didn't make me feel too good.

I knew a lot of musicians, but I wasn't sure how many of them would help if asked. I wasn't sure who would even believe me. I wouldn't have blamed them if they didn't. If I hadn't had my own direct experiences, I wouldn't have believed myself either. Hopefully, our team would grow, but for the moment, the entire team was sitting in my house.

I asked Michael what would've happened if Sifu hadn't rescued me. He said I would have been rendered into a deep state, like hypnosis. After that, he didn't know. The Phaser was trying to reverse my personal phase by causing me to become fearful. It definitely worked. I was scared like never before and that made it easier for him. I could feel myself losing control as I descended deeper and deeper into his gaze. Michael said it usually takes years to reverse a person's phase. Done over time, we don't realize it's happening. With me, the Phaser was doing it all at once.

Apparently, the Phaser was about to put headphones on my ears. I could feel their power as he approached. He dropped them when Sifu came to rescue me. Sifu, thinking they were mine, brought them back to the house. With Isis and Uncle Clyde at the ready, Michael put them on to see what effect they had on him.

Because Michael was totally aware and unafraid, the headphones had little effect, but once he purposefully changed his mental attitude, he began to slip into a deep trance. Isis and Uncle Clyde watched closely as his awareness began to slip away. At the last moment, they brought Michael back by singing and playing Music for him, or more accurately, they played *at* him.

Their experiment confirmed that awareness, feeling, and real Music are the keys to beating the Phasers, and as Isis made clear, love is essential. It is when we are unaware, living with lower ideals, or playing uninspired Music that the Phasers launch their sneak attacks on us. Before we know it, our lives have changed in ways that are often imperceptible until it's too late.

Somewhere along the line, the Phasers began to focus on Music, realizing they could reach their goals faster by doing away with her. In this way, they could attack humanity as a whole instead of individually. It was a crazy concept, but there were too many incidents that seemed to confirm its truth. Music herself told me that people don't feel her anymore and that we'd forgotten how to listen. It was starting to make sense.

I thought about the many times I'd relinquished an

ambition or good idea because someone had talked me out of it or because I'd lost focus for some other reason. I could remember countless gigs where I felt uninspired and hadn't given it my all. I wondered how many times I'd been purposefully thrust out of phase. One thing I knew for sure, even though the Phasers may have been involved, I had no one to blame but myself.

Michael recognized the effects of the Phasers decades earlier and had begun searching for a way to combat them. Knowing he would need help, he searched for suitable pupils. My friends and I were three of them. Jonathan was another. He found that younger musicians made the best students but were also the most vulnerable to the Phasers' influence.

Everything Michael told me caused more questions to form in my mind. I also wanted to fill him in on all the things my friends and I had discovered. Michael said we would find time to share all our thoughts and ideas as time unfolded. First, he wanted to continue discussing the plan they'd begun working on. He seemed to have an urgency to get started. How to get started, I wanted to know.

"How do we stop them?" I asked.

Isis replied, "We already told you. It's actually very simple. So simple, it's difficult."

"Then what we do?" Ali asked.

"Feel!" she answered. "Feel deeply, honestly, and as much as possible. Hug each other. Speak to each other. Recognize and respect each other. Sing together and play with Music together. Ze most important of all: love each other and love yourself."

"Right!" Michael remarked. "Music brings people together,

not only to feel, but to agree on what we feel. That is powerful! And that is why Music is an important force for the Phasers to demolish. It is extremely important that we continue to feel Music."

"We gots to feel each other, too," Uncle Clyde added. "Even from a distance. Feel one another."

"That does sound simple," I remarked.

Uncle Clyde stood up.

"Maybe it do fo' you, but society as a whole done lost touch. Most people ain't got time for feelin' no more. We too busy. We done forgot how to do it. Those who do remember get prescribed a pill so they can forget again. Now that's a shame, ain't it? Don't do that, son. Don't eva' be afraid to feel, and neva' be afraid to show how you feel."

"Hai," Seiko added. "People call me weak if I show my feelings."

"You definitely ain't weak," Uncle Clyde said, waving his finger at his young pupil.

Seiko hit her drum three times. The sound was dull and muted.

"My drum!" Seiko said. "It still no sound right. No feeling. Out of phase, I think."

"Jonathan!" Michael called.

Jonathan hopped up immediately and grabbed the drum from her.

"Place it outside," Michael instructed. "It may be infected."

"Bye-bye, drum. I hope to see you again," Seiko moaned.

Jonathan carried it outside and closed the door behind himself. I was curious. I looked at Michael and pointed at the door. He explained.

"Everything is a vibration. It does not matter what you

call it or what it looks like. Phasers are peculiar. Somehow and for some reason, they have figured out a way of reversing the phase of some vibrations but not others. It is not difficult to understand as a concept, but it is dumbfounding how they do it with Music. I do not totally understand it."

He furrowed his brow and shook his head. That was the first time I ever remembered hearing him say he didn't understand something. He usually had all the answers. It was frightening.

Michael continued, "We change our own vibrations all the time and we can even change someone else's. You see, ideas are vibrations. Change your mind and you have changed your vibration. Persuade someone else to change their mind and you have changed their vibration."

"But Michael," I asked, "can you really change someone else's mind? Don't they actually do it on their own?"

"Exactly!" he answered. "And it is the same with the Phasers. I do not think they can change your vibration without your permission."

"Do they need our permission?" Ali asked. "At my church, the bell did not ring. I give those men no permission to do that."

"Wes ze bell moving?" Isis asked.

"Yes," Ali answered.

"Are you sure it was not ringing?" Michael asked.

"Oh! I see. Maybe it ring, but I did not hear it? Is that what you are saying?"

"Yes."

"I did not think of that."

"When we begin to act in ways we know are inappropriate, we give permissions we do not realize we are giving. We open ourselves up to many invasions."

Ali, Seiko, and I lowered our heads. We understood completely.

"How do we stop them?" I asked.

"Stop giving permission," Michael answered.

It sounded easy, but I knew it wasn't.

"What about my drum?" Seiko asked.

"I don't know," Michael answered. "It may be infected somehow. If so, we do not want it in the house."

Ali spoke with concern. "But Jonathan. Do he get infected?"

Michael answered, "Jonathan does not seem to be affected by the Phasers. His brain is wired differently. He is good to have around."

I wanted to be like Jonathan. I felt inspired.

"Michael, I'm ready. Just tell me what to do. When does our training start?"

"Right now!" Sifu answered.

Abandoning his position in the doorway, Sifu walked across the room and stood above me. He carefully folded his Kato mask and placed it in his back pocket. I had no idea what his intentions were, but I cast my suspicions aside. We needed to act and I was ready to begin. I looked up at him and nodded.

"Stand up!" he ordered, taking a step back.

The headphones fell to the floor as I wobbled to my feet. My legs were weak and tingling from sitting too long, but the pain in my knee had drastically diminished. I took one last sip of juice and steadied myself.

"Okay. I'm ready."

"Show me your fighting stance!" he ordered.

"I don't fight and I'm pretty weak right now," I answered.

"Pretend you do and pretend you're not," he responded.

It took a moment but I understood.

Recalling an episode from *Kung Fu*, an old television show starring David Carradine, I adjusted my weight and raised my hands in front of my chest. I closed my left hand into a fist while keeping the other hand open palm up. I didn't know what I was doing, but I hoped my acting would help me pass the test.

Sifu looked me up and down before responding in a gentle tone.

"Very good. You're a natural. This is going to be easy for you and fun for me. You can drop your hands."

I was proud of myself. I'd faked my way through. My arms were sore, so I was happy to lower them to my waist. As soon as I did, Sifu slapped me in the face—hard!

"First lesson!" his voice boomed. "Never drop your guard!"

I didn't like my first lesson.

Pre-Pair

◆

Never underestimate the power of doing something wrong.

First lessons are often the most memorable. Mine lingered in my mind as well as on my left cheek. Afterward, we were dismissed for the rest of the day. I retreated to my room to allow my body and my ego to heal.

As soon as I lay down, I recalled the events that had transpired over the last twenty-four hours. I'd been chased, kidnapped, and rescued. I'd lost new friends and found old ones. I learned about a group of people who were attempting to bring humanity down by eradicating Music. And now I was being told it was time to start combating them, but I didn't know how we were supposed to do it. I was curious as to what other preparations were in store. So far, I'd only been slapped in the face. It was a whirlwind of a day. After all I'd been through, I sure didn't feel ready for a battle.

I sank deep into the mattress, clinging tightly to my

mother's handmade quilt. It felt like only minutes had passed when I was awakened by Sifu's valiant voice at the brutal hour of six A.M. The announcement echoed from the other room that we'd be starting in thirty minutes. I hurried out of bed and walked straight to the kitchen for a satisfying cup of juice. I never liked the flavor of toothpaste mixed with juice, so I'd formed the bad habit of quenching my thirst before taking care of my dental hygiene. (I keep telling myself that I will reverse the order one day.)

Other than Sifu, I seemed to be the only one awake, or at least the only one up and about. I hadn't seen anyone as I walked into the kitchen. The door to the bathroom was open but it was empty. I glanced back into the living room but still didn't see anyone. Where was everybody? Someone had to have slept on the couch. A blanket was still lying on the floor. Not even Sifu was present.

Being careful to keep my noise to a minimum, I grabbed my cup and quickly walked back to my room to get dressed. Maybe everyone was outside and I was running late? It hadn't felt like thirty minutes had passed, but I knew how time could seem to fluctuate when I was sleepy.

I'd just closed my bedroom door when I realized I'd felt very little pain during my walk to and from the kitchen. My legs moved easily and my arms didn't hurt at all. I still had a few scrapes, but they no longer hurt unless I pressed on them, which, for some reason, I kept doing. No amount of sleep could've made me feel so good so quickly. I knew something must have happened, or more accurately, someone must have done something.

Years ago, I'd witnessed Michael and Uncle Clyde heal a man who'd been hit by a car. They'd done it, primarily, by singing to him. The man was bleeding and unconscious, but after a few minutes, he was sitting up fully awake and alert. Somehow his wounds had been miraculously healed. It was more than amazing, but at the same time it seemed very natural. I've never seen anything like it before or since.

As I maneuvered around my room, I thought about how I rarely appreciate feeling healthy. It only enters my mind after I've been sick or injured. I spent the next few moments standing alone, celebrating my body and appreciating it for all it had been through and had provided me. Sifu's voice invaded my thoughts.

"Twelve minutes!"

I didn't know what I was getting dressed for, so I put on my usual attire—sweatpants and a T-shirt. With a few minutes to spare, I brushed my teeth and put on my shoes. As I entered the living room, I found Sifu sitting in Michael's chair. Knowing we were alone, I quickly recalled that he liked jokes, so I tried one of my own.

"Let me see your fighting stance," I said with a smile.

"You're looking at it," he answered without changing his position.

"What do you mean?"

"My fighting stance; this is it."

"But you're sitting down."

"Very observant. You *are* the chosen one. I see why Morpheus likes you." At least he was smiling now.

"Very funny," I answered, recognizing his reference to *The Matrix*. "But how can you—"

Sifu interrupted, "Why would I ever get into a fighting stance? Wouldn't that put my opponent on guard by letting him know I was ready to fight?" I hadn't thought of that. "Like cheese to a mouse . . ." He held his thumb and index finger close together. "I want to lure my opponent in. I want to look inviting, like an easy target. I never want to give him a chance to prepare. And then, by the time he realizes it's a trap, bang! It's too late!"

Before I could react, he sprang out of his seat and thrust his fist into my face, holding it mere millimeters away from me. I could feel the heat. Fortunately for me, he stopped just short of impact. How he'd made it across the room so quickly was startling. I barely saw him move. I stood frozen, unable to move. He smiled. I looked down and noticed his foot on top of mine, preventing my retreat. I looked up. He nodded and slowly backed away, retaking his seat. His point was clear.

"That was amazing!" I remarked.

"I know. Sit down." I guessed he wasn't interested in compliments.

Sifu didn't look intimidating. Actually, the contrary. He looked like the type of person a bully would pick out of a crowd. He was tall, skinny, and wore glasses. His reddish-brown hair and pale skin made him stand out. Sifu seemed to embrace his vulnerable demeanor. I think he liked how it gave the illusion that he was weak, which clearly worked to his advantage.

Choosing Sifu as a target would be a huge mistake for any bully. Sifu had tremendous power and speed for his size. I'd witnessed both. I couldn't understand how a man so thin could generate so much force. Curious, I took my seat on the couch and waited. After about a minute of awkward silence, he began.

"It's like a finger pointing away to the moon." He pointed his right index finger at an imaginary object in the sky.

I thought I heard someone laugh. I looked around but saw no one. *Must have been my imagination.* I aimed my attention back at Sifu, recognizing his reference. He must have been a movie enthusiast, this time quoting Bruce Lee's character in *Enter the Dragon.*

Having seen the movie multiple times, myself, I continued the dialogue.

"Don't concentrate on the finger or you will miss all the heavenly glory."

That was one of my favorite movies, but I didn't know what it had to do with anything—unless he was merely trying to find a sneaky way to slap me again.

"You are blind but not deaf," he remarked.

Now I was really confused and had no idea what he was referring to. He was also using a fake Asian accent. I started to ask about it, but he beat me to the punch—almost literally.

"Do you work out?" he asked.

"Yes. Well, not as much since I moved to Nashville, but I used to play a lot of sports."

"I can tell. You look pretty fit," he responded.

He was right. I was fit. But I had a hunch that he was luring me in, baiting me again. The fact that he had given me a compliment raised my suspicion since the last one had resulted in a slap to my face. *Like cheese to a mouse.*

There was a phone book lying on the side table. I guessed he'd brought it in from the kitchen drawer. He stood and held the book in front of his chest with both hands.

"Hit it," he instructed. "As hard as you can; hit it!"

He wanted to test my strength. *Here's my chance.* I would

show him how much power I had. I hadn't thrown many punches in my life, but I felt that I could deliver a pretty good blow. All he had for protection was a phone book three inches thick. With all of my weight on my rear foot, I balled my fist and cocked my right hand way back.

Sifu warned, "Don't miss."

I smiled and threw my blow before I felt he was ready. I hoped it would add to the shock. My fist made a loud smack as it hit the surface. Sifu rocked back and actually looked surprised.

"Wow!" he said. "That was amazing! You must lift weights."

I should have noticed the trace of sarcasm in his voice and the slight smirk on his face, but I was too proud.

"No. I've never lifted weights, but like I said, I do work out a bit." I inadvertently puffed up my chest.

Sifu handed the book to me. I should have been smarter than to take it. He instructed me to hold it against my chest as he had and to really brace myself. I stood with my left foot forward, holding the book firmly with both hands. Realizing it was my turn to take a blow, I bent my knees and steadied myself. I was nervous.

Sifu placed his right fingertips lightly against the book and told me that he would hit it without pulling his hand away first. I looked down. His hand was open and relaxed. *No problem.* I straightened my legs and relaxed. That was my next mistake.

"Remember, I'll punch it from right here." He tapped the book with his fingertips. "I won't pull my hand back at all. Ready?"

"Of course," I answered, cockier than I should have been.

Sifu smiled, and before I knew it, I was flying backward through the air in slow motion. I landed on the table behind me, knocking it over. The wind had been completely knocked out of me. I lay on the ground unable to breathe.

I shook my head, wondering what had just happened. Then I felt something move underneath my legs, and whatever it was, was laughing. To my surprise, Seiko poked her head out. She'd been hiding beneath the table under a blanket. If it weren't for the table, I would have landed on top of her. She was laughing hysterically. I was totally confused.

"You okay, Victa-san?" she asked, trying to control her laughter.

I rolled onto my side and lifted my legs off her. Because I still hadn't caught my breath, I couldn't speak. I leaned back and stared at the ceiling.

"Blind! I told you," Sifu said.

"Yes, my brother, but not deaf."

It was Ali's voice. I raised my head in time to see him stand up from behind the couch—the same couch I'd been sitting on.

"Seiko, you almost gave us away. And brother, you almost stepped on me when you go to the kitchen." He was laughing, too.

My couch was placed in the middle of the room, which meant I had to walk behind it to get to the kitchen. I remembered seeing a blanket lying on the floor when I'd first walked by. Thinking back, it was a very lumpy blanket. I hadn't considered that someone could be hiding underneath. Sifu helped me back onto the couch.

"What's going on?" I asked, still struggling to catch my breath.

"You must learn to see," Sifu answered.

"I thought *I* was the blind one," Seiko teased.

"I can see," I answered.

"Tell me what you see," Sifu said.

"What do you mean?"

"Look around."

I sat up and glanced around the room. At first, I didn't notice anything out of the ordinary, but then, there in the corner, I saw Uncle Clyde standing motionless between my bass guitar and the bookshelf. I could have easily seen him . . . if I had only looked.

"I don't believe it," I said. "I must have walked right past you a few times."

"Yes, you sho' did. I could've reached out and grabbed ya. But keep looking. You ain't done yet." Uncle Clyde came over and took a seat next to me.

I stood up, fully alert, and spun around slowly in a complete circle. Partway through my second turn, I saw a book fall from the same bookshelf Uncle Clyde had been standing next to. I glanced up and noticed Michael lying on top. It was remarkable how he managed to make himself look so small and invisible.

I pointed. Michael hopped down effortlessly. I was reminded of how fluid his movements were. I'd seen him hop fences, bound up and down hills like a deer, and run without breaking a sweat. I smiled as I walked over to him.

"I like this game. It's fun," I remarked.

"This is no game," Michael answered. "Look behind you."

I turned and saw a pair of dark sunglasses staring at me merely inches from my face. Horrid images of Phasers flooded my mind. I screamed instinctively. Michael caught me as I fell backward and gently lowered me to the ground. I looked up at Isis, who was dangling the glasses above my head. Somehow she'd quickly and silently snuck up behind me without me noticing. That was a bit alarming.

"I can usually hear you coming from a mile away," I told her while trying to hide my embarrassment.

"Yes, my dear, and zat's exactly why you didn't hear me now."

It made sense. Her approach was usually preceded by the sounds of bells and ankle bracelets. This time, I hadn't heard anything. She either wasn't wearing them or had secured them somehow. Because of that, her presence was not on my radar.

I felt ashamed. It seemed like no matter how hard I tried, I could do nothing right. I lay flat on my back and exhaled heavily. Sifu, recognizing my emotional defeat, offered some encouraging words.

⊕

"Never underestimate the power of doing something wrong."

I thanked him. He could tell that I didn't fully understand. He walked closer and stood above me. I looked up at him from the floor, ready to be chastised.

"Hey! Lighten up, dude. Babies fall, but they get back up every time. It's through falling that they eventually learn to walk." Sifu helped me to my feet before continuing. "So, if you want to improve at anything, be accepting of your mistakes. Believe it or not, even I make mistakes. I know it's

hard for you to believe, but I am human . . . sometimes."
He smiled and winked. "Seriously. Even a slingshot has to
pull backward before it can propel forward." I looked at Ali.
Our eyes met. Sifu continued. "Making mistakes is okay.
Embrace it, accept it, and learn from it. Repeat that enough
times and, like my punch, you will no longer have to pull
back at all."

Sifu returned to his normal position in the bedroom
doorway as Michael reclaimed his usual chair.

"Find a seat," Michael said.

Seiko, Ali, and I took our seats in front of him.

"Now, everyone, listen and pay attention."

He waited for Isis and Uncle Clyde to take seats before
he continued. Uncle Clyde sat next to Seiko. Isis knelt on
the floor. Although he gestured to all of us, he directed his
comments to me.

"What we just did should not have worked. This is your
home, and even with your eyes open, you did not see. We
took very little time hiding ourselves. We grabbed a couple
blankets, hid behind your bass . . ." He gestured with his
hands as he spoke. "Uncle Clyde helped me onto the bookshelf while you were standing right over there pouring your
juice." He pointed toward the refrigerator. "Yes. You *can* see,
but you chose not to. You did not use your awareness. Even
without paying attention, you should have noticed us."

He was right and I felt embarrassed about it. It was *my*
house. I knew it very well, but it was that familiarity that
caused me not to see. The fact that I knew my home meant
that I no longer paid attention while I was there. I'd become
too comfortable. That was why they could hide in plain sight.
I only paid attention to where I was going. I lowered my head.

"Don't waste time feeling bad about it," Michael offered. "This could have happened to any of us. Believe me, you are more aware than most."

"I don't feel that way."

"You are focusing your energy in the wrong direction. Turn your attention toward gratitude. Be thankful for the lesson and make a point to be better from now on. You can do it. We need you to do it. We have to remain aware from this point on. All of us!"

"Thanks, you guys. That was eye-opening, literally." I motioned to my friends and back to Michael.

I would no longer be caught with my eyes closed, especially while they were open. I looked at my friends. We nodded in agreement, taking in everything Michael said.

He continued, "When we enter a new place, we look around at everything. But after a few days, or sometimes after only a few minutes, we fall into patterns of looking at the same things over and over. We quickly develop blind spots. This demonstration should be a wake-up call."

"What do we do next?"

"How do you feel?" Michael replied, continuing his habit of answering a question with a question.

Ali answered first, stating that he felt guilty for being part of the lesson at my expense. Seiko added that it was fun even though she wouldn't have done any better if she had been in my place. I spoke last.

"Well, I was embarrassed at first, but now I feel good. I feel like I'm awake, reenergized. Thank you all for the lesson."

"You are very welcome," Michael answered. "It is always good to say thank you." He pointed at me. I nodded. "Do you know why I asked you to thank your bass years ago?"

I wanted to respond but I didn't have a good answer. I thought about the first time I thanked my bass as well as the effect it had on both me and my instrument. It made me feel closer to it. And as strange as it may sound, I would say that my instrument also felt closer to me. Feeling a bit self-conscious, I didn't respond.

"One day, you will learn to speak your mind, my child," Isis stated. "I hope it come soon."

"I teach him," Seiko replied.

"Yeah, yeah, lil' girl. You sho' ain't got no problem doing that," Uncle Clyde said with a laugh.

I looked at Seiko. Although I didn't always like what she had to say, I was envious of her audacity to say whatever was on her mind. Michael raised a finger.

"When you honestly thank someone or something, you inadvertently or purposefully give a part of yourself to that person or thing. The more you do it, the stronger and more permanent the bond becomes. Think about it: a team is always stronger than the individual players. So even before you play, pair up. Pair with your instrument. Pair with your audience. Pair with Music. Do it *before* you start a task. In other words: the best way to prepare is to **pre-pair**."

Wow! I didn't say it out loud, but I wanted to. I only knew one person in the world like him. He had a very special way with words. He knew how to use them to their full extent. He was also wise enough to insert a pause after saying something he knew needed time to sink in. I needed lots of pauses.

"Victor, your bass had been waiting years for you to recognize it. That is why it jumped on your shoulder as soon as you reached for it. It was out of gratitude."

"Michael, you're amazing!" I couldn't hold it in. "I never told you that story. I know that I didn't. How'd you know about that?"

"You have no idea all the things you have told me."

I hadn't told anyone that story. I could never fully understand how he always seemed to know things he had no way of knowing. But, again, he was correct.

Years ago, I had spent close to thirty minutes thanking my bass. It was the first time I'd ever done it. It was a sincere and powerful moment. Once I was finished, I reached down to pick it up, and it leapt off the bed onto my shoulder. I was stunned. I stood there in shock, hunched over the bed with my right arm stretched out. The bass should have slid down off my shoulder, but it didn't. It felt lighter than usual. I also felt lighter than normal. It may have been my imagination, but it felt as if my bass was thanking *me*. I actually said "You're welcome" out loud.

Michael allowed my thoughts to play out before he continued. "I want you all to thank each other. Right now! Say it out loud if you feel it."

We spent the next few minutes thanking and hugging each other. From across the room, I thanked all the instruments in my house. It was amazing how such a simple act could be so gratifying.

"Close your eyes and magnify your feelings," Michael instructed. "We have shown each of you how to do it." I could sense Michael pointing at me. "I showed you myself a few years ago. Do you remember?"

"Yes, I do."

Not long after I'd first met Michael, he showed me how to isolate a feeling and move it around to different parts of my body. This technique, he told me, could be used for relaxation or healing. Moving the feeling was not as difficult as I would've imagined it to be, but moving it was only the beginning. As Seiko and Ali had proven, a feeling or a thought could be sent across the room.

Michael was full of unbelievable techniques, and although I'd learned many of them, I hadn't continued to practice. I'd gotten lazy, plus I thought I would never see my teacher again. Now that he was here, that all of them were here, I felt thankful. I closed my eyes and focused on gratitude.

Almost immediately, I felt a warm sensation in my upper body. I allowed the feeling to spread down through my legs. Before I knew it, my whole body was filled with an abundance of warm *thankfulness*.

"Now, keep going. Make it bigger," Michael instructed.

My attention was split between what I was trying to do and guessing what he was going to ask us to do next. I wondered how well my friends were doing. Michael told us not to worry about each other, but I couldn't help it. I was having a very hard time staying focused.

"Isis, help him," I heard him say.

Immediately, I heard Isis whisper in my ear.

"Do not wrestle with your thoughts. Only notice that you are thinking zem."

I hadn't heard her approach, but I felt a light tingle in the middle of my forehead as if she'd touched it with a feather. Breaking the rules, I opened my eyes and saw her sitting on the floor at least six feet away. Her eyes were closed. I looked at Michael. He nodded.

I closed my eyes, took a deep breath, and did what Isis had suggested. Surprisingly, it worked. *Noticing* that I was thinking seemed to place me on the outside of the *act* of thinking. My thoughts were still active but they no longer controlled me. It was as if I could see them in the distance. As my thoughts weakened, the feeling of gratitude grew.

I emptied my mind and sat with the feeling for a while, allowing it to spread throughout my body. Once I was comfortable, Michael asked me to do something I'd never done before. He asked me to split the feeling into three pieces and to send one piece each to Seiko and Ali. The last piece, I was to keep for myself. I did what he asked before I allowed myself time to think.

I envisioned my gratitude as a large ball of golden light. Next, I sent the ball through the room until it was right between my two friends. Splitting the ball into two pieces, I watched it explode over them. As if on cue, Seiko gasped and spoke something in Japanese. Uncle Clyde whispered back to her in the same language.

"Yes!" Michael said. "Feel it."

We sat, feeling the sensations for at least an hour. It felt as if the whole room was filled with powerful energy. It was wonderful. Michael offered further instructions, as well as gentle comments whenever he felt us losing our connection. Although I had a sense of self, I felt connected to everyone else in the room.

With my eyes closed, I used my imagination to glance around the room. We were all surrounded by a yellowish glow. The glow filled the whole room but was brighter around each of our bodies. The thought that I was making it all up persisted, but that was okay. Michael often told me to make it *up,* stating that was much better than making it *down.* I was good at making things up. It was reality I had trouble controlling. Gradually, the line separating the two was thinning.

A familiar melody flowed through the air. I recalled the sound from years earlier. It was Uncle Clyde playing his harmonica. Although he played quietly, I could totally feel it.

The beautiful sounds amplified the resonating feeling in my body, or maybe it was the other way around. Either way, the tingling in my body grew. I hadn't felt this way since I'd heard Michael sing to some animals late one night in the woods. He often did things that would be labeled as crazy, but now I know that he was preparing me for something larger. As Uncle Clyde continued playing, Michael began to whisper.

"It's time to begin. We must keep our eyes open even when they are closed. My young pupils, you do not fully understand what is going on and there is no time to fully explain. But understand this: If Music is in danger, we are all in danger. That is a threat to the whole world. Not many realize it, and even fewer are brave enough to do anything about it, but we are here.

"Music brought us together, and we will act together. We have to stay linked. To succeed, we will not"—he paused and took a breath—"we *cannot* always physically be together, but through Music we will be united. We can recall this feeling. We *must* recall this feeling. You will know when the time is right. Isis, Clyde, do you have anything to add?"

"You told 'em straight. I ain't got nuthin' to add."

"I do," said Isis.

I heard her stand up. I didn't know if I was supposed to or not, but I opened my eyes again. Isis walked to the middle of the room and spread her arms. She spun in a slow circle as she spoke.

Music continued quietly in the background. I glanced at Uncle Clyde, who was sitting with his eyes closed and his hands in his lap. His hands were empty. I looked around and noticed that everyone's hands were empty. *Wait a minute. Where is Music coming from?*

"My children," Isis began. "We have been chosen. Mother Music has spoken, and like good children, we have listened. We have the knowledge, the ability, the wisdom, the desire, and now, we must have the strength. Most importantly, we have each other. We are family."

She retook her seat. I remembered listening to her years ago. When she spoke in her most serious tone, her accent vanished. On this day, she was very serious!

"Okay!" Michael concluded. "The time is now!"

Music faded. Everyone opened their eyes and looked around at each other.

"Wait!" Ali said. "Who was playing?"

"I know," I remarked, "I thought Uncle Clyde was—"

Just then, the front door opened. We all turned to look. It was Jonathan. I was happy to see him, but I didn't like what he had to say.

"Michael, get ready! They're here."

Time Signature

✦

Time is a suggestion, not a rule.

Jonathan told us *they* were here. I wanted to know who *they* were, but Jonathan closed the door behind him, choosing to stay outside. *They* couldn't be that bad, right?

"Michael, who's Jonathan talking about? Who's here?"

"Phasers," he answered. "Jonathan has been waiting for them all morning."

"Phasers? Coming here?" Seiko cried out.

I was just as alarmed. "What do we do? Should we sneak out the back door?"

Seiko grabbed Uncle Clyde who didn't appear to be worried at all. He actually had a smile on his face. On the other hand, Ali was wide-eyed and looked like he was just as nervous as I was. Isis? Well, she was being Isis. She stood nonchalantly in the middle of the room, twirling in a circle with her eyes closed. Her ankle bracelets were in full effect, rattling along and resounding with her every move.

"Isis, this is no time for dancing," I told her. A smile was her only response.

"Maybe it is, son," Uncle Clyde replied.

"What do you mean? Phasers are coming."

"Phasers are *coming*," he said, emphasizing the word. "So, dat means dey ain't here yet, ain't dat right?" His accent was in full effect.

"I guess you're right," I answered.

"It also means ain't nothing wrong yet, right?"

"Uh, yeah. I guess so," I replied again, although it still didn't calm my nerves.

"It also means yo' problems is in yo' head, and you projecting yo' imaginary problems on da *now*, ain't dat right?" I nodded. "Listen, son. One of these days you'll realize dat problems only exist in de future, and da future is all in yo' mind."

"Or in ze imaginary past," Isis chimed in.

I was being bombarded by accents. And I realized that both of theirs came and went depending on the effect they wanted to have.

"Dat's right," Uncle Clyde confirmed. "Time ain't nothing but a series of events. Events come and go, but *now* is always what it is. Things is always better right now. Remember dat. The time is always now. Just repeat dat phrase when things seem bad."

"The time is always now," I articulated.

"Ze past is history. Ze future is a mystery. But now is a gift. Zat is why it is called ze present."

"That's cute," I told her.

"Oh no, son. It's more than cute. Dat's how it is. Jus' keep sayin' it over and over: 'Now is a gift.' And at the same time, do yo' best in every moment. Doing yo' best and keeping yo' awareness on the beauty of *now* allows you to put yo' stamp on the current time. Yo' stamp is yo' fingerprint, and yo' fingerprint is yo' signature. Put yo' signature on the *now* and then carry it forward. Dat is how you create time."

"So, are you saying that I determine what my future will be by deciding what the current time is right now? Is that right?"

"Exactly! You got it! Only you can decide what the current moment is. Put yo' stamp on it. Put yo' signature on the current time. Dat's what we call a **time signature**."

"Whoa!" My eyes widened as I let it sink in.

Michael pointed at me. "Grab your bass, I may need you to play."

I picked up my instrument and took a deep breath. Hoping it would give me confidence, I repeated Uncle Clyde's phrase in my mind: *The time is always now.*

"Ali, go sit at the keyboard," Michael instructed as he looked around. "We need a drum for Seiko."

"It's outside," Sifu said. "You want me to get it?"

"No. Seiko, take this garbage can."

"Garbage can? I don't play garbage can," Seiko objected.

"Good! Play Music then. You know how to do that, right?"

Michael smiled as he handed her a small plastic pail. Seiko didn't appear to be happy, but she took it anyway.

"Listen!" Michael instructed. "You are sitting around waiting as if you need an instrument to play Music. Look at Uncle Clyde and Isis; we do not need anything. You see,

Music is who we are, and playing Music is an attitude, an awareness, an experience. We live in that place continuously. It is time for you to understand that."

Isis continued to twirl.

Michael was serious. I was more familiar with his whimsical approach. In the past he answered every question with a question and took his time guiding me toward my own conclusions. This time around, his tone was commanding and his expression was somber. He spoke with conviction and urgency as if there was little time.

Isis stopped spinning and stood to Michael's left. Uncle Clyde rose to his feet and stood just behind Michael and to his right. The three of them stared at us. We sat silently and listened diligently as Michael continued.

"If you listen closely, all the instruments in this house sound the same. They are silent. They do not make a sound until we touch them. That should make it clear where the Music is really coming from. Music comes through you, not the instrument. Be musical first! Join with her! Feel her! Most of all, stop waiting! Even if you never touch an instrument in your life, be musical! We cannot afford to wait any longer."

The three of them stood still staring at us. We stared back.

"Do it now!" Michael ordered.

Seiko readied her plastic pail and Ali placed his fingers on the keys. Just as I lifted my hands, Michael signaled for us to stop. At first I was confused, but then I realized that he wanted us to be musical *before* we played our instruments. I wasn't sure how to do that. I looked at my friends. They were also confused.

"What does it feel like to play Music?" Michael asked.

I closed my eyes and imagined playing the bass.

"Do not play the bass!" he ordered. "Play Music! Like actors in a play—they do not wait until they get onstage to get into character. They are already in character while back-stage putting on makeup."

"Dat's right," Uncle Clyde added. "We needs y'all to be musical now. Don't wait 'til the show starts."

I considered a different approach. Many years ago, Michael told me that one of the reasons children learn so quickly is because their imaginations are incredibly strong and vivid. According to him, the brain doesn't know the difference between imagination and reality, or *so-called* reality, as he so often called it. Adults often use their imaginations for the purpose of worrying, so Michael gave me a different strategy. He guided me to use my imagination to create a special *sacred* place that I can visit whenever I choose—a place that is delightful and safe and where I am in complete control at all times. He even had me place an individual marker near the entrance so that I can always find it easily. I was instructed to use my sacred place often and to always keep it tidy.

I imagined myself walking down a winding trail that led to a beautiful entryway covered in multicolored florae and flowing ivy. A few weeds scattered to my left and right reminded me that my place was underused. As my trail ended, I walked through my entry and found Music await-ing me. I welcomed her. Surprisingly, I could also feel the presence of Seiko and Ali.

I opened my eyes and looked to my right. Their eyes were closed. I wondered if they were imagining their own sacred places. Regardless, we were joined in Music. I could feel it.

"Well done," Michael said. "Keep that feeling."

I watched Michael as he turned toward the door just before Jonathan appeared from outside.

"Okay, here we go," Jonathan announced.

Jonathan closed the door behind him, standing just inside with his hand near the knob as if waiting for someone. Michael picked up my acoustic guitar and laid it on the floor in front of him. Then he took a seat in his chair. Uncle Clyde stood next to Seiko, who sat with the plastic pail between her feet. I could see Uncle Clyde's harmonica sticking out of his breast pocket. Ali sat next to the keyboard with one hand positioned on the keys. I strapped on my bass even though it wasn't plugged in.

I didn't know what was about to happen. Everyone stared at the door except Isis, who continued dancing with her eyes closed. Ali, Seiko, and I were the only ones who appeared to be concerned.

Slowly, Isis stopped spinning and faced the door with her arms spread in a receiving posture. Her palms were open and facing forward. She looked peaceful but ready. I sat peacefully, but I was definitely not ready.

"Come in," Isis said in a gentle whisper.

I didn't know who she was talking to until, almost immediately, a knock came at the door.

Jonathan grabbed the knob and looked back at Michael. He nodded. Jonathan pulled the door open to reveal two nicely dressed men holding briefcases. I was happily surprised. They didn't look menacing at all. They were smiling and appeared pleasant, not how I expected Phasers to look. I relaxed.

"Hello. May we help you?" Jonathan asked.

"We have a great deal for you today. We are passing

through your neighborhood with an exclusive offer, an offer of a lifetime. For just one penny—"

"Passing through our neighborhood?" Jonathan interrupted. "Our neighborhood starts way over there." He gestured to his left, then to their car. "You're not passing through. You just entered the neighborhood. I saw you drive up and park right here."

"That's correct, sir. We're starting with you. And because you are the first, we will give you and everyone in your household a special bonus." They opened their briefcases in unison. "For just one penny—"

This time, Uncle Clyde interrupted. "Ninety-nine songs fo' a penny? Dat's yo' deal, right?"

"Exactly! I see that you're already aware of it," the Phaser replied.

"Yes, I is." Uncle Clyde looked around the room. "So tell me this. How you gonna split a penny ninety-nine times?"

"It's a promotion, sir. Times are difficult for musicians these days. We're just trying to—"

"Yeah, Times *is* difficult, but it's just a phase, ain't that right?" Uncle Clyde raised an eyebrow and nodded.

Jonathan snickered. The men turned their heads, looking at each other and then back to Uncle Clyde. They didn't look happy. They took a step forward toward the open door.

Michael picked up the guitar and stood up. He began playing the guitar as he slowly walked toward the men. It was a gorgeous song I'd never heard before. It caused my skin to tingle. The men took a step back. Even in the midst of that tense situation, I was aware of how good Michael made my cheap guitar sound.

One of the men began to reach into his breast pocket. At that moment, Isis also began walking toward the door, simultaneously singing along with Michael's Music. The melody was vaguely familiar although I couldn't understand the language. Her voice was enchanting. I didn't want her to ever stop. The man froze for a moment before lowering his hand.

Then, as if choreographed, the two men closed their briefcases and slowly backed away, walking backward all the way to their car. It was a strange visual. Neither spoke a word or showed any expression, whatsoever. Once they drove away, Jonathan nodded and closed the door.

Jonathan turned around and smiled. Michael and Uncle Clyde joined in with laughter. Seiko, Ali, and I sat with blank stares. The men appeared to be harmless. A little strange, yes, but definitely harmless.

"Phasers?" Ali asked.

"Yes," Michael replied, still laughing.

"We won dat sparring contest, didn't we?" Uncle Clyde joked.

"Yes," Isis concurred. "Zey tried, buy zey couldn't match us."

I had been enthralled by her singing and wanted to know more about the song.

"Isis, your voice is beautiful. I don't remember ever hearing you sing."

She smiled. Then it hit me. The melody she sang was the same one I'd heard as I was being hypnotized by the man on the street. I remembered hearing it just before I was rescued. Her singing helped break the spell. At the time, I had no idea where it was coming from. Now I was sure it was her. I looked at Isis with adoring eyes. She stretched out her arms. I ran into them. "Thank you. You saved me!" Tears began to flow.

"You're welcome, my child. I wouldn't let those bad men harm any of my children."

"What did you do? How did you break the spell?" I asked.

"I sang to zem," she replied.

"You sang? That's it?"

"Oh no. I loved zem, too."

"What do you mean?"

Her reply was simple but wonderful.

"Music is good. Love is good. Music and Love together is ze best!"

Ali responded, "Music and Love put together. Wow!"

"Zat's correct. Everything is more powerful with Love inside."

"You's right," Uncle Clyde added. "It's the best way to treat bad people. You don't have to like 'em. You don't always have to be nice to 'em. But it helps everything and everybody if you love 'em."

"Everybody needs Love," Michael added.

"But wait," I interjected. "What about the salesmen? Are you sure they were Phasers? They seemed like nice people. Why did you guys treat them like they weren't?"

"Yeah," Seiko added. "Ninety-nine songs—that's a good deal, right?"

I laughed. Michael didn't.

He leaned the guitar against the wall and walked over to us. His eyebrows narrowed. The room became quiet. Michael motioned to Ali, who joined Seiko and me on the couch. Michael knelt down as close to us as possible, making it clear he was about to say something we should never forget. We sat huddled together, pre-paired to listen.

"The only reason it sounded like a good deal is because it

was not *your* Music they were selling. Imagine recording an album. You pour your soul into each song as if they are your children. Then, because you do not know any better, you sign those songs away for someone else to own. The songs are still important to you. They will always be important to you. They are your offspring, worth more than any amount of money, but you no longer own them. You will never own them again. As a matter of fact, your kids will never own them. Instead, a record executive's kids will eventually own your songs. And then"—he lowered his head and shook it side to side—"someone sells your kids . . . for a penny."

"Ahhh," Seiko groaned.

I hadn't thought about it like that. Whoever composed the songs the men were selling, or, more accurately, giving away, probably had no idea it was happening. Even if they did know, they could do nothing about it because they no longer owned them. I'd learned long ago that if I ever wrote a song, I should make sure to retain the publishing rights. I guess that was what Michael was referring to. I'd learned a similar lesson years earlier from my aunts and uncles.

While at a family reunion, I had asked my mom and her siblings to teach me an old gospel hymn I'd heard them sing to my grandmother during her final days. I was hoping to record the song for a future project. Before they would teach it to me, my aunts and uncles gathered around and questioned me as if I had to first pass a test. I didn't understand. They'd known me my whole life. Why not just teach me the song?

My relatives made it clear that the song was sacred and that they wouldn't just give it away to anyone—not even me. I thought about it. They didn't own the song; they didn't write the song; nor were they going to get paid for it. They wanted to know how the song was going to be used, who was going to play it, and why I wanted to learn it in the first place. They wanted to protect the sanctity of the song, ensuring it was not used for money or fame, but only for the purpose of placing Music in people's hearts. I realized, at that moment, that I didn't think that highly of my own music. It was a great lesson. A part of me woke up that day.

"I understand that," I told Michael. "Somebody is getting ripped off, that's for sure, but that doesn't make them Phasers, does it? It's not the salesmen's fault. Aren't they just trying to make a living? Were they really—"

This time, Seiko interrupted me.

"They were Phasers!" she said adamantly.

"What?" I asked. "How do you know?"

"No footsteps!" she answered.

I thought back and realized she was right. The men were wearing hard-soled shoes, but they made no sound.

"Seiko, you're amazing!" Ali exclaimed.

"Of course she is," Uncle Clyde said, proudly placing his arm around her. "I knew she was special the first time I saw her."

Seiko sheepishly looked up and flashed a gratified grin.

"What causes them to have no footsteps?" I asked, using Seiko's phrase.

"We don't know," Uncle Clyde answered. "Maybe it's 'cause everything they do is out of phase."

"Zey are very strange. Like ghost, zey come in many different forms, and most of ze time, you don't even see them."

"Yeah," Uncle Clyde added. "They used to take they time. Now they actin' fast, like they on a mission."

"What we gonna do?" Seiko asked. "How we stop a ghost?"

Sifu responded in his own way. "Just because someone's a ghost doesn't mean they know how to fight!"

"You have one-track mind," Seiko told him. "All you think about is hit somebody."

Sifu smiled and made a fist. We could hear the sound of his knuckles popping from across the room.

"Listen," Michael said, "Phasers have been around for centuries. They are not usually seen, but their presence is definitely felt. Affecting Music is only one way they get to us. They also influence our thoughts and decisions. Think about it. The actual pitch of Music has been changed. The quality has been drastically reduced. We know Music causes children to learn faster and broader. So, what is their solution? To take Music programs out of schools. Yes, Phasers do influence us, but we make our own decisions. When is the last time any of you have listened to a complete record?"

Jonathan, who had been sitting quietly, looked at me and winked. It had been just a few days earlier that we had listened to both sides of the record he had just purchased. We even read the credits together. I was happy about that. I started to mention it to Michael but chose to refrain instead. I was not proud of the fact that it was the first time I'd done it in almost ten years.

When I was a kid, my parents would put on an album and turn off the lights. We would listen to the whole thing as a family. Sometimes we'd listen to two or three albums in a row. Like Jonathan and me, we'd also read every word on the album jackets. But that was a thing of the past. I doubted there were many people who still did that.

I felt ashamed. It had been a long time since I'd purchased a vinyl record. I'd reduced myself to only buying single songs from the Internet. I rarely go to concerts anymore unless I can get in for free. How could I call myself a musician when I refused to pay to hear musicians play? What happened to me? Had I been phased? The answer had to be yes!

Uncle Clyde chimed in. "They actin' different now, Michael. They gettin' bold."

"And more powerful," Isis added.

Michael continued, "They definitely seem to be growing in every way. They are even allowing themselves to be seen. They were never this daring before."

"That's right," Uncle Clyde said as he looked at me. "They showed up to yo' house. They seems to got ants in they pants now."

"Zer numbers have increased, much more zan before. Maybe it's zer collective power zat makes zem zat way. But we have collective powers of our own."

"Maybe Sifu is right," Seiko commented. "Kiladi, why you don't pound them like you did that man in Shinjuku Station?"

"Oooh! Now you're talking. I like the way she thinks," Sifu responded.

"No, Baby Girl. This is totally different. That man was a bully. The Phasers, they something else. Pounding ain't gon' stop them."

"It can't hurt to try," Sifu suggested with a sly smile.

Michael added, "Phasers do not usually operate in a physical way, so they do not respond to physical opposition. We have to take a different approach."

"We must love them, right?" Ali asked.

"Yes, but it'll take more than that."

"What do you mean?" I asked.

"Music told you that she was ill, right?"

"Yes." Ali, Seiko, and I responded almost in unison. I wondered if they'd had conversations similar to mine.

"Why did she say she was sick?" Michael asked.

"Because we don't feel her," I answered.

"And we don't listen to her," Ali added.

Seiko chimed in, "Yeah, we only want to tell her what to do. Men always tell women what to do."

"We need to tell the Phasers what to do. How do we beat them?" I asked.

"Like we already told you," Michael answered. "Listen! Feel! Play! But it has to be real."

"And love them, too," I added.

"It sound too easy. Is that all there is to it?" Ali asked.

"No, my child," Isis responded. "Now more zan ever we also need to live an honest life. Music won't respond to us in ze same way if we don't. If we look at some of our past musicians, we will see zat it's true."

Ali began to cry. He dropped his head and covered his face. For a moment, all was silent.

Isis sat next to him, placing her arms around his neck.

Ali spoke through his tears. "I'm sorry, Essah. I knew I was wrong. I couldn't help it. I tried not to take, but I couldn't stop myself. I needed the money. It wasn't much, and I only use for good things. Please believe me." He buried his head on Isis's shoulder and started sobbing again.

"No worry, my baby. Ze past is ze past. Ze time is always now."

I thought about my own life and had to admit that I'd also begun to stray. Basically, I'd become bored and unmotivated. I'd lost my drive and made many excuses. I had recorded a major television show with a banjo player and had also completed a couple small tours. I'd even been mentioned in a local magazine. Instead of being driven by the experiences and the music, I'd become addicted to the compliments. When I didn't get them, I felt as if my audience was wrong. I knew that I was a good bass player, but I'd become dependent upon hearing it. I didn't realize it at first, but the little success I'd found had begun to steer my ego in the wrong direction.

I didn't want to admit it, but I'd also become driven by the money. It only took a few well-paying gigs to shift my focus. Rather quickly, the income became more important than the music. As soon as the gigs slowed down, my morale dropped. I waited for the phone to ring. I blamed everyone else for my lack of work. I did little to help myself. The thought of helping others never crossed my mind. Not being as forthright as Ali, I kept quiet. Regardless, I was reminded, once again, that my thoughts are never mine alone when I'm with Michael.

"The ego," he said, "is a powerful thing. It can be both helpful and harmful. Your ego is your fingerprint. It is an individual stamp that declares you as unique and special. But *everyone* is unique and special. Everyone has their own stamp. As soon as you assume your uniqueness to be better than someone else's, problems will arise."

"You can be sure about dat," Uncle Clyde agreed.

Isis added to the conversation. "Actually, Life tries to correct ze problem long before you recognize it exist. But sometimes we don't listen. By the time we realize ze problem, it can be very difficult to reverse ze situation."

"Dat's right," Uncle Clyde added in his usual vernacular. "If'n you let yo' ego cross the line, yo' whole life will start to accelerate . . . downhill, dat is."

"That is the only way to pick up speed while coasting," Michael added.

"Downhill!!" they said in unison. Both of them started laughing.

Surprisingly, Jonathan raised his hand as if he wanted to make a comment. We all turned to face him. The room became silent as we awaited his words.

"You don't believe in yourself because you don't know who you really are. You think that you're not good enough, so you need other people to tell you. That's okay. I'm happy to tell you if that's what you want to hear. But it won't be real until *you* know it to be true. It's not who you think you are that keeps you from getting there. It's who you think you aren't. It doesn't matter what anyone else says. You are always enough."

Although he spoke softly, his words hit hard. I felt as if Jonathan was speaking directly to me, and I'm sure my friends felt the same. Ali avoided eye contact. Seiko buried her head in Uncle Clyde's chest. I searched for a way to change the subject.

To avoid further scrutiny, I decided to make a quick exit into the kitchen. I was surprised by the lack of pain in my knee as I stood up. I sat back down and asked a question.

"Michael, my body was hurting when I went to bed. I feel much better now. Did you do something or was it the stuff Sifu put on my skin?"

"Like I told you before, all healing is instant. You are either sick or you are well."

"I remember hearing that, but I know you did something. What did you do to make me better?"

"You are already a healer. Your body heals itself all the time. In this world, it just takes time to do it. So, you do not need to be a master of healing. You need to be a master of time."

Michael had told me those same words years ago. I was hoping for a different answer this time, but I guess he felt I needed to hear it again. He'd told me that I already knew everything I needed to know. Whether that was true or not, I was happy to have this opportunity to learn from him again. Uncle Clyde made it very clear.

"That's right, son. You's a lucky boy. Most of Michael's students only see him once, and only fo' a few days at most. You had him fo' a long time, and you still gettin' a second chance. Michael must see something in you. Make sure you listen to him this time."

Michael rarely liked taking credit for anything. He didn't want me to think that I had to rely on him. He often delayed the truth just to keep me guessing. In that way, I would have to think for myself. He wanted me to realize my own power. He wasn't fond of teachers who were so invested in their teaching that they neglected to invest in their students.

I looked at Michael sheepishly. For some reason, I felt like I was taking advantage of him. I looked away.

"Now that I think about it," Uncle Clyde laughed as he continued, "it ain't the way he teaches; it's the way he don't teach that screws people up. You might not be so lucky after all."

"Don't listen to that old man," Michael retorted. "Sometimes he don' knows what'n he's talking about."

"I's de only one you eva' needs to listen to, son. And Michael, if'n you's gon' try and talk like me, at least say somethin' useful." Uncle Clyde was smiling heavily.

That was the way I remembered those two, always cracking jokes with each other. Seeing them act so serious lately was uncharacteristic and made me realize the severity of our situation. I relaxed as they had, causing me to feel comfortable enough to ask a question that had been on my mind for a long time.

"Hey, you guys. I'm curious about something I've heard both of you talk about—time! Michael, you said I need to master it. Mastering time? Is that really possible?"

"Of course it is," Michael answered. "Like choosing a time signature in music. Time can be whatever you want."

"What do you mean?"

"People do it all the time without realizing it."

"How so?"

"What happens to time when you are doing something you really enjoy?"

I thought before answering.

"Time seems to go by really quickly when I'm enjoying myself, but it slows down when I'm bored."

Ali chimed in. "Sometime hours pass like minutes and other time it go slow like molasses."

"Exactly!" Michael responded. "And when you are in a car accident?"

"Time stop," Seiko answered immediately. "I remember my father driving. Car crash into us. I see everything in slow motion. My drink come out of my cup; glass fly through the air; at same time I see other driver's face. He have very scared look. Woman on side of road holding baby. She watching whole accident and our eyes meet each other. I see everything at same time. Very weird."

"Yes! That's it!" Michael said. "What makes time change like that? Whose decision is it?"

"I see your point," I responded. "Somehow, we make the change. Our perspective changes unconsciously, I guess."

"Right! Unconscious and on purpose."

"Michael, do you say we can change time whenever we want?" Ali asked.

⊕

"Time is a suggestion, not a rule."

Michael had a way with words. It sounded simple, but I still didn't understand.

Uncle Clyde tried to help.

"Listen kids—you are in charge. Time is bound by you, not the other way around."

"Can you teach us?" Ali asked.

"Another time," Michael answered. "We have work to do."

"Michael, please, one more question?" I asked.

"What is it?"

"Why did you come back?"

He answered in a serious tone. "I needed *you* this time."

"What do you mean?" I asked.

He pointed to his friends. "For decades, we have shared our knowledge with people all around the world. Most people do not adhere to our teachings. Something we were

doing was not working. That is exactly why I quit teaching."
He scratched his head. "People get inspired for a while, but
then Life takes over. After a while, they barely remember
we were there. You were different. Your instincts were strong
and you responded to them. That is why I sent many teachers, and also why I stayed around for so long."

"Long? You were barely here two weeks," I reminded him.
It was Uncle Clyde's turn to speak again.

"Think about it. You saw me fo' jus' a few days, and
Isis for jus' a few minutes. Think about all you learned in
that short time. To have Michael fo' more than a day was a
gift, son."

"I guess I didn't realize how lucky I was."

"It is true," Michael said. "I do not stay in one place for
long. Once I left you, I found more receptive pupils and
checked in on others. I always kept tabs on you, though. I
needed to see how fast you were developing."

"Or if you was developing at all," Uncle Clyde joked.
I think.

"Really? You were watching me? How did you do it?"

"I did it in my own way."

I didn't understand what he meant.

"Well, how did I do? Was I a good student?" I asked.

"I had to speed you up a bit."

"By sending Jonathan?" I asked.

"Exactly!"

"That's amazing! So you planned it all along?" I looked
at Jonathan. He smiled. Michael continued.

"Sort of. Actually, I needed you to learn from each other.
I needed both of you to grow. You see, the best way to continue developing is to teach what you know. Your lesson was

to teach him. His lesson was to teach you without you realizing it."

"Whoa! It makes sense now. I was supposed to be the teacher, but sometimes I didn't know who was teaching who."

"You were really good," Jonathan remarked. "But you needed a boost. We were moving along pretty well until Music disappeared from the paper."

"I never showed the paper to you."

"You didn't have to. I knew."

Michael responded, "I told you, Jonathan is special, but he still has more to learn."

"I've never seen it disappear like that before," Jonathan said.

"Neither have I," Michael replied. "It let me know I had to get both of you out of there immediately."

"Wait a minute," I said. "I got myself out. I had to run for my life!"

"Partially true. You are an adult. Jonathan is still a kid. There were some things you needed to see and do for yourself. Experiencing the Phasers firsthand was necessary. It helped prepare you for what is coming next."

"Next? You mean there's more? I could've died."

"Again, partially true. But we made sure you did not."

This time, Sifu spoke up.

"Yeah, bud. How do you think you made it back here? Don't forget who rescued you."

"Don't get me wrong. I appreciate it. We all do." I looked at my friends. "I just wish you would've showed up a little sooner."

"A lot sooner," Ali corrected.

"Geez! They're never satisfied, are they?" Sifu responded,

smiling at Michael. "If I hadn't scared that guy away, where would you be?"

Sifu seemed a bit arrogant, the macho type, which I didn't like. It seemed like his solutions always involved a competition, which he needed to win. And like Michael, he seemed to have the uncanny ability to read my thoughts.

"Listen, bud. People who are looking for problems often find them, and I don't mind if they find me. I love solving problems. The sound of one hand clapping is a beautiful sound. Two hands sound even better."

"You can't just beat up everybody," I countered. "There's always someone bigger and badder, right? Do you really expect to win every competition?"

"Competition? What competition? I have no competition! Therefore, I never lose."

"Isn't that arrogant?"

"Oh no," he replied, pointing a finger in my direction. "Don't mistake confidence for arrogance. Listen carefully." He leaned in close. "When you play your own game, no one can ever beat you."

He had a point.

Ali, sensing the tension, changed the subject.

"We come from all over, three different lands. How you guys know where we were?"

"I would never leave you, my child," Isis told him.

"I know, Essah. I could always feel you. I knew I would see you again." Ali grabbed her by the hand.

"You were my responsibility," Michael said, nodding to me.

"And I had the girl," Uncle Clyde concluded.

"I was looking for you!" Seiko shouted. "Why you no come get me?"

Uncle Clyde held her close. "Aw, Baby Girl. Everything is all right now, ain't it? We's together again."

"But how?" Ali asked. "How you know where we were?"

"Were you in Virginia, too?" I asked, addressing Michael.

"Don't worry about it now," he answered. "Just know that we are all connected. It is imperative that we remember that. Right now, we need to prepare for our next visit. Today was easy. We may not be so lucky next time."

I didn't like the way that sounded.

"Okay. What do we do next?" I asked.

"We play Music. But first, come with me. We need to get a new drum for Seiko."

"*Yatta!* A new drum for me."

Seiko hopped up and bounded to the door like a little kid. Michael instructed Sifu to get the van.

"Okay," Sifu answered. "But first, another lesson."

I didn't like that idea. Sifu left his position in the doorway and walked toward me. I recoiled in my seat.

"Don't worry," he said. "I just want you to be safe out there. I can't babysit you kids forever. The more relaxed you are, the easier it is to feel the Phasers. Here's an easy relaxation technique."

Sifu asked Ali and me to stand side by side in the middle of the floor. With everyone else in the room, I didn't think he'd pull the same trick as before, but I was still reluctant and kept my seat. Ali rose to his feet immediately. I hesitated. Seiko was instructed to stay where she was and to pay close attention. This time I wasn't the only participant, so I finally gave in and stood beside Ali.

Sifu told us to face him, relax our shoulders, and take five slow deep breaths. I could feel the relaxation starting right away. My chest rose up and down as my shoulders drooped toward the floor. Next we were instructed to open our eyes as wide as we could, blink them rapidly fifty times, and then allow them to slowly close on their own. I did as he instructed, paying close attention as I counted. At fifty, my eyelids were tired, so allowing them to drop was easy. As soon as my eyes were closed, Sifu slapped both of us at the same time—this one more painful than the first.

"What was that for?" I asked, holding my jaw.

Sifu smiled and raised two fingers. "Lesson number two: Don't trust anyone!" I'd fallen for it again.

Seiko ran over and grabbed Sifu by the arm. She didn't look happy. At least a foot and a half shorter than him, she looked up, pointed a stiff finger, and gave strict instructions.

"No fair, Sifu! Next time, you slap me, too!" She released his arm and stormed out the front door.

"Ooh . . ." Sifu responded with a satisfied smile.

"I like this girl."

Won for All

◈

Sometimes remaining silent is the best way to lead.

I'd learned long ago that Michael did everything for a reason. He didn't make a move unless there was a purpose and a lesson attached to it. This day was no exception.

"Let's go. We need to arrive at the music store before ten A.M.," Michael announced as he walked out of the kitchen.

Sifu went outside to start the van. I looked at the clock.

"Michael, it's almost ten o'clock now. The store is twenty minutes away."

"Do not tell me that," he answered. "And stop looking at the clock!"

Instinctively, I looked at the clock.

"I said, do not look at the clock!" he reiterated.

Michael walked out the front door without saying another word. Ali and I followed. Seiko was already beside the van, bouncing up and down with excitement. Michael turned around, waiting for Ali and me to catch up. Once the four of us were together, he gave strict instructions.

"From this point on, pay attention and do not look at the clock!"

Ali put his hand over his watch. "You want me to take it off?"

"No!" Michael replied.

"There's a clock in the van," I reminded him. "Do you want me to put a piece of tape over it?"

"No! Just don't look at it!" he answered.

"Why?" I asked.

Michael barked, "Because I said so!" I flashed a puzzled look.

"Just kidding," he answered with a sheepish grin.

"Good, 'cause that was a silly answer," I retorted. "What's the real answer? Why shouldn't we look at it?"

"Choice!" he answered. "Do it, or not, because of your decision and willpower. You always have choice. Take this time to exercise it."

"Choice. That's it?" Ali asked.

"No! *Now* is always the time. Looking at your watch pulls your awareness away from the present. Pay attention to everything that is happening now. Look around and ask yourself, 'What am I missing?'"

"'What I am missing?' I like that," Ali stated.

"Right!" Michael replied. "Plus, when most people look at their watch, the next thing they say is rude."

Not trusting himself, Ali took off his watch and placed it in his pocket.

We got into the van and buckled our seat belts. Sifu sat

behind the wheel and Michael in the front passenger's seat. I sat in the back, which had a direct view of the clock, making it difficult not to look at it. I followed Michael's order, though, and chose to look in the opposite direction, paying attention to things I usually ignored. I could tell that my friends were doing the same.

We drove in silence, which was quite satisfying, until we were jolted forward as Sifu rounded a corner and slammed on the brakes. A terrifying funnel cloud was spiraling toward the ground. I didn't know what to do. Like my friends, I sat frozen in shock.

Neither Seiko, Ali, nor I had ever seen a tornado before.

The massive swirling cloud had appeared out of nowhere. Darkness filled the sky in front of us, although we could see blue skies to our left and right. We could feel the power of the wind as it began to shake our vehicle and rattle its doors. I felt the intensity escalate inside the vehicle. Sifu put the vehicle into reverse and prepared to step on the gas, but Michael raised his hand.

"Don't move!" Michael whispered, keeping his hand in the air.

After a short pause, he lowered his hand and sat back.

"Maybe it won't see us."

That's an odd comment, I thought. How could the tornado see us, or not? I literally feared for my life, and I wasn't the only one, I'm sure. I could feel myself beginning to panic. But as we sat there, the tornado turned slightly to our left and glided right past us as if it hadn't seen us. *What?* (We found out later that the twister had quickly dissipated without causing much damage.) We were lucky . . . or *was* it luck?

I knew that Michael was, let's say . . . different. He always had his own rationale, but what sense did it make telling Sifu not to move? What was going through his mind as we watched our possible demise pass by so closely? I had to know. His response was eye-opening and beautiful.

"This is a momentous occasion and we are on a grand mission. I cannot believe Music would bring us all together just to tear us all apart."

For some reason, it made sense, like something my mother would've said.

In spite of our unexpected interruption, we arrived at the store in (what felt like) the usual amount of time. Michael removed his seat belt and opened the door. Sifu stayed seated and kept the engine running.

"What time is it?" Michael asked, exiting the vehicle.

He spoke and acted calmly, as if we hadn't almost died. I was still a bit shaken up. Although I had been hyperaware a few minutes earlier, I realized I still hadn't glanced at the clock.

"Can we look?" I asked.

"Sure, if you choose to," he answered without turning around.

9:56 A.M. That was impossible. I looked at Ali. He pulled out his watch and checked it. The time was correct. We'd done a twenty-minute trip in eleven minutes. As far as I could tell, Sifu hadn't driven any faster than normal. I hopped out of the van, catching up with Michael. My friends followed.

"How'd you do that?" I asked.

"I didn't do anything," he replied as he walked.

Seiko grabbed him by the arm.

"Michael, tell us. How you change time like that?"

"Time did not change; you did."

"What does that mean?" I asked.

"You paid attention. That's all."

"Of course, I paid attention. We almost died."

Michael stopped walking and turned to face us. He took a deep breath and offered one of his simple answers.

"Yes! Literally! You paid attention. You paid with energy. Energy was your currency. You see, when you give energy to attention, you literally 'pay' attention. Nothing is free. You must give to get, but you must first get in order to give, which means you can only give what you have already gotten. When you fuel attention with energy, attention becomes more potent. The best way to add energy is through emotion. Add that potency to the *now* and the *now* will expand. In simple terms: pay attention to *now*, and it will pay you back with more time."

He turned and continued walking through the parking lot. I stood, trying to make sense of anything he'd just said.

"Michael!" I yelled.

He stopped and turned. I ran ahead and asked another question.

"But Michael, sometimes it's the opposite. Sometimes time passes really fast. When I'm having fun, hours go by but it feels like minutes. Why does that happen?"

Michael responded quickly, seemingly without thought.

"It happens *because* you are having fun. During that time, you are *not* super focused on everything; you are gently focused on one thing only—the task you are trying to accomplish. If the task brings you joy, time will compensate. You forget to eat, and you are not hungry. You forget to drink, and you are not thirsty. Time recognizes your enjoyment and rewards you by passing unnoticed. You see, pay attention to everything at once, and time slows down. Have fun with moderate focus, and time zooms by rapidly. Although your awareness has a lot to do with it, time has a mind of its own and can change whenever it wants. But remember . . . time is always on your side. That's the simple answer."

There was nothing simple about it. I desperately wanted to understand, but I needed more time. Ironically, there was none.

Michael hurried through the parking lot. He was on a mission. I wanted to know what it was, but my mind was still occupied. I contemplated while I walked.

Whenever I'm running late, I will not give any attention to the idea of being late. I will do my best to be as efficient as possible and I will definitely not look at the clock. But when I want time to speed up, I will have fun. I smiled at the thought.

Michael slowed his pace as we neared the entrance of a megastore. A cacophony of musical instruments, similar to an orchestra tuning up, blared through the walls as we approached. There was a line of people outside and we could feel their excitement as they waited to enter. Michael stood for a moment with his eyes closed. His knitted eyebrows conveyed his discomfort.

"Preposterous!" he whispered in disgust. He opened his eyes and, disregarding the long line, continued in. We followed.

The store was in the heart of Nashville. It was a new chain that was popping up all over the country. We'd arrived during the second week of their grand opening. I'd never been to a music store that large. It felt like I was on another planet. Orange seemed to be their favorite color. The walls and carpets and every fixture in the store were in a variety of orangey tones. It actually made me thirsty.

"Michael, I don't have any money," I warned him.

"That's okay. I don't think we'll need it," he responded.

I didn't understand how we were going to buy a drum without money, but I suppose I didn't need to know. There were a lot of things I didn't understand about Michael. He operated in his own way at all times. I kept quiet and followed as he proceeded forward. Seiko, full of excitement, pranced in front of me.

Michael breezed past the entrance counter and right up to the nearest instrument he could find. He picked up a ukulele (without asking) and instantly began producing beautiful tones. I'd never heard him play that instrument before, but as he'd previously made clear, he didn't play instruments; he played Music.

His ability to play any instrument no longer dumbfounded me. If a sound can be produced, I guess it can be called Music, right? But Michael's ability to play all instruments as well as he does is still so incredible to me. I'd witnessed him achieve the impossible many times before, and there, in that store, another astounding experience was about to unfold.

Without tuning it first, he began gently plucking the ukulele. The instrument was barely audible with all the extraneous noise in the room. Then magic happened. Michael continued playing without increasing his volume. Like smoke filtering through a room, his Music slowly consumed everything and everyone.

Seiko, Ali, and I looked at each other. We were the first

to notice, but soon after, the people adjacent to us quieted their voices and began looking in our direction. They, too, were becoming mesmerized by the beautiful sounds. Reacting to the quieted voices around them, those who were slightly farther away instinctively softened their voices and began listening, first looking around in all directions before zeroing in on the source.

I watched as resonant ripples of Music flowed through the space. Like the effects of a pebble thrown into a pond, the concentric rings of Michael's Music expanded larger and wider, embracing everyone in the building. I could sense the sound emanating from him in all directions. I looked at Ali. His eyes were closed. Recalling an earlier lesson from Michael, I stood up straight, corrected my posture, and took a deep breath. With my eyes slightly out of focus, I looked at Michael again.

It was faint, but I could see waves flowing through the room, passing through everything they came in contact with. The feel of the store was completely altered. Customers and employees stopped what they were doing and looked to see what was happening. The whole building had become silent except for the beautiful sounds of Michael. If the walls could talk, they wouldn't have said a word at that moment. Michael and Music had slowly taken control of the whole building.

A crowd formed around Michael, Ali, and me. Seiko squeezed through and joined us in the center. She'd found a djembe somewhere in the store and began playing along. I was shocked by her gentle touch. I looked at Ali with my mouth wide open. We'd heard her bang on her drum in the back of the car, but this was much different.

With her eyes closed and her game face on, Seiko provided the perfect accompaniment to Michael. She handled her drum with the consummate elegance and artistry of a seasoned professional. The control and skill she displayed was evident even to the untrained ear. She played in a way that seemed far too experienced for someone her age. The crowd turned their attention toward her. Her childlike appearance added to the spectacle.

Seiko kept her beat steady, only offering slight accents in the spaces between Michael's phrases, in the same way one might respond with "amen" to a preacher. Their musical dialogue felt natural and effortless. No one would have guessed it was the first time they'd played together.

Onlookers jostled for position to get a better view of the kid playing the drum. We could hear comments circulating as they discovered she was a girl. "Go, girl, go!" a woman shouted. Seiko, "the little drummer girl," as she was instantly dubbed, had captured the hearts of everyone.

They continued playing for a few more minutes. Michael smiled and nodded at Seiko like a proud father. I was proud, too. I wished Uncle Clyde were there to see her.

Gradually, the Music faded into silence. Michael stopped playing but kept his hands floating silently above the instrument. Seiko followed. It was a dramatic finale. The audience stood motionless, holding their breaths, frozen in anticipation of Michael and Seiko's next move.

Michael seized the moment. In slow motion, he pulled his right hand away from the ukulele and raised it in the air. The whole building watched in silence. Then, with everyone's attention on him, he turned quickly and motioned toward Seiko. The crowd erupted simultaneously with screams

and applause. Seiko covered her smiling face in embarrassment. Ali hugged her hard. I glanced at Michael.

"That was incredible."

"Seiko was incredible," he replied.

Seiko was lost in the middle of the crowd with Ali by her
side. Michael walked in the opposite direction, easing his
way through the people until he stood on the outside of the
circle. I followed.

"You don't like crowds, do you?" I asked.

"I don't mind crowds. I just don't need them," he answered.

It was a good answer and I knew what he meant. Michael
never asked for a crowd, but whenever one formed around
him, he made the most of it. On this day, he directed all the
attention to Seiko. Somehow, he had played in a way that
made her stand out. I wanted to ask him how he'd done it,
but there were other things I wanted to know first.

"Michael, I saw what you did. You took control of the
whole store as soon as you walked in and you did it with
a ukulele, the quietest instrument you could have chosen.
How'd you do it?"

"Thank you. You could've done the same thing," he
answered calmly.

"I don't think so, not like that."

"I'm sure you remember the ten elements of Music. I
just used all of them, some of them more than others."

"Dynamics!" I said. "You used that one, for sure."

"Exactly!" he responded, turning to face me. "I used
dynamics to quiet the room, but I also used feel. If you
noticed, when we first walked in, the room had a particular
feel to it."

"Yeah, loud and louder," I joked.

"Right." He laughed. "I cut across that with a different feel, a different pulse even. The rhythm of the room was pretty fast, so I played slowly. The dynamics were loud and hard, so I answered with soft and quiet. I was also articulate and to the point. I chose an instrument with a tone that was different from any other sound in the room. I used notes and phrasing to create a simple melody that could quickly be learned by the subconscious. Everyone in the store memorized it whether they realized it or not. If my Music hadn't contained enough space, I may have added to the chaos instead of reducing it. Of course, I wouldn't have known what to do without having first listened. You see, I used all the elements of Music to achieve my goal, but it was how I used the elements within the elements that really drew them in. My technique worked pretty well, don't you think?"

I laughed and gave a thumbs-up.

The elements within the elements. I'd heard about that from Jonathan just a few days earlier. I was anxious to hear Michael expound upon the subject.

"Do you mean, like, you can find *dynamics* within *notes*, and *tone* within *space*?" I asked.

"Exactly! For example—"

"Wait!" I said as I spun around to alert my friends. "Ali, Seiko, come listen to this."

I needed reinforcement. Because I was sometimes slow to grasp Michael's concepts, I hoped they would be able to help. Also, I figured they were overwhelmed by the crowd. This would give them an excuse to break away. I was right.

"Thank you, my brother," Ali said. "They give the little girl no space to breathe. Everybody want to talk to her."

"Yeah!" Seiko added. "'Little drumma girl. Little drumma girl. You so cute.' They say it over and over." I could tell it made her happy, although she tried not to show it.

A few other people followed them over. Having heard Michael play, they were also curious to find out what he had to say. A store employee was among our small group. I'd noticed him earlier. He was dressed in bright orange and wore a wide smile on his face. He was the only one who'd greeted us when we entered the store. I wondered how he would respond to Michael's eccentric teaching style. Michael, in his best *Michael* way, confused us all.

"As I was saying, like family members, all the elements are related. For example, the mother can be found in the daughter, and the father in the son. But both parents can be found in both offspring. They are made up of the same DNA. They affect each other. A group of people get together and all is well. Change one person and it can change the whole feel of the room. Do you understand?"

Most of the people walked away baffled. I was used to Michael's methods. I trusted he would make it clear sooner or later. The only one remaining besides my friends and me was the young employee. He seemed intrigued but remained silent.

"Good," Michael said. "Now that they are gone, we can continue."

"What you mean? Why they have to go?" Seiko asked.

"They did not have to go," Michael answered. "But the fact that they did let me know that what I have to say is not for them. They will get their education elsewhere."

"Oh, I get it," I added. "When the student is ready, the teacher will appear."

"Not exactly," Michael replied. "That is not entirely

accurate." He pointed at each of us, including the employee. "The teacher is always present, but the student is not always wise enough to see. Here is a more accurate statement: When the student is ready, he will recognize the teacher."

Michael winked. The rest of us looked at each other with eyebrows raised. The store employee took a step closer, making it clear that he was ready.

Michael continued, "Music stores can be breeding grounds for abrasive energy. That's why Phasers like to come here."

The store employee wrinkled his brow, so Michael addressed him directly.

"Think about it, Brandon."

The employee was surprised to hear his name. He looked down to see if he was wearing a name tag. He wasn't. I patted him on the shoulder. "You'll get used to it," I told him. He shook his head. My friends and I smiled. Michael continued, looking at Brandon.

"You have only been open eight days, and you can already see a rise in musical problems at the store. Instruments have mysteriously gone silent. Heads on four of the drums are broken. Two fuses and three speakers have blown. And just the other morning, you found two guitars hanging on the wall with broken strings."

"Wait a minute. How did you know that?" Brandon asked, looking around as if searching for hidden cameras.

Michael ignored him and kept speaking.

"What did we hear when we walked in today?" He didn't wait for an answer. "I will tell you. It was chaos. There was plenty of noise but barely any Music. That is not a welcoming environment for anyone, especially if you have to work here all day.

"On a good day, you will be lucky to hear some Music coming from the pianos, but they are usually squashed by the other screaming instruments. Imagine if the employees knew how to do what I just did. They could keep order in the store at all times."

"I wish I could do that," Brandon replied.

"Stop wishing and do it" was Michael's response. "It would be a great way to discourage the Phasers."

"What are Phasers?" Brandon asked.

"Bad people who don't like Music," Seiko answered.

"There is a movement," Michael continued, "to diminish or end Music altogether. Phasers are carrying out the mission. Their effects have been seen and felt for centuries all around the world. They have been frequenting your store since you opened."

"Were they here today?" Ali asked.

"Of course. I'm not sure Music could sound so bad without them." Michael chuckled. "Actually, there was only one. I'm surprised you didn't see him walk out when I started playing. He was the only one in the building wearing headphones."

"Wait!" Brandon perked up. "You mean the guy in the suit is a Phaser? I've noticed him before. He comes here a lot. He never buys anything. He doesn't even talk. It's like he avoids us. When we walk toward him he walks the other way."

"I wish he had walked the other way the other night. He almost killed me," I commented.

"Really?" Brandon said. "He tried to kill you?" His eyes widened. "Should I call the police?"

"No," Michael answered. "You can't get arrested for wearing headphones. I can show you a better way to make them go away."

Michael pulled a guitar from the display and handed it to Brandon. We found out later that the guitar was Brandon's primary instrument. He must've wondered how Michael knew. Michael seemed to know everything. I was happy to be in his presence again. I hadn't realized how much I missed the many miracles that surrounded him. To him, they were common occurrences. I was excited at the prospect of witnessing another one.

"Listen," Michael instructed, motioning with his arm.

We glanced around the room, paying attention to all the sounds emanating throughout the store.

"What do you hear?" Michael asked.

Noises seemed to come from every corner of the store. We took turns answering, describing, in detail, all the sounds we noticed.

"Do you think the musicians can hear each other?" Michael asked.

"Yes. I think so," Brandon answered.

"If so, why are they *not* playing together?" Michael hunched his shoulders and then raised his right index finger. "I ask you this: In a room full of people, do individuals talk to themselves, or do they talk to each other? I will answer for you: people talk to each other. So, then, why do musicians play by themselves? I will answer that also. It is because they are not listening to each other and are not conscious of speaking with their instruments." Michael shook his head slowly. "That is why there is chaos in this room once again. Brandon, put an end to this nonsense."

Michael pointed at Brandon and then to the guitar. Next, he leaned back and folded his arms. Brandon looked at us for help. I shrugged my shoulders. Seiko readied her drum, but Michael raised his open hand. He wanted Brandon to do it alone.

"I don't know what to play," Brandon grumbled.

"Consider that a blessing," Michael responded. "Imagine if your audience already knew everything you were going to play; they would be bored and you would be disappointed. Use the element of surprise to your advantage, even with yourself."

I could see from the expression on Brandon's face that his brain was working in overdrive. But he was a bold one. He rolled with the punches and did the best he could without too much hesitation. Instead of backing down or retreating altogether, Brandon persevered and listened before he spoke.

"That guy's in one key . . ." He pointed to his left. "And he's in another. Hmmm, which key should I choose?"

Michael remained silent, his arms still folded. Brandon's eyes surveyed the room.

"Okay!" Brandon whispered. "Most people like blues, so I'll play a blues. I'll use Mixolydian and throw in some pentatonic and blues scales, or maybe I'll make it a minor blues. Should I play a shuffle? Or no, I'll do it in a funk style so that—"

"Stop! Stop!" Michael interrupted. He unfolded his arms and stepped forward, tapping Brandon on the forehead. "You are thinking too much. Theory is for the practice room, not the stage. Just listen like you were before. The room will tell you what to say."

"I don't know how to do it," Brandon responded out of frustration. He lifted his head and looked at Michael. "Can't you just tell me what to play?"

Michael replied, "Yes, I can and I already did. Stop thinking *what* and start thinking *why*. If your desire is true, it will bring about the *how*. Think back: How did you feel when I was playing?"

Michael gently tapped Brandon three times in the chest just above his heart. Brandon closed his eyes and took a deep breath before replying.

"I remember hearing soft, beautiful sounds. It made me feel calm. I wanted to know where it was coming from."

"Soft and beautiful got your attention and pulled you closer," Michael said. "Do any of these sounds grab your attention?" He waved his hand again, motioning across the room.

"Not in a good way," Brandon answered.

"How do they make you feel?"

"They actually push me away," Brandon responded.

"Perfect! Now you know how *not* to play."

Michael stepped back and nodded as if giving permission.

"Well, as an employee . . ." Brandon looked over his shoulder. "I'm not allowed to play while I'm working."

"You're not working right now. Play!" Michael ordered.

Without hesitation, Brandon fingered some chords. Michael stopped him right away.

"Listen!" he ordered. "Do not play the guitar. Play Music!" Michael reached over and detuned three of the strings. "There! That should help. Take what you hear, turn it into what you feel, and express *through* the guitar."

Brandon was in shock. He looked at me. I shrugged my shoulders, offering no help.

"Do not think. Tell me what you hear," Michael instructed.

"I hear clutter," Brandon said. "I want to turn it into music, but I don't know how."

"Life is choices. Stop choosing ignorance. Do it now . . . or not!"

Michael folded his arms again. His face was stern. Brandon took a frustrated breath.

"Try easy," I whispered.

I took a deliberate slow and relaxed breath. Brandon took the hint and followed my example. He placed his hands back on the instrument and tilted his head. Then, he responded with wisdom (and a bit of theory).

"I can do this." He took another breath. "I *will* do this." He shook his head. "No. I *am* doing this!" His confidence grew with each statement.

"Very good," Michael said. "Bring it all together—soft and beautiful."

The air-conditioning unit produced a little buzz in the key of B-flat. The ringing phone consisted of two notes, an A and an F. Brandon began softly playing a chord incorporating all three notes. Ali whispered in my ear, "G minor 9." He was correct. Michael gave an inquisitive but impressed look. I agreed. Brandon had made an interesting chord choice.

Brandon played with his eyes closed, his head swaying gently back and forth. Michael pointed at him and then to his own ears, letting us know that Brandon was really listening. Without looking, Brandon quickly and effortlessly retuned all three strings. Michael looked at Ali and me, raised an eyebrow, and nodded. We were all impressed.

Brandon's lowest note of the chord was a G. While playing, he seamlessly moved that note up a step, then up another half step, which turned the chord into a B-flat major 7. It was a very musical transition. The people closest to us responded to the change in tonality. The pleasant quality of the new chord drew people closer. Brandon's eyes were still closed, so I wasn't sure if he noticed, but Michael definitely did and began whispering instructions.

"Very good, Brandon. Now, amplify the volume gradually. Slowly . . . slowly . . . very good. Without losing your connection, open your eyes and look around the room. Notice the change you are causing. Now respond to it. Yes. You see the guitarist glancing in your direction. With intention, play to him."

"How do I—"

"Do not think *how*! Just make it happen!"

Brandon smiled as he looked around the room, pleased with his progress. The other guitarist nodded and gave him a thumbs-up, and then added melodic lines to Brandon's chords. Ali pointed at a keyboardist who had unconsciously begun playing along with the two guitarists. Michael nodded to us and winked.

"Now," Michael continued, "because I already used the soft and beautiful approach, I want you to go in a different direction."

Brandon instantly (and musically) switched back to his original chord and began adding more rhythms.

"Perfect," Michael said. "A strong groove will definitely get the bass player's attention."

A bass player looked in our direction. Brandon, feeling the excitement, altered his rhythms, making them busier and more intricate. Michael responded right away.

"No! Do not change your part. Adding fills will make him listen to you. You don't want that. You want him to feel you. Just keep it steady."

If there is such a thing as a minor miracle, this was surely one. Right there in the store, there were two guitarists, a keyboardist, and a bassist playing together, and all four of them were in different sections of the store. Michael nodded at Seiko. She repositioned her drum and joined the jam.

Seiko's rhythm helped propel the groove throughout the building. Patrons began nodding in sync even before they realized they were listening. It was amazing how easily it happened.

"Now," Michael said, "we can start the countdown. Ten, nine, eight, seven . . ."

Ali and I looked at each other. We had no idea what was going to happen. Once Michael reached the number three, he pointed at the store's office. At the count of "one," the door opened and the store manager looked out. Brandon turned back around but kept playing. The expression on his face was clear. He expected to be reprimanded.

The manager walked toward us with an angry scowl. His agitation was evident, but I noticed his attitude change as he approached Brandon from behind. His expression became that of surprise with a hint of curiosity. He started to reach for Brandon's arm but slowly retracted his hand. An interesting thought rolled through my mind.

⊕

"Sometimes remaining silent is the best way to lead."

The manager joined our small group, which was becoming larger as customers made their way toward the wonderful sounds. Standing directly behind his employee, the manager listened with one folded arm and the other hand under his chin. After a few moments, he nodded to himself and began strolling around the store. Gradually, his expression turned to that of surprise and satisfaction. When he came back to our area, he stood in front of Brandon and gave two raised thumbs. Big smiles shone on both their faces.

After a few more moments, Seiko began slowing her pattern little by little. Her gradual ritard brought the jam to its natural conclusion. The manager broke the silence with applause. Everyone else joined in.

The musicians made their way to the middle of the store and joined in a loving group hug. Celebrating their camaraderie, the audience gave a second round of applause. The newly formed ensemble linked arms and took a bow.

As the crowd dispersed and the store returned to normal, the five new friends continued talking. I stood back, enjoying their electrifying energy. I couldn't remember ever being that excited after a jam that I hadn't participated in. Then I realized their jam hadn't sounded like a jam at all. Theirs sounded like a song. Michael, who seemed to always know what to say, explained it perfectly.

"Most jams are sporadic and formless," he told me. "Musicians often jam with the intention of showing how good they are, waiting for their chance to solo. These musicians played as if they wanted to show how good everyone else sounded. They listened and made room for each other. There is no way for it not to sound good when you play with this kind of attention and intention. Imagine if all children learned how to incorporate a band mentality into their daily lives. The world would be as harmonious as the song they just created."

Ali joined in. "My church always feel the best when we all sing together. There is so much joy in everyone."

"All for one and one for all," I remarked.

"Yes!" Michael added. "When we work together, everyone wins."

Instantly, I saw the familiar phrase in a new light.

"All for one and **won for all**," I repeated. It sounded the same but took on a whole new meaning.

"Imagine," Michael continued. "What if politicians were required to learn to play an instrument? World summits could become world jam sessions."

"Now that would be cool," I said joyfully.

"Yes. We all become true brothers," Ali said.

"And sisters," Seiko added.

We shared a laugh.

The store manager had pulled Brandon aside. I couldn't hear what was being said. After a few minutes, the manager approached Michael.

"That was pretty amazing. I've never seen anything like that in my store."

Michael looked at me and winked. I could tell what he was thinking. *You have never seen this in your store? Whose fault is that?*

"Are you the manager?" Michael asked.

"Yes, I am. I usually don't permit my employees to play while they're working, but that sounded so good, I decided not to stop them. Brandon told me you taught him how to do that. I'm prepared to offer you a teaching job if you would accept."

Michael responded with a typical Michael answer.

"I am honored. I would be happy to teach here, but I like to teach from the top down. So, I would need to start with you. Are you okay with that?"

The manager hesitated. Michael glanced at me out of the corner of his eye before continuing.

"For this store to succeed, the aim to make money will need to take a back seat to the goal of fostering relationships. You start that by recognizing who your customers are as well as your employees. You have a special kid here." Michael pointed at Brandon. "If Brandon didn't have a brain of his own, I may have needed to teach him, but because of his intelligence, I did not have to teach him anything. I guided him; that is all. That is the key. People with assumed authority assume that others cannot think for themselves. Can you imagine a music store being managed by a businessman who has not played a note of Music in over three years?"

Michael leaned forward, tilted his head, and raised an eyebrow. The manager leaned back and responded with a stutter.

"Y-y-yes. Um, yeah. Well, anyway, thank you. Keep in touch."

"From the top down," Michael prodded.

The manager turned and walked toward his office. Michael had touched a nerve in him. I could sense the thoughts swirling through his mind. He stopped midstride and faced Michael once again.

"I'm gonna have to rethink my 'no jamming' policy." He looked in the air as if reliving a memory. "I may start jamming again myself."

"You will not regret it," Michael assured.

The manager nodded at Brandon. Brandon flashed a big smile.

"Hey," Michael called out. "This drum. She really likes it. How much is it?"

The manager surprised us all (everyone except Michael, I suspect). He walked back over and extended his hand to Michael.

"The drum? It's hers. She can have it."

Michael reached for his hand, but Seiko beat him to it. She grabbed the manager's hand and shook it vigorously while also bowing up and down.

"*Domo arigato gozaimasu!*" Seiko repeated over and over.

She knelt down and clutched the drum to her chest, rocking it back and forth like a baby. The rest of us, including Brandon, took turns thanking the manager.

Once the store manager returned to his office, Brandon told us that he could sense a difference in him. In Brandon's words, the manager's energy had changed. He couldn't explain it but said he could feel it. He'd been contemplating quitting the job but now felt like things would get better for him and the rest of the employees.

"I will hold him to it. I will make sure he jams with us," Brandon said with a hopeful look.

Brandon gave Michael a hug and the rest of us a wave. "I'll never forget this day," he said as he bounded off to help a customer (with a smile, of course).

People change after meeting Michael. Like him or not, you are better after being in his presence. His influence has lasting effects. He alters energy, and in most cases, no one realizes he's doing it. He spoke in a way that caused the store manager to think, and more importantly, reevaluate. Michael prefers this method. In his mind, direct answers often end a person's search, while answering a question with a question enhances the learning process. Michael leads his students in ways that help them find solutions on their own. It is a brilliant teaching method—one I hope to learn.

The store had returned to normal—well, better than normal. Although the customers filled the building, all the sounds were quiet and musical and the overall energy was peaceful. Seiko was beaming, holding her drum as if it were a precious baby. Just then, the manager came out of his office looking concerned.

"Hey! Did someone turn off the Internet?"

Slowly, all the musical sounds faded into static. Then the lights flickered.

"Oh no!" Michael whispered to himself.

I'd never heard him sound alarmed. It freaked me out. My whole body tensed. Michael's head turned toward the front door.

"He's back," he said in a soft voice.

Instantly, the whole store went dark. The front door swung open. I was startled. A beam of sunlight flooded in. I raised my hand, gazing through my fingers. My eyes adjusted to see a dark shadowy figure standing in the open doorway. Even though the sun silhouetted him from behind, I could see the red blinking light from a distance.

I was starting to really dislike headphones.

A Storefront

◈

If you can't convince them, confuse them.

Twenty seconds is a long time when you're scared. The lights came on after what seemed like an eternity. All appeared normal except that Michael had suddenly vanished. I glanced in all directions but he was nowhere to be seen. He'd been standing right next to me a moment earlier and I hadn't heard him move. Strangely, the man in the doorway had also disappeared.

The store activity quickly resumed. Brandon ran over to us looking serious and scared. He wanted to know if Phasers had caused the power outage. We nodded in affirmation. The four of us may have been the only people in the store who realized the severity of the situation. The store manager casually walked back into his office. Even he was oblivious. I was sure Michael recognized the danger, but we didn't know where he was.

Brandon said that he would search the back of the store. It was possible Michael had gone out that way. Seiko, Ali, and I cautiously walked toward the front door. It was closed. I looked at Ali. He nodded. I opened the door, stepping back in the process as if there might be an unwanted surprise awaiting us. We met Sifu as he ran toward us from the outside. We were happy to see him.

"Have you seen Michael?" I asked.

"Wasn't he with you?" he responded.

"Yes, he was, but the lights went out and he was gone when they came back on."

"I don't hear no footsteps," Seiko added. "He just disappear."

"We must find him, my brother. He may need our help."

"I agree," I said. "But let's do it together. We don't want to get separated like we did before."

"Right! Stay together," Sifu ordered. "I'll run ahead to see if I can find him. Remember: stay together and be careful."

We stepped back inside and met up with Brandon. He hadn't seen Michael anywhere. We were concerned but decided not to alert the manager, knowing he wouldn't believe us if we told him about the Phasers.

We needed to act on our own but were unsure of what to do. Brandon said that he might be able to take his lunch break early. If so, he would have an hour to help us search for Michael. We asked him to check while we figured out a plan.

Brandon ran to the manager's office, leaving the rest of us confused and staring at each other. I replayed the sequence of events in my mind. *The manager asked about*

the Internet. The instruments in the store began to sound differ-
ent. Michael made a comment. The lights went out. There was
someone at the door. The lights came on. Michael was gone. The
images were clear, but they didn't all make sense. Where was
Michael? I wanted to continue searching, but I'd become
paralyzed with indecisiveness. Brandon returned and broke
our silence.

"We have one hour. What's the plan?"

We glanced around at each other. We hadn't made a plan.

"Y'all haven't come up with anything? What have you
been doing? A Phaser shows up and your friend is missing
and you're standing around like you don't care." Brandon
was right and we knew it. "You can stare at each other if you
want. I'm going to find Michael." Brandon started to walk
away but Ali grabbed his arm.

"No. We go together."

"Okay. Where should we start?" Brandon asked, looking
at me.

I still didn't have an answer. My mind was racing but
getting nowhere. Seiko spoke up, providing direction for our
group.

"We find each other from across the world. We can find
Michael in Music City. He not far away."

Something she said centered my mind, triggering a bit
of clarity.

"Music! They told us that Music brought us together."

"That's right, my brother. They say they connect through
Music. Maybe we can do it, too."

"Right," I continued. "Maybe we can connect to Michael."

Brandon appeared puzzled.

"Connect through Music? What are you guys talking
about?"

"Shhhh!" Seiko put her hand over Brandon's mouth. "They talk, you listen."

Again, she gave me a clue without realizing it.

"Seiko! That's it! Listening! We have to listen to Music. She told me that."

"What? Who told you that?"

Seiko put her hand over Brandon's mouth again.

"We explain later," Ali responded. "Right now, we must listen to Music."

Customers were quietly mingling around the store, but no one had resumed playing. The phones and cash registers must have needed time to reboot because they were also quiet. In the midst of the stillness, my thoughts became clear.

I instructed everyone to close their eyes and listen until they could hear every sound in the room as Music. Brandon looked at me. I told him to do it immediately before he allowed his mind to form questions.

We stood motionless. To the untrained ear, all was silent. To the four of us, Music was all around. Every footstep provided rhythm. Every voice created a melody. The sounds of the lights and air-conditioner added harmony. I welcomed Music with open ears and an open heart. My body began to tingle. The phone rang. I opened my eyes. My friends were smiling. Although their eyes were closed, I could tell that their ears were as open as mine.

I took a deep breath. I could feel something happening. The four of us were bonding together with a deeper connection. It's difficult to explain, but an unseen force was bringing us closer together. It had to be Music. I listened harder. The feeling decreased. I listened easier and the feeling magnified. The tingle in my body increased. I spread my arms, opening myself to the sensation. A feeling of assurance surfaced.

"Michael is not here. He's not in the store," I said.

I didn't know how I knew, but I knew I was right. I suggested we go outside, close our eyes, and listen again.

Once outside, Music was even more vibrant. All the noises blended together, creating a symphony of sounds that were not only pleasing; they also provided information. We could hear the highway, the schoolyard, and the wind as she whistled through the trees. Every sound carried a message.

I asked everyone to close their eyes again and to point in the direction where they felt Michael was. Brandon said he had no idea where he was. I told him to guess. When we opened our eyes, we were all pointing in the same direction. We were shocked.

I noticed a blinking crossing signal in the direction we had pointed. It was a welcome sight and sound. We ran toward the light, hoping to get there before it stopped. The light fell silent just as we arrived.

"What now?" Brandon whispered.

A bird alerted in the distance. We turned our heads in unison.

"We go that way, my brother. In my country we say, 'Birds always tell the truth.'"

Ali was sure of himself, so we followed him unquestioningly, running in the direction of the sound. We stopped at the next corner and listened. The bird had moved. We continued in the same direction and found a large hawk sitting high atop a tree. As if leading us on purpose, the hawk waited for us to gather before flying away. Again, we followed.

Rounding the next corner, we came upon a black van parked on the side of the road. I froze. Brandon, not responding to my fear, kept running ahead with Seiko close behind. They were reacting to something else.

The hawk was perched low on a fence post across from the van. As I ran to join my friends, the side door of the van slid open. I slowed my approach until a pair of thin but muscular legs stretched out of the door.

"Sifu-san!" Seiko yelled.

"You kids need a ride?" he asked, poking his head out the door.

We relaxed and ran toward him. The beautiful hawk ascended, resting on a limb just above our heads. I took a closer look. *A red-shouldered hawk.* As my friends began conversing with Sifu, my attention began to drift. My mind journeyed through the past as my eyes locked onto the wild bird sitting just above me.

Years earlier, I'd had an incredible experience with a similar-looking hawk. With Michael at my side, we induced the hawk to descend from a tree and land on my arm. As the bird drew closer, its sheer size became more than intimidating, but it radiated a captivating nobility that comforted me. The experience was both scary and beautiful at the same time. Michael was adamant that we could communicate with animals if we would simply learn to tune in to their frequency. On that day, he proved to be right. I pondered whether this was the same hawk who was staring down at me now. As soon as the thought appeared, the bird nodded its head toward me. Maybe it was just my imagination.

I was happy to be reunited with Sifu. I felt safer, but I also had questions. Had we found him or had he found us?

Was the hawk involved? Michael could communicate with animals, but did Sifu have the same ability? I was about to ask when a song grabbed my attention from inside the van. I hadn't realized that the radio was on until Debbie Gibson pulled me closer.

I climbed in the van, recognizing the song from my CD collection. It was from Gibson's *Electric Youth* album. I'd heard it many times, but this time something was different. The song spoke as if it had something to tell me. I listened.

Without effort I recognized the key as B major. Subsequently, the chord progression formed in my mind. But instead of letters, as I was accustomed, I visualized the progression in a form known as the Nashville Number System.

As the song played, the chords scrolled through the air: 3 minor . . . 4 major . . . 1 major . . . 5 dominant. The progression repeated: 3 . . . 4 . . . 1 . . . 5. Music was sending a message. The progression: 3, 4, 1, 5. The key: B. It hit me like a ton of soft bricks. *My street address! 3415 B Pelham Avenue. That's where we'll find him.* I was certain.

"Sifu! Take us to my house. Now!"

"Yes, sir!" he replied, springing to his feet.

I hopped into the front passenger's seat. My friends climbed in the back. A tiny object fell out of Sifu's pocket as he strapped himself in. It appeared to be a small flashlight. I picked it up with the intention of handing it back to him but realized it had a red lens on the front. I flicked the switch. The light began flashing. Sifu snatched it out of my hand and quickly turned it off. He shoved the light into his pocket and drove off without saying a word.

Sifu acted suspiciously. His movements while snatching the light weren't carried out with the same finesse I'd become accustomed to from him. This time his movements were jerky, as if he'd been caught in the act. I stared at him but he wouldn't look back, not even a glance. Something had made him uncomfortable.

A sinister scenario played out in my mind as we traveled across town. I never found out if it was true or not, but I still have my suspicions. I didn't know Sifu that well, so I wasn't sure about him. Michael is the kind of person who could've and would've orchestrated something as outlandish as what I was thinking. So, it is possible. Here's my theory:

Everything that happened in the previous hour, including finding Sifu, had been set up and orchestrated by Michael. The power outage at the store: it was all a front, **a storefront**, you might say.

Somehow, Michael was able to get the sounds of the instruments to fade into static, and somehow, he arranged for the power to go out on cue. It's possible the store manager was working with him. The Phaser who appeared in the doorway . . . he wasn't a Phaser at all. Based on the fact that Sifu was still carrying a blinking red light, it was most likely him. We never saw his face. And while we were preoccupied, Michael snuck out the back door—rather quickly, I might add—and went to my house. I was sure that's where we would find him.

I realized my theory was wild and left a lot of unanswered questions, but isn't that what a theory is? But if true, what could Michael's motives possibly be?

The whole ordeal was scary. We were genuinely worried about Michael. Once I was sure he was safe, I wouldn't worry anymore; I just needed an explanation. I looked at

Sifu. He turned up the volume on the radio and kept his eyes on the road.

As I sat there quietly contemplating the situation, my curiosity turned to admiration. Michael was a teacher—a strange teacher, yes, but there were reasons for everything he did. And there was always a lesson involved. If my crazy theory was true, the reason behind it would soon be made clear. I was sure of that. So, I decided to keep my thoughts to myself (for a while). I knew that my inquisitive nature (and my ego) would not allow my suspicions to stay hidden for long.

Regardless of what really happened, I was sure we'd be seeing him in a few minutes. As always, I had many questions. I knew he'd have answers, although they'd likely be disguised as questions. Michael showed me that knowledge is more valuable when discovered by the pupil, and more potent when the student becomes *one* with the knowledge. I used to quote him continually until his voice popped into my mind one day: *"If you really like what I say, learn it so well that it becomes what you say. Then you can quote yourself."* I am still working toward that.

At the music store, I'm pretty sure Michael's disappearance was his way of helping us find confidence in ourselves so that we'd be forced to make our own decisions. Well, "force" is not the right word. We always had a choice. Anyway, Michael's plan worked. Thinking back on the events, it became clear that he composed the entire incident so that we would find the courage to make our own choices.

In the midst of and despite all the confusion—a grand opening, static, a power outage, a reappearing Phaser, and a disappearing Michael—my friends and I worked together to find our own answers. We even used Music to find Michael. We hadn't found him yet, but I knew we would, and I was sure he would say that Music used us. I was fine with that, too. The main point was that we didn't allow the confusion to impede us. He must have orchestrated it all. That is his way.

✛

"If you can't convince them, confuse them."

We arrived at my house and I hurried out of the van, opening the rear door for my friends. Brandon chuckled as he stepped out. I gave him an inquisitive look. He covered his mouth and continued walking. I hurried past him and ran into the house. The door was unlocked, and to my surprise, nobody was home. I searched each room and called for Michael. No answer.

"He is here. I know it," Ali whispered.

Remembering the trick they'd played on me earlier, I looked on top of the bookshelf, under the bed, and in the closet. Still nothing. Seiko's new drum was sitting near the couch, which solidified our notion that Michael was close.

I reminded myself to listen and immediately heard a single chirp from a bird. I looked outside the kitchen window and saw a large footprint on the edge of the driveway. I ran outside to get a closer look. A very clear human track sat in the center of a small mound of dirt near the base of a tree. I was proud of myself for having noticed the footprint from such a great distance. Years earlier, I'd learned about animal tracking from Michael and was eager to show my knowledge to my friends.

I called them outside. The track was made by a shoeless left foot. Each toe was distinct and could be clearly seen in the leaf debris. I pointed out how tiny mounds of dirt on the left outside edge of the track indicated the direction the person was going, and how the spread toes suggested a person controlling their balance. I even showed them how there was more pressure on the toes than on the heel. They were impressed, which boosted my ego.

As I continued my lecture, a large rock dropped from above, scarcely missing my head. I slowly looked up. There . . . directly above our heads . . . sitting in the tree . . . in plain sight . . . was our teacher . . . Michael.

"Very good. You found me. Well, with the help of my raptor friend. We've been enjoying the show."

"You've been sitting there the whole time?" I asked.

"Yes."

I lowered my head, shaking it side to side.

"Funny!" Michael continued. "You neglected to notice the bird chirps until you went inside the house. Interesting! You did not expect me to be outside, so you did not pay attention. You walked right past me. I could've dropped rocks on each of your heads. Your friend here was the only one who looked up."

Brandon surprised us with his response.

"I actually saw you, Michael. As soon as I got out of the van, I saw you sitting up there in plain sight. You put your finger to your lips, so I didn't say anything. I tried not to laugh."

"Thank you," Michael answered, looking down at Brandon. "You are my favorite. The others are blind and deaf." He and Brandon shared a laugh.

With a high-pitched squawk, the red-shouldered hawk transferred to the same limb Michael was resting on.

"You see? He's laughing, too," Michael joked as he petted the bird on top of its head.

I wanted to ask a question, but Seiko spoke first. She was not happy with Michael and didn't hesitate to let him know.

"Michael, this no time for play games!"

Michael hopped out of the tree, landing in the center of our circle. The hawk also descended, choosing a branch just above Michael's head.

"This is the perfect time, Seiko," Michael responded. "Games are great teaching tools."

"But Michael," I said, "we were worried. We thought something had happened to you."

"Something is always happening to me, but that is never a need for worry."

"We're happy you are safe," Ali remarked. "But what happened after the lights go out?"

Michael gave a surprising answer.

"I will tell you what happened. The four of you started listening."

"Listening?" I asked.

"Exactly! What did the other people do once the lights came back on?"

"They stand there. They do nothing," Seiko answered.

"Right," Ali added. "Everyone act like nothing is wrong. Only Brandon, he sense something. My new brother."

Ali grabbed Brandon's hand and raised it into the air.

I also felt proud. The four of us had recognized a problem. Not only that, we took action. I doubt anyone else even realized Michael was gone.

"We did well, right, Michael? Are you proud of us?" I asked.

Once again, Michael put my ego back in check.

"Yes. You did very well until you saw the track. You allowed it to control your focus and boost your ego. Once that happened, you stopped looking and listening—all of you. You allowed Victor to pull you away from wide-angle awareness into a very narrow focus. There is a time to narrow your focus, but this wasn't it. All of your senses were absorbed by the track. If your goal was to find me, you succeeded, but you chose a dangerous method. We can't afford to let that happen again."

I was trying my best, but it seemed like I was always a half step away. Again, I lowered my head in shame.

"You see, Brandon noticed me right away because he has never been to your house. Like a child, he took in everything as new. He looked all around, right and left, up and down. The rest of you are blind because you know the place too well. You have focus points, which create blind spots. One of your focus points is right there." He pointed to my front door. "As soon as you pulled up and looked at the door, that was it. Life was over. Life did not start again until you went inside. All I did was find a blind spot and sit in it. You were so blind I actually climbed down the tree to make the track." He pointed at the ground. "I knew I could get you with that. It was all too easy."

"I'm sorry, Michael. It was my fault. My ego did take over. I wanted to show my tracking skills."

"It doesn't matter now," he replied. "You still passed the test."

"Test?" I questioned. "This was a test?"

"It is all a test as well as an experience," he answered. "If you learn, you succeed."

"We no want test. We worry about you," Seiko scolded.

"No time to worry. We have more to do."

"More test?" Ali asked.

"More training," Michael replied. "But first, I need to find Jonathan. Has anybody seen him?"

"No," I answered. "We looked everywhere. The house is empty."

Michael turned his head, yelling Jonathan's name in all directions. We'd already searched the whole house. I didn't think there was any need to call for him. I turned in a complete circle anyway, my eyes scanning the trees.

Then, the ground beneath my feet began to move. I jumped. I looked down and noticed a human hand sticking out of the ground. Our circle widened. The hand was attached to an arm. Ali grunted an African word I'd never heard but, nonetheless, understood. Brandon fell backward yelling, "Snaaaake!"

To our surprise, Jonathan slowly rose to his feet. He'd been lying right beneath our noses under a pile of leaves and twigs. It was amazing! I must have been standing on him when I was showing everyone the track. Jonathan confirmed my suspicion.

"You're heavy," he remarked.

"Wow! This is crazy," I responded.

"And potentially dangerous," Michael admonished. "As I said before, your familiarity conditioned you to have blind spots. Now, I quickly conditioned you to only look up. This is exactly how Phasers work. They condition you to stop paying attention. Then, before you know it, your whole life has been diminished. When that happens, you diminish. Mediocrity, or less, becomes the norm. The sad thing is that many people never notice."

It was a valuable lesson. Jonathan was covered in dirt and leaves. We helped brush him off and return the ground cover back to normal. Michael waved good-bye to the hawk and motioned for us to follow him inside. Michael and Jonathan hurried in. The rest of us took our time, looking in all directions.

Once inside, we found Isis and Uncle Clyde sitting on the couch. Once again, I shook my head side to side. I wanted to ask them where they'd been hiding, but Michael had other plans.

"Let's go. We have one more exercise for you."

As if on cue, Sifu walked through the door. My anxiety level skyrocketed. I was not fond of his lessons.

I'd already failed two of them.

All-One

◈

All people need to be loved.

Apparently, this time I was not about to get slapped. But I was sure it was going to happen one way or another.

We were headed downtown to continue our training.

"Michael," Brandon said, "I have to get back to work. My break is almost over."

Michael simply replied, "Stay here with us."

Brandon didn't argue. I think he'd spent enough time with Michael to realize he could fix any problems that might arise from being late.

There were nine of us inside the van. Michael handed instruments to four of us. His choices were suspect. Seiko was given the same plastic garbage pail she'd used earlier. Ali was handed a ukulele. A kalimba was chosen for Brandon, who said he'd never seen one before. Having grown up listening to the band Earth, Wind & Fire, I knew exactly what it was.

A kalimba, a beautiful instrument, is also known as a thumb piano. Although the body can be formed in many different shapes, the instrument is usually constructed as a flat and hollow box, small enough to be comfortably held in both hands. Attached to the body is a group of thin metal tines lined in a row. Each tine is a different length, producing a different pitch when plucked with the thumbs. I wished I'd been chosen to play the kalimba, but instead I was given a violin, which I did not know how to play.

There were four different instruments. The only commonality was that we each held one that was unfamiliar to us for the most part. Seiko wasn't given a real instrument, but at least her garbage pail resembled a drum. The instruments were also relatively quiet, which seemed totally ineffective for playing outside.

In Nashville, it is customary to take in the vibe by cruising down Broadway on foot or with the car windows open. When the weather is nice, you can enjoy an array of sounds as they filter out of the open doors and windows of each venue. The outdoor party atmosphere attracts thousands of tourists who flood the city daily to experience its musical magic.

As Sifu turned onto Broadway, we were instantly engulfed in the mayhem. The bustling of people and cars slowed our travel. Just as we made our final approach to Third Avenue, a car pulled out, leaving us the perfect parking space. That was a good sign.

We exited the van and stood on the northwest corner of Third and Broadway. Sifu and Jonathan immediately walked away in opposite directions.

"I guess they already know what it's gonna sound like," I joked. Michael didn't laugh.

We gathered together and quietly waited for instructions. No one said a word. Ali, Seiko, Brandon, and I looked at each other and then at Michael, who was merely staring back. His face was calm. Isis and Uncle Clyde stood silently on either side of him. I looked up the street in both directions. Jonathan was out of sight, and Sifu was at the corner of Fourth Avenue, leaning up against the wall with folded arms. The noisy hustle and bustle of Broadway proved no match for the screaming inside my head. Impatient, I broke the silence.

"What do you want us to do?"

It had been years since I'd heard him say it. With one word, memories flooded my mind and chills consumed my whole body.

"Play!"

I smiled. I knew what that meant. The word was literal. Michael wanted us to start playing immediately. There was to be no talking, no tuning up, no discussion about key signatures or grooves, and absolutely no hesitating.

Michael never understood why musicians talked so much before playing. According to him, the more musicians know, the more useless questions we ask. *What key? What feel? What form? Who wants to start?* We never have to ask how to start a verbal conversation, so why do we have to talk before starting a jam? Dancers, for example, simply allow Music to move them—no questions asked.

Ready to start our musical conversation, I held the violin like a bass and plucked the four open strings. The intervals were different than on my bass and the instrument was out of tune, so I found two notes on the same string and repeated them in a steady rhythm.

Brandon waited a moment and then plucked a few notes on the kalimba. It was in a different key, so I immediately adjusted. He fumbled around, exploring the instrument before finally settling in on a part. Once he did, I could tell that he was a natural on that instrument. He looked at me and smiled.

Now that Brandon's part was established, Seiko joined the conversation. Sitting down with her legs crossed, she hit the pail once with precision. She waited, then hit twice more, continuing to add beats until her part was complete. The fact that she was playing a garbage pail didn't seem to hinder her musicality at all.

It was evident that repetition made it easier for each of us to join in. It provided an open invitation, just as a simple greeting invites someone into a conversation. I looked at Ali, making sure not to change my part so that he could easily find his. He was listening with his eyes closed, so I did the same.

Without testing the ukulele first, Ali played a three-note arpeggiated pattern. He used a triplet rhythm that perfectly complemented Seiko's groove. I opened my eyes in amazement. His eyes were still closed. Immediately, we all sounded much better.

I was shocked. We actually sounded good. We hadn't discussed anything and we were successfully playing music. Because of the surrounding noises, we huddled together. We didn't care whether anyone else could hear us or not, we were enjoying ourselves. Music was certainly happening on the corner of Third and Broadway.

None of our teachers' expressions had changed and they offered no further instructions, so we kept playing. We played for fifteen or twenty minutes before Michael tilted his head.

"What?" I asked, continuing to pluck the violin.

"How long are you guys going to keep talking about the same thing?"

Immediately, Ali began singing. Not lyrics or words, I don't think, but what sounded like an African chant. I loved it. The feel of his voice made me want to dance.

"Yes. Yes," Isis remarked in a gentle tone as she extended her arms and began to sway.

A young couple stopped to listen. A gentleman bobbed his head and began singing along with Ali. His girlfriend danced in circles around him. They both wore big smiles. They didn't stay long but left four dollars on the sidewalk as they walked away. Seiko immediately grabbed the bills and put them in her pocket. I laughed.

Once the couple left, our song came to its natural ending. Michael told us to start another. This time he wanted us to turn up the Music without turning up the volume. I wasn't sure what he meant.

Without asking, Seiko played a different pattern. She lifted the pail off the ground and held it between her knees, which gave it a different sound. It also allowed her to strike the pail harder without increasing the volume. *Soft but intense,* I told myself. *Just like Curtis Mayfield.* Michael looked at me and nodded.

Brandon reached for my violin. Michael hadn't specified rules, so I gave it to him. He handed the kalimba to Ali, so I took the ukulele. Although I hadn't played one in a long time, I felt more comfortable with it.

Ali launched into a beautiful and elaborate African

melody. I was impressed. Brandon's expression showed his appreciation, too. He joined Ali by plucking a rhythmic pattern while moving the note around randomly. It sounded amazing! Because his rhythm was so solid, it made every note sound good. I thought about singing, but I was too self-conscious. I knew that I would involuntarily compare myself to Ali, which is always a useless endeavor. Instead, I played simple chords.

Michael moved next to me and nodded to Uncle Clyde and Isis, who took Brandon and Ali by the arms, pulling them in separate directions. Michael instructed them not to stop playing. When they were about ten paces away, Michael spoke to me.

"Can you hear Seiko?"

"Yes," I replied. "She's sitting right next to me."

"Stop listening to her. Pay attention. *Feel* her energy instead."

I looked left and right. Uncle Clyde and Isis were whispering to my friends. I suspected they were being given similar instructions. I looked down at Seiko. I could hear her easily, but I could no longer hear the others. I looked at Michael. He looked back at me. I didn't know what to do, so I stopped playing. Michael didn't like that.

"You see a girl. You see a drum. You hear a beat. Three separate things. Make them one!"

I was confused. I think Michael enjoyed keeping me that way. I didn't know how to do what he was asking. I looked at him and shrugged my shoulders.

"When a person is talking, do you listen to the person, their mouth, and their words separately?"

Instantly, I understood. I held the ukulele to my chest

but didn't play. I listened to Seiko and changed my focus. All of a sudden, I could hear the spaces between each beat. Her groove seemed to widen. I no longer heard a drum or a rhythm; I heard Music. She *was* the Music. I inadvertently responded by swaying back and forth. Michael took a step back. I took a step inside, where Music surrounded me. I could feel her on all sides. Again, Michael spoke one word.

"Play!"

He didn't just say it; he commanded it. I didn't feel like he was commanding me exactly, but as if he had total command of the word itself. He infused power into it, and when the word was spoken, the power also flowed into me. Michael didn't want me to play the ukulele; he wanted me to play Music. It was my time.

Without thinking or searching, I closed my eyes, allowing Music to flow through me. Paying attention to the feeling rather than the notes, I released my energy through the instrument. I heard Seiko gasp. She felt it, too. There was no longer any separation. Seiko, Music, and I had become one.

"Now," Michael whispered. "Do not forget about your brothers."

I had forgotten about them. My two friends were far away and their instruments were soft. The surrounding noises made it nearly impossible to hear them. I raised my head, but Michael told me not to look. He also told me not to listen but to *feel* them instead.

Years earlier, Michael had taught me how to amplify soft sounds that were difficult to hear. He'd asked me to keep time with a quiet metronome while a vacuum cleaner and a television were running. I had to listen through the sound of the appliances to audibly pinpoint each beat of the metronome. Surprisingly, I was able to do it. Unsurprisingly, it was difficult at the current moment.

Michael wanted me to join with Brandon and Ali just as I'd done with Seiko. With all the surrounding noises, it was nearly impossible for me to hear the plucked violin and kalimba. I was instructed to listen with my feelings more than my ears. I took a frustrated breath. Michael placed his right thumb on my right temple and his fingers in the center of my forehead. His touch was gentle, but I could feel his energy. Intuitively, I closed my eyes. His words resonated through my mind as he explained.

"Know that we are **all one**. It is only when we refuse to *listen* that we feel all *alone*. Understand this: it is impossible to be alone except by thinking it so. Therefore, do not think it! If we listen with our whole being, we can transform 'aloneness' into 'all oneness.' Now, pay attention to your feelings and use them to connect with your friends."

Michael removed his hand, but my eyes remained closed. I mentally reached out with my energy. Almost immediately, I felt them. I could also feel what they were playing. Brandon was ten paces to my right, which put him twenty paces away from Ali on my left. There should have been no way they could hear each other, but in the midst of all the downtown commotion, the four of us were totally in sync.

It was enlightening. When I used my ears only, I could scarcely hear Ali and Brandon. When I reached out with my feelings and my intention, jamming with them was much easier. When I welcomed Music as the fifth member of our ensemble, playing together was not only effortless but also gratifying. Being joined in Music caused us *all* to become *one* unit. I suspected my friends were feeling the same.

I looked in both directions. My friends were standing far away from me, with Isis and Uncle Clyde standing by their sides. Seiko's head was down, but I could tell that she, too, was connected. Everyone was smiling (including Music). Once again, Michael gave me instructions.

"Your brothers, pull them to you."

I didn't know what he meant and I told him so.

"Brandon and Ali, make them come to you," he answered.

"How?" I asked.

I think this was the most agitated I'd ever seen Michael become.

"How . . . How? We do not have time for *how*. *Why* I might accept, but *how*?"

He walked in circles, looking around as if he wanted something.

"Stop playing!" he ordered. "Stop! Stop, I said! Stop!"

Seiko stopped abruptly. She looked frightened. I felt the same but tried to appear calm.

"Michael, I'm sorry. I just didn't know what—"

He raised his index finger and held it in front of my face. His eyes were closed. I was confused. I didn't know what he wanted me to do.

"Stop thinking!" he yelled.

Ali and Brandon stopped playing and ran over to us. Isis and Uncle Clyde walked.

"What's going on?" Brandon asked.

"Do not talk! Nobody talk!" Michael ordered.

He stood for a full minute. He didn't move so we didn't either. His face was serious and his eyes were still closed. Our eyes were open, but we kept our mouths shut. Then, Michael spoke.

"Victor! Choose someone!"

"What do you mean?" I asked.

"Choose someone. There are hundreds of people on the street. Pick anyone you want."

"You mean, like—"

"Do it!" he shouted.

"Okay. Okay," I responded. "The woman in the red blouse."

"The one behind me or the one across the street?" he asked.

I looked over Michael's shoulder and saw another woman wearing a red blouse walking into a store. I looked at Michael. His head was down and his eyes were still closed. The woman across the street was the farthest away. Not knowing Michael's plan, I chose her. My friends' astonished faces made it clear what they were thinking. We were about to witness the impossible.

"The woman across the street," I answered.

Without opening his eyes, Michael forcefully grabbed the ukulele from me. With his eyes still closed, he raised his head to the sky and began playing.

"Do not look at me. Look at her!" Michael ordered.

We turned to look. Almost immediately, the woman in the red blouse slowed her pace, stopped walking, and stood still. She tilted her head to the side as if listening, or maybe remembering something. Without apparent reason, she changed her direction and increased her pace. She wove her way through traffic and crossed to our side of the street. Reaching the sidewalk, she made a right turn and headed in our direction.

Somehow, Michael seemed to be drawing the woman to him. I was dumbfounded. There was no way she could've heard the ukulele from across the street. I was standing right next to Michael, and I could barely hear it.

As she came closer, Michael stopped playing and opened his eyes. He handed the ukulele back to me and walked over to the woman. She appeared a bit startled. After a very short conversation, the woman covered her face and began sobbing. She turned to walk away but stopped. Michael waited. She faced away. A few seconds later, she turned around. Michael opened his arms and she ran into them. He hugged her firmly for a full minute and then whispered something in her ear. She lifted her head, dried her eyes, and walked away with a smile and a slight bounce in her step.

Michael walked back to us. We wanted to ask what he'd said to her, but everyone kept silent. Isis gave Michael a hug and whispered something to him. Again, we didn't ask. Michael pointed at me.

"Your turn!" It was more an order than a request.

I didn't hesitate. I acted before doubt crept in. My skin was tingling because of what I'd just witnessed. I made sure the tingling didn't stop. I glanced across the street. My eyes acted on their own and zeroed in on a man walking in our direction. I spoke swiftly.

"The man across the street! Walking this way! Blue jeans! Yellow shirt! Blue hat!"

I was sure of myself. I didn't really know what I was sure about, but I started playing anyway. I never thought about what to play; *why* to play was my main focus. I wanted to do what Michael had done. My eyes were open, but I saw him more clearly in my mind. The image was vivid, the feeling was strong, and my desire was pure. Like a prayer, I played for him.

My memory is vague, but I was told that the man immediately turned left and crossed the street the same as the woman had to Michael. I remember the man standing in front of me. He seemed as confused as I. Caught by surprise, I became nervous and handed the ukulele back to Michael. I didn't know what to do or say, so I did nothing.

"Where is your sax?" Michael asked the man.

"It's at the club," he answered.

"Bring it tomorrow. Right here. Midnight."

"I'll be here," he replied.

The man turned and walked away. He was scratching his head. Why he agreed, I don't know, and he probably didn't either. Did he know what would be happening tomorrow night? I doubted it. I didn't have a clue either.

"Michael?" Ali asked. "How did you know he was a musician?"

"Yeah, and what instrument he play? How you know that? You have special power?" Seiko asked.

"Of course I do! Mystical Magical Michael. That's what they call me."

"What do you mean?" I asked.

"Yeah. Right. Special powers," Uncle Clyde answered with a laugh. "It's called eyesight. Dat's all it is. The man was wearing a neck strap."

"Stop it, Clyde. You're blowing my cover," Michael chortled.

We all laughed. Michael turned toward Ali.

"Okay. Back to work. Ali, it's all yours."

Michael handed the ukulele to Ali. Ali pushed it away, choosing to continue playing the kalimba. Michael raised his eyebrows and nodded.

Over the next few hours, my friends and I honed our

skills. Michael stopped providing direction or even tips. He seemed fine leaving us to our own devices. He showed no concern as to whether we succeeded or failed, but he did tell us not to treat our failures as failures.

"Always treat everything as progress on the journey toward greatness, but remember: the journey is never yours alone. Think about it: If you call someone's name, it is their choice to answer, or not. You job is to call the correct name. But if they do answer"—he looked at me with a smile—"make sure you have something to say."

The ultimate demonstration came from Uncle Clyde. With the sun receding behind the buildings, it became increasingly difficult to make things out clearly. He removed a harmonica from his pocket, and with one long exhale, blew a three-note chord that lasted close to a minute. Once the chord faded into silence, there were three people standing in front of him. We were beyond amazed, of course, and didn't keep quiet about it. I'm sure our gasps could be heard above all the surrounding sounds. Michael acted as though Uncle Clyde's accomplishment were commonplace and proceeded to invite the three new strangers to the apparent gathering the following night. Of course they agreed.

Seiko shouted Jonathan's name and spun around. I followed her gaze to see Jonathan running up. Amazingly, she had recognized his footsteps with her back turned. Ali, Brandon, and I looked at each other in shock. We still weren't used to her uncanny ability.

"Michael," Jonathan said, "all looks good. I haven't seen any Phasers, but I did find a few participants. We should have a good team tomorrow night."

"Dat's good, son!" Uncle Clyde answered. "Michael

found a saxophonist and I recruited two singers and a dancer. Da kids, dey wuz pretty good, too."

I was anxious. Something was going to happen tomorrow night, and I had no idea what it was. Judging by Uncle Clyde's dialect, he didn't seem too concerned. If there was going to be a jam session, I knew we would be part of it. That's what we were training for. We just didn't know what kind of jam it was going to be.

Sifu appeared just as our parking meter expired. A policeman walked over holding his ticket book in his hand. Sifu gave him a disparaging look. The officer immediately put the book in his pocket and walked away. We stared at Sifu.

"What?" he responded. "I have powers, too. Yours makes them come. Mine makes them go."

Sifu unlocked the van and we climbed inside. Isis, who had been quiet most of the day, whispered to Michael, "It won't be this easy tomorrow. They'll be here, for sure. We have to get it right this time."

Michael took a deep breath and nodded. I had a pretty good idea what they were talking about. It was a quiet ride home until Seiko, the outspoken one, asked a question that had been on our minds.

"Michael, what you say to that woman?"

His one-phrase answer was enough.

✥

"All people need to be loved."

Rebelation

◆

*If you venture down the rabbit hole, at least venture
down the rabbit whole.*

There was no good reason to have awakened so early. We'd
been given the rest of the evening off, so I went to bed early,
but I'd barely slept. I laid awake most of the night in anticipation of what the next evening had in store. Knowing how
Michael worked, I contemplated the idea that nothing was
going to happen. But that was highly improbable. Although
I was sure that something big was on the horizon, I was also
sure that I would never be able to anticipate what it was. He
liked to keep us guessing.

Michael was up early, too. I found him sitting in his chair
with his eyes closed. He appeared to be either sleeping or
meditating. I'd never seen him sleep, so I assumed it was the
latter. I left him alone and went into the kitchen. Through
the kitchen window, I saw Sifu in the backyard executing

what appeared to be some type of martial arts exercises. His slow flowing movements and lightning-fast strikes were both graceful and explosive, like a combination of a crane and a snake. I couldn't look away.

I watched through the window for ten minutes or more until he stopped. He faced the trees with his back to me. Keeping his legs straight, he bent at the waist and placed both palms flat on the ground. In slow motion, he rose back up and slightly bent his legs. In one quick motion, he turned and threw a pine cone, hitting the window right in front of my face. I jumped back and retreated to the living room. Michael was waiting for me.

"Forget something?" he asked.

"Oh, right," I responded. I'd forgotten my juice.

"Bring two," he said.

I walked back into the kitchen and glanced through the window, but I didn't see Sifu. I walked closer and looked all around the backyard. *He must have left.* I turned to get my juice and noticed the refrigerator door wide open. *I must have forgotten to close it.* I retrieved the carton of juice and closed the door only to find Sifu standing behind it. I jumped again, dropping the container of juice. Sifu caught it before it hit the ground.

"Always keep your eyes open, even when they're closed," he said with a snicker.

I reclaimed the juice, continuing to stare at him as I walked away. I didn't know whether to be angry, embarrassed, or impressed. Actually, I was all three. I filled two glasses and went back into the living room. Michael hadn't moved. I handed him a glass and sat down, quietly sipping my juice.

Michael stared at me. I was uncomfortable.

"Go ahead. You can ask," he said, obviously aware I had been holding my tongue.

I wanted to ask him about the power outage at the store, but I didn't know how to begin. I finished my juice and took a breath. Michael, who hadn't touched his drink, handed it to me.

"No. That one's yours," I said.

"No! It is not. I had you get it for you."

Outsmarted again. He knew me better than I did. With another sip of juice, I mustered up enough nerve to start my inquiry.

"Michael, have you ever lied to me?"

"Absolutely! All of Life is a lie."

"Have you ever told me the truth?"

"Absolutely! All of Life is the truth."

"What does that mean?"

"What I tell you is neither true nor false. It is up to you to choose one."

"Or both," I added.

He looked surprised.

"Very nice! You are my favorite student today."

That made me feel good . . . even though it was only seven in the morning.

I lost my nerve. I never asked the real question. Maybe I didn't need to.

Sifu walked in and stood over me. I looked up hesitantly. He winked.

"It's time to get started. We have a lot to do," he said.

I wasn't ready to start anything, especially with him. I'm sure my expression showed it.

"This is serious and necessary," Michael added. "It is important for all three of you, but you are the only one awake, so we will start with you."

"It's easy," Sifu said. "I just need you to sit down and close your eyes."

"Oh no! I'm not closing my eyes. 'Lesson number two: Don't trust anyone!' I'm not falling for that again."

I sat back, increasing my distance. Michael tried to help.

"This is about energy! You will need it for tonight."

"Oh no. The last lesson raised my energy enough. You saw what he did to me."

Sifu laughed and clapped his hands.

Ali, who was asleep on the floor, rolled over and began to stir. He was a heavy sleeper.

"What's going on?" he asked.

"Training time again," I answered.

Ali wasted no time. He rose to his feet, folded his blanket, and sat next to me on the couch.

Seiko, who I thought was still asleep, stormed into the room.

"What you guys doing?"

"I think we're about to get slapped," I answered.

"Not without me," she said.

"Don't worry. I won't let that happen again," Michael assured.

I trusted Michael but not Sifu, and I told him so. Michael instructed Seiko to have a seat. He spoke in a calm tone and we gave him our undivided attention. Well, honestly, my attention *was* divided. I kept one eye on Sifu.

Michael made us aware that Sifu's art was not much different than ours. We were astonished.

"Listen, and listen closely," Michael instructed. "Your art is Music. Sifu's is Wing Chun kung fu and was invented by a woman. So, you can say that, like Music, his art is also female. Both can be used to move people with little force."

Sifu smiled and held up a fist. Michael continued.

"You see, Wing Chun descended from the Shaolin monks, or as a musician might call them, the *She-aeolian monks.*"

Ali and I looked at each other with our mouths open. In music theory, "aeolian" is the technical name for the sixth mode of a major scale. It is also called the natural minor. Michael, as always, added to our thoughts.

"Aeolian is a feminine scale, while major, or Ionian, as theorists call it, is masculine. Sifu, being very masculine, uses a feminine art form, which completes the circle—yin and yang."

According to Michael, Sifu understood Music in ways that relate to the human body. Ali had already explained to me the relationship between a guitar and a female body, but Michael took it a few steps further.

For example: muscles can be viewed as "music-cells," and arteries as "art-with-ease." Apparently, a double French horn is based on the body's intestines, a saxophone mirrors the esophagus, and a flute relates to the part of the throat referred to as the windpipe. Michael could tell that our minds were swirling, but he wasn't finished.

"Wing Chun contains three empty-hand forms, each containing 108 different movements. 108 times 2 is 216, which is half of . . ." He looked at Ali.

"432," Ali responded.

"Music! Scientific tuning," I added.

"A human heart beats an average rate of 72 beats per minute, which equals how many beats in an hour?" Again, Michael looked at Ali.

"4,320," he answered.

"432 again," I proclaimed.

"All day long," Sifu remarked.

"Sifu," Michael asked, "do you have anything to add?"

"Always," he answered, taking a step closer to us. "Before scientists caught up, monks already knew that the sun was the center of the solar system and that it gives Life to all that surrounds it. They also knew about the powerful sun in the center of the human body." He formed a fist and hit himself in the stomach. "The solar plexus! This is the source!" Sifu took a step back, providing space for his words to sink in.

"Now," Michael continued, "listen closely to Sifu. He will teach you a simple meditation. Follow his explicit directions. You'll be glad you did."

"Okay," I responded. "I'll do it if you say so, but I'm not going first. I don't want to get slapped again."

"Don't worry. I won't let it happen," Michael assured.

Seiko rose to her feet, walked over, and stood directly in front of Sifu.

"I told you. Me first!"

Sifu looked at me out of the corner of his eye.

"I like her!" he said with a smile.

"This is serious! No more jokes," Michael affirmed.

Michael left the room, leaving us alone with Sifu. I watched from the couch.

Seiko was instructed to sit on the floor with her legs crossed. Sifu told her to face her palms up and rest the back of her hands on her bent knees.

"Perfect. Close your eyes and relax," he instructed.

That's the part I didn't like. I was glad to be watching.

After a few minutes of normal breathing, Sifu taught Seiko an alternate technique called reverse breathing. It involves pulling your stomach in slightly while inhaling through your nose and then allowing your stomach to expand as you exhale through your mouth. I tried it from the couch. It was counterintuitive, but not difficult. We listened closely as Sifu continued with instructions.

"Lightly place the tip of your tongue on the roof of your mouth, just behind your teeth, as you inhale. Release it as you exhale. Continue this process, slowly, and relax as you meditate on your breathing."

He slowed his speech and knelt down in front of her. Sifu balled his hands into fists and pointed the first two fingers of each hand as if he were about to shoot twin guns. I was afraid for Seiko. I leaned forward and started to say something. Sifu looked at me and slowly shook his head. His expression was serious. I sat back and kept quiet.

He pointed his fingers downward, lightly touching Seiko's open palms, then inhaled slowly and held his breath. His face tightened and his lips pressed together. The veins in his arms began to bulge. Ali and I looked at each other and back at Sifu. With his fingers in her palms, we watched Seiko's body expand as if she were being filled with air. A few seconds later, Sifu exhaled, released his fingers, and stood up. They were done. The whole process took less than two minutes.

Seiko looked at Sifu and raised her eyebrows in astonishment. Something had happened and she seemed pleased about it.

"You're done," Sifu told her. He looked at me. "Your turn."

I pushed Ali off the couch and onto the floor.

"He volunteered to go next," I said.

"Okay, my brother." Ali chuckled. "I go next."

We watched Ali go through the same process. He responded in the same way. Seiko watched through joyful tears. Once he was finished, Ali returned to the couch. With a wide-eyed look of wonder, he placed his hand on my shoulder, assuring me all was okay.

"Wow! Powerful! Very powerful!"

Seiko nodded in agreement.

I hadn't meditated in a long while, but seeing that it had only lasted two minutes each and no one had gotten slapped, I was actually eager to get started. Without being asked, I took my place on the floor.

"You know the routine," Sifu whispered.

I pushed away my fear and closed my eyes. Sifu reminded me to relax and to reverse my breathing. I did my best to relax. Sifu knelt in front of me. My body tensed. As soon as his fingers touched my palms, a jolt of electricity shot into my hands. I jerked my hands away and opened my eyes.

"Relax," Sifu whispered. "Just relax."

I looked down at his hands; they were empty. I looked up at Ali.

"It's okay, my brother. Really. It's okay."

I took a deep breath and closed my eyes again. The electricity returned, starting in my palms and then drifting up into my arms. It continued through my chest and down into my lower stomach, where it settled and circulated in an area just below my navel. It was weird, but that was only the beginning. Next, the visions started.

A yin-yang symbol appeared in front of me. A treble clef was in the top half and a bass clef in the bottom. The symbol began rotating slowly, allowing me to notice the treble clef becoming a bass clef as it turned upside down. As the yin yang picked up speed, rotating faster and faster, the clefs combined, turning into one clef consisting of both clefs at once. It's difficult to imagine and even more difficult to describe. The clef kept spinning as it turned from vertical to horizontal. Now lying flat, it spiraled downward like a tornado—wide at the top and narrow at the bottom. Instantly, I found myself sitting atop the clef, spinning around and around, looking down into the funnel. The funnel also spouted upward. I sat in the center. All was calm. All was peaceful.

Sifu's electricity ended and so did the vision. I opened my eyes and my mouth at the same time. I pushed Sifu's hands aside, hopped to my feet, and grabbed a pen and a napkin. I had to write it down while it was still fresh in my mind.

"I see it now. Come look!"

Ali and Seiko ran over to me. I drew a bass clef on the napkin. I then spun the clef upside down and drew a line through it, turning it into a treble clef. They noticed it right away and gasped in unison. I wasn't finished.

"Guys, we've been seeing them flat on the paper our whole lives. They're not flat."

I drew a spiral reminiscent of a tornado going down the page.

"This is what they truly represent," I explained.

I held the napkin flat in the air and spiraled my finger down underneath it.

"Music is not flat," I repeated. "It spirals in all directions. That's what the symbols are showing us. The top of the bass clef is the bottom of the treble. Middle C. That's where they meet. We can travel through the spiral as far as we choose to go—like Alice in Wonderland."

"Yes, my brother, but we can go down or up the rabbit hole."

Sifu offered a clever comment.

✛

"If you venture down the rabbit hole, at least venture down the rabbit whole."

Although it wasn't totally logical, I understood completely.

"I feel more whole than ever," I replied.

"Me too," Ali concurred. "Sifu give us extra . . ." He couldn't find the word. "Extra *something.*"

"Who is Alice?" Seiko asked. "And what hole we going down?"

We laughed. She didn't. Michael walked in and looked at my drawing.

"Interesting," he remarked. "Looks like you received good information."

"Just one more thing," Sifu said.

He sat down in Michael's chair. Only important information ever came from that chair. I was curious about the wisdom he was going to impart. We took our seats across from him.

"Listen," Sifu said.

He sat silently, staring at us. We expected him to continue but he didn't. We waited. All was quiet. After a minute, he spoke.

"Tell me what you hear."

"It's quiet," I responded. "I don't hear anything."

"That's because you're an infant!" Sifu exclaimed.

Seiko laughed. I didn't.

Sifu proceeded to quickly name at least twenty things he could hear at that given moment. It was an eye-opener (or maybe an ear-opener). I could hear the same sounds, but only after he'd brought them to my attention. It was a revelation. Seiko didn't look impressed at all. I wanted to ask what she'd heard, but Sifu continued.

"The best exercise I could ever give you is this one: Sit, just sit!" He rose up out of the chair and plummeted back down for effect. "Sitting inside is good, but outside is better. In either case, sit and observe. Use all of your senses, including your feelings and intuition. Believe it or not, sitting outside in the *same* place every day will cause you to learn even more."

"What do we think about when we sit?" Ali asked.

"Nothing," Sifu responded. "You don't have to think about anything. If you are quiet and really listening, what you need to know will show up. How it shows up is not up to you, so stay quiet and aware."

"How much we do it?" Seiko asked.

"Do it as often as possible," Sifu answered. "And when you're too busy, do it even more."

He stood and began to walk away but turned to offer a final comment.

"That is all for now, my grasshoppers"—he pointed at me—"unless you want to show me your fighting stance again."

"No, thank you," I responded, recoiling into the back of my seat.

Sifu returned to his usual standing position in the doorway. Michael reclaimed his chair, closed his eyes, and waited
as if gathering his thoughts. He exhaled slowly before he
began.

"Tonight—"

Isis burst in through the front door.

"Michael! Come quick! It's Jonathan!"

Michael hopped up, but Sifu made it out the door first.
I followed Michael. Once outside, I saw Sifu running down
the street. Michael ran to the end of the driveway and
stopped, so I stopped, too. Michael's back was to me. He
raised his head slightly and appeared to close his eyes. He
then took off running in the opposite direction from Sifu. I
followed.

"Victor, stay here," Isis ordered.

"No, Isis. I can't."

"You must!"

"No!"

I ran in the direction of Michael. Ali remained with Isis.

"I'll be careful!" I yelled.

As I reached the cross street, I saw no one. There were
multiple roads in front of me and I didn't know which one
to take. I had three choices: left, right, and center. A fourth
choice came to mind. I could go back home. I didn't like
that choice. I pushed fear aside and took a step forward.
Instantly, I heard a familiar sound. *The hawk.*

I turned left and ran as fast as I could. From a distance, I
saw Michael crouched on one knee at the edge of the street.
He was gazing into the woods. He raised his hand behind
him, signaling for me to stop. I slowed but kept walking
toward him. He waved again. I kept walking.

As I reached him, he pointed forward. I looked through the trees and saw three men standing in the middle of the woods, thirty yards away. Though the trees obscured my view, I could tell they were standing in a triangle formation facing outward. Something was lying motionless at their feet. I shifted my body and altered my view. My stomach dropped.

"Jonathan!" I whispered.

Michael held a finger to his lips. I stared ahead and spotted Sifu standing off to the side of the men. He kept his distance. I assumed he could easily take on three men, but he held his position for some reason.

"What should we do?" I whispered.

"Go get some instruments," Michael answered.

That sounded like a dumb idea, but I kept quiet.

"Phasers," he said. "Instruments! Go get them!"

I'd once seen Michael heal a man by singing to him. I wanted him to do something like that right then. It would surely be faster than going to get instruments, but I did as he asked.

"Okay," I answered.

"Hurry!" he snapped.

I backed up slowly and ran quickly to my house. Isis, Seiko, and Ali were on the porch with instruments in hand as if waiting for me.

I halted at the edge of the driveway. *Wait,* I thought. *We're supposed to be musical without instruments.* Something wasn't right.

"Where's Uncle Clyde?" I asked.

"He's not here," Isis answered.

I turned around. They followed. We made our way to

the end of the street and turned left. We were stunned to find Michael and Sifu walking toward us carrying Jonathan's limp body between them. I ran ahead to help. We transported Jonathan to my house and laid him down in my bedroom.

"What happen to him?" Seiko asked, fighting back tears.

"Phasers," Michael answered as he knelt by the bed.

"But I thought—"

"So did I," Michael interrupted.

"Phasers are changing," Isis commented. "They are getting stronger and bolder."

"Is he alive?" Ali asked.

"Yes," Michael replied. "But he's weak. I don't think he'll be able to go with us tonight. Someone will have to stay here with him. We'll be down two."

"That's not good," Isis responded. "We will need everyone tonight."

Isis's accent had vanished. This was not a good sign. I wanted her accent back, but more so, I wanted answers and I wanted them now!

"What's going on tonight, Michael? You haven't told us anything and now Jonathan is hurt. Tell us what's going on!"

"Later. Let's talk about it later."

Michael was sitting on the edge of the bed. He leaned forward to stand, but I placed my hand on his shoulder, keeping him seated. He smiled. Sifu placed his hand on my shoulder. I didn't budge. Michael glanced at him and shook his head. Sifu relaxed.

"No, Michael, I want to know now. Tell us what's going on tonight."

"I said later!" His tone hardened.

"I said now!" I was determined.

Michael slowly rose to his feet. He was at least six inches taller, which allowed him to look down on me. He glanced at Isis and back at me.

"You disobeyed me, Victor. I told you to stop. You didn't listen. I repeated the order, and you repeated by not listening. I told you not to talk. Again, you didn't listen."

Isis walked over. She was at least six inches shorter than me. I looked down at her.

"I also told you not to go," she admonished. "You didn't listen to me either."

Ali and Seiko stood motionless, their faces frozen with fright. But for once, I wasn't fearful at all, and I wasn't backing down.

"You're wrong, Michael. I listened to both of you. I just didn't obey either of you."

"Listen to me, Victor—"

This time, I interrupted.

"No. You listen. I love you both. I respect you both, but I'm my own person, and I can make my own decisions. I don't need you telling me what to do all the time."

"So . . . ," Michael leaned close and tilted his head. I held my ground. "You love me, but you don't need me to tell you what to do anymore. You're capable of making your own decisions. Is that right?"

I thought before I answered.

"Yes, that's right."

"Okay."

Michael turned and walked toward the door. I could sense my friends' bodies stiffen. Again, I didn't budge, refusing to even turn around. I heard Michael pause at the door. He stood for a moment, turned around, and walked back over to me. I turned. With his face inches from mine, he asked an interesting question.

"'I love you both,' you said. Do you know what Love is?"

That was a strange question. I could feel the heat of his breath, but I didn't move away. Feeling stronger and more confident than ever before, I answered.

"Yes, I do."

Of all the brilliant and magnificent things I'd heard him say, I'd never heard him speak about this subject. I don't know why, but I asked a couple questions of my own.

"Have you ever fallen in love, ever? Or is that a problem for you?"

Michael turned his back and took a few steps away. He took a deep breath and lowered his head. Even from behind, I could tell that his eyes were closed, as if recalling a sensitive memory. Turning to face me again, he raised his head and spoke from a distance, this time, in a much gentler tone.

"I do not just fall, I dive in headfirst and allow it to consume my whole being. Love is never a problem, but how you respond to it can surely cause one."

Michael crept slowly toward me, the power in his voice increasing as he spoke.

"Love is the most powerful and precious thing on this planet. Love is never wrong! I fall in love with Music, instruments, people, flowers, buildings, thoughts, food, smells, sights, feelings, memories, and everything I can." He pointed his finger at me and spoke in a demanding tone. "The only reason we fear anything is because we love something else. Even Fear points back to Love. So, it is never a problem for me to fall in or out because I can never get enough. Love is the essence of what we are made of. Love is who we are!"

He calmed himself and continued.

"'I love you' is a statement, but it is also a question. All statements are questions. Everything in Life is a question. Life itself is a question. It is actually the *only* question. It is the question you are asking and answering yourself. Tell me, Victor: What is that question?"

I remained silent. Michael leaned forward. I remained motionless. He shook his head in disgust and turned away as if leaving again. And at that moment, I completely understood his point.

"Your actions, right now, are asking the question," I stated.

He paused at the door for what felt like an hour but was actually just a few seconds. Tenderly, he turned and stared at me. A tear ran down his cheek.

"I guess I did teach you something," he whispered.

"I thought you didn't teach?" I responded with a wink.

He wiped his face and pranced over to me.

"Don't change the subject," he said with a smile. "What were we talking about?"

"Love!" Seiko shouted.

"No, we were talking about the question," I corrected.

"Ai, right," Seiko replied.

Now, it was my turn to ask the questions.

"Tell me, Michael. What *is* the one question all of Life is asking?"

"Life asks nothing. Life is the question, but she allows you to ask."

"And answer," I added.

Michael smiled. I continued.

"And that question is . . . ?" I asked with a raised eyebrow.

"The same one we are always asking," he responded.

"And that is . . . ?" I repeated.

"Who am I?" Michael answered.

"That's it?" Seiko questioned.

"I don't understand," Ali remarked.

"Victor, tell him what you were thinking when I was about to walk away."

I turned toward Ali and spoke with certainty.

"I knew that Michael wasn't leaving. He was just testing me. I remembered how scared I used to get whenever I thought he was leaving. I decided not to feel that way this time."

"Who decided?" Michael asked.

"I did!"

I answered emphatically, pointing at my chest. Michael stared at me with an inquisitive look. And with his stare came my complete enlightenment. Time took an intermission as thoughts waltzed through my mind.

It was clear. The questions and answers were unconscious and unspoken, but in each moment, I had decided who I was going to be in response to Michael's actions. I realize now that we are always asking and answering, and our response is a declaration of who we are. In this instance, I knew exactly who I was. Michael was proud of me and so was I.

Michael took a deep breath. He looked at Isis. She nodded. He looked at Sifu. He nodded. Michael leaned forward, raising both hands toward me in slow motion. Seiko gasped. Something was about to happen. Once again, I held my ground. Michael stared. I stared back, choosing not to blink. Then, Michael gave in, his frown transforming into a giant smile.

He quickly grabbed me and gave me the biggest hug I'd

ever received from him. I didn't understand. He hugged me so tightly, rocking me back and forth, that I couldn't move my arms. Isis was cheering, "I knew it! I knew it! I knew!" She came over and hugged me, too. I looked at her. She was crying. Sifu hugged me from behind. There were three people hugging me and then there were five. I don't know if Seiko or Ali knew why—I sure didn't—but they joined in anyway.

"Okay. Okay. Okay," I said, finally breaking free. "Tell me what's going on."

"You graduated!" Michael announced.

"Graduated? What do you mean?" I asked. "Graduated what?"

"You don't need us anymore."

"Zat's right."

"Wait a minute. What do you mean? You're not leaving, are you?"

"We're not going anywhere. We still have a job to do, but you've claimed your power."

"Yes. We've been waiting for zat."

"I've claimed my what?"

"Listen, bud," Sifu said. "Keep your head on straight. You don't have power like me yet, but you might get there someday . . . in another lifetime or two."

Sifu held up a fist. I gave him another hug. He didn't resist. I was no longer afraid of him.

I finally understood what they meant. By rebelling against my teachers, I'd found my own understanding. And even though I'd disobeyed them, I was 100 percent sure of myself. They were proud of me for that. It had taken years, but finally, I *had* claimed my power. I could feel the difference. It was a revelation.

"It's more like a **rebelation**," Michael responded.

I laughed. He winked.

I remembered back to the few times Michael had acted like he was leaving me. I had panicked each time at the fear of abandonment, feeling as if I could not manage on my own. I realize now that he was asking me a question. Michael was always asking questions. This time, though, something was different. I could feel it. My confidence level was at an all-time high and I knew that it was here to stay. Although I was finally standing on my own two feet, I still wanted Michael to stick around. I wanted all of them to stay, and I wanted them to know that.

"Because of you guys, I'm a new person. I have a real relationship with Music and I see the world through clear eyes. Most of all, I know who I am and I love who I am. Michael, I *really* appreciate you. You've taught me . . . No!" I corrected myself. "You've *shown* me how to be a better me and also demonstrated how to lead others toward being a better them. But still, I don't want you to leave." I glanced around the room. "I don't want any of you to leave."

"We know that," Michael replied. "That's what makes it beautiful. Even though you don't need us, you still want us to stay."

"Yes, my child. Zat is most wonderful. You have reached ze ultimate pinnacle of our relationship—of any relationship. We are very proud of you."

Although I was honored to hear them speak of me in this way, there were other important things I needed to know.

"Okay. Thank you, but enough of that. We still don't know what's going on tonight! You haven't told us yet!"

I looked at Isis and then at Michael. Michael nodded and responded.

"I'll tell you all right now. Come! Let's go into the living room."

"What about Jonathan?" Seiko asked.

"Don't worry about me. I'll be all right."

The weak voice came from the bed. We turned to look. Jonathan flashed a reassuring thumbs-up.

That was a good sign.

M-Pulse

⊕

No method is sometimes the best method.

That was the first time I'd ever been rewarded for *not* listening. I wasn't sure what had just happened. Being with Michael was often like being in school. The difference? A lot of students don't like their teachers and can't wait for their lessons to end. It was the opposite for me. *Now that I'm a graduate, where do I go from here?*

Michael sat silently, waiting for the rest of us to take our seats. Sifu stood in his usual spot while Jonathan remained in the bedroom. Isis and Ali brought water for everyone and orange juice for me. I hadn't seen Uncle Clyde all morning.

Michael took a small sip of water. He licked his lips and pulled his long dark brown hair behind his shoulders. Slowly filling his lungs with air, he began speaking. His tone was serious, indicative of the importance of the evening.

"We know what we know." Michael slowly raised a finger to his temple. "And we do what we do." He held his open palms in front of him. "Separately that is not enough." His words were slow and deliberate. He looked at each of us intently. "Tonight, we must *do* what we *know* and *know* what we *do.*" He kept his left hand open while the other touched his temple.

He held his position for a moment, allowing his words to sink in. Then, raising his head to the sky, he stretched both arms in the air and gradually spread them wide.

"The musical ozone is being depleted around the world, but starting with this dear city, we will nourish the atmosphere, much in the same way trees replenish the air with oxygen. Tonight is when we bring it all together. Tonight, we *must* bring it all together."

I didn't understand why tonight was so significant. There'd been a big buildup and I was ready to know why. Michael was good at keeping me in the dark, but he also made it clear that I was in charge of turning on the light. That was his way of teaching: from confusion to clarity, puzzlement to perspicuity, chaos to candor, and turmoil to tranquility. I kept quiet, hoping we would quickly move from listening to lucidity.

"**M**usic's **pulse** has begun to weaken. Life will change if she can no longer take physical form. We cannot allow that to happen. We are part of a long lineage of people chosen to continue this age-old battle. Your religions and fables have hinted at it since the invention of the written word.

"The Arthurian legend of the sword in the stone has been around for generations, but what is it really about? Here's a clue. Move the letter *s* from the beginning of each word and place it at the end. The story's alternate meaning will be revealed."

I closed my eyes, rearranging the letters in my mind. Michael continued just as the words became clear.

"That's right. 'Words' and 'tones.' Could the story actually be urging us to decipher the meanings from the vibrations? Remember: after many others attempted and failed, it took an innocent young boy named Arthur to free the sword from the stone. Upon his success, the boy was instantly heralded as the new king. For those who choose to see, the message is clear: *Art* is king!"

As always, Michael's words vitalized and thrilled me. Like young Arthur who had been protected and tutored by Merlin, a magician (or maybe a musician), Seiko, Ali, and I had been mentored by wizards of our own. They'd sought us out, taught us, and protected us. Now they were preparing us for an adventure. Although I was apprehensive, I also felt motivated. I grabbed my two young friends' hands and gave them a squeeze. Like King Arthur, I hoped we, too, would be victorious.

Michael repositioned himself on the floor. He folded his legs into lotus position and closed his eyes. He sat for a moment before continuing.

"Music City is a special place, but 'Music' is quickly being consumed by the 'City.' Nashville's small-town feel is diminishing fast, too fast. Over the years, Phasers have been very successful in the fields of education and religion. Music is the last stronghold. We cannot afford to lose her." He gestured toward us. "This is where *we* come in."

Isis moved over and sat next to Michael on the floor. Holding each other's hands, they stretched out their free hands toward us. We joined them on the floor, forming a circle. The five of us held hands and sat in silence. I could feel the energy as we waited for Michael to continue. He spoke in a hushed tone.

"In ancient times, there was a hidden society of scholars called the Essenes. They were the holders of high knowledge and were known to have taught many people, including some of your religious figures." He looked at Ali. "They were much like Essah and the Elders. Only the lucky few, or should I say, the *worthy* few are allowed to learn from them. You are fortunate to have been accepted by Essah." He looked at Isis. "If she agrees, I suggest you continue with her."

"You are always welcome, my child," Isis replied, looking at Ali.

"That says a lot about you, Ali. The knowledge of the Essenes is alive and well with Essah. It is also alive and well right here. It is not a coincidence that 'Tennessee' spelled backward is 'Essene net.' There is an invisible attraction that subconsciously draws people here. Like a butterfly." He gazed at me. "Once you are caught in the net, it can be difficult to escape."

I was stuck on the spelling part. Trying to do it in reverse caused my attention to drift. I knew there were a bunch of *e*'s and *n*'s, but I could never remember where to put them. Seiko, sitting to my right, elbowed me in my side, nudging me back into the room.

"In your musical theory, the two notes that define a chord are the third and the seventh. In the state of Tennessee, the first two digits of every zip code are also three and seven. Think about it: each zip code can be viewed as a dominant chord. The whole state may be trying to lead us back to the *one*."

As always, my skepticism kicked in.

"Can't it just be a coincidence?" I asked.

"Of course it can. But as in 'cooperation,' a 'coincidence' is a 'co-incident,' a 'co-relation,' and a 'co-laboration.' It is also a coincidence that there are twelve months in a year and twelve notes in your music system. There are seven days in a week and seven notes in a scale. A major scale contains five whole steps and two half steps. The major part of your week has five workdays, leaving two days that make up the weekend, although there is nothing weak about it. I could also say that your five-day workweek is equal to a five-note pentatonic scale, but that would just be another coincidence, right?"

I didn't have an answer, so Michael continued.

"A soprano is 'super analog' and 'alto' means 'to alter.' To be spiritual means to be in the spirit reality as well as in the ritual of the spiral. Your acoustic is nothing more than a chaos stick, and it is also a coincidence that your first bass was a Univox—'one voice,' not to be confused with the 'universe.' You can blow up the world with an atomic bomb or you can heal the world with an 'A-tonic' bomb. To blast the world with love, our choice is a Cupid bomb. That, my friend, is called Music!"

He became animated and I became aggravated. Although his use of words was clever, I was ready to move on to another topic.

"Okay, Michael, I get it!"

He had his own ideas.

"Wait! There's more! Much of your musical terminology

comes from Greece. Is it a coincidence that Greece sits in the Ionian Sea? In scientific tuning, 256 hertz equals the note C. Speaking of Greece, why is Nashville called the Athens of the South? Maybe it's because it is exactly 256 miles away from Atlanta. Coincidence? Of course! When Plato wrote about Ancient Athens and Atlantis, was he referring to current Tennessee and Georgia? I don't know. It's all Greek to me."

Michael's information was super interesting. He was also speaking super fast, too fast for me to keep up. Unfortunately for me, he had no intention of slowing down.

"Using the base-two binary system, two to the eighth power equals 256. In scientific tuning, that is the note C, which puts the note A at 432, a magical number. Is it a coincidence that 432 multiplied by 432 equals 186,624? Ali, what is that number?"

"Wow! The speed of light," he answered without hesitation.

"Yes!" Michael continued. "That is a coincidence. Here is another. 432 times 2 equals 864. Ali, please tell us."

"The diameter of sun—864,000 miles," he answered.

"432 divided by 2—"

Ali didn't allow him to finish.

"216. The diameter of the moon—2,160 miles."

I was blown away by Michael's information as well as Ali's knowledge. My eyes widened. The coincidences kept occurring.

"432,000 times half of 432?"

Michael looked at Ali, who thought for a moment before answering.

"Um, maybe 93 million and something."

"Very good," Michael complimented. "And what is that?"

"The distance from Earth to sun."

"Exactly!"

"Michael, that is amazing!" I exclaimed.

"No, it is just a coincidence, but just in case you were wondering: Twice a year, on the equinox, the earth receives equal periods of twelve hours of sunlight and twelve hours of darkness for a total of . . . 86,400 seconds."

I think he slowed down for my benefit. I answered with excitement.

"864! 432!" I was proud to have come up with it on my own.

"Precisely!" Michael stated. "And that"—he played a drumroll on his leg—"brings us to the reason we are here tonight."

Finally! I'd been waiting. I was filled with anticipation. My mind raced. So much had happened in so little time. I'd traveled to Virginia, become a teacher, lost my student, found new friends, and lost them, too. We'd been followed, chased, kidnapped, and taken to my house only to find out we'd really been rescued. We learned about Phasers and had been training to combat them. I still didn't really know who they were or how to stop them, but I had gotten slapped a few times. There was so much I didn't know. The one thing I *did* know was that whatever was going to happen was going to happen tonight. It had all come down to now. And finally, we were about to find out why. Filled with curiosity, we sat, quietly, waiting for Michael to explain.

We waited.

. . . and waited.

. . . and waited some more.

Finally, Michael rose off the floor and sat in his chair. Viewing that chair as the dominion of knowledge, I leaned forward with expectation, but Michael sat silently. Sitting on the floor became a challenge for me, so I returned to the couch. My friends followed. We sat there for five more minutes at least. Michael hadn't budged. I reclined on the coach, afraid to make a sound, and waited.

I was fading into dreamland, when all of a sudden, Michael and Isis turned their heads. I snapped awake, noticing a thin beam of sunlight shining through the window and down onto the floor. The window sat high on the wall—too high for me to reach, so I'd never paid attention to it. The ray of light cast a small circle on the floor a few feet away from where Michael was sitting. We watched with fixed attention as the beam inched its way across the room. Michael sat erect, his full attention directed at the illuminated golden circle.

Isis, still sitting on the floor, silently removed her necklace. A small clear crystal dangled from the thin chain. She placed the crystal in her open palm and laid her hand on the floor a few inches away from the light. Her movements were slow and graceful, flowing like a beautifully choreographed dance. We leaned forward in anticipation, realizing something was about to happen.

We watched as the beam crept closer and closer to Isis's open hand. The light, moving ever so slowly, seemed to stall until we noticed it touching her finger. Michael leaned forward. I was transfixed, and I could sense everyone's excitement.

Isis wiggled her fingers as if enticing the light to come closer. To our delight, we watched the beam finally connect with the crystal, instantly filling the room with colors. We found ourselves, literally, on the inside of a rainbow. I couldn't control myself. I stood up, spinning in circles, bathing in the colorful aura. My body felt warm. I could tell by the joyful looks on their faces that my friends were just as enthralled.

I didn't want the feeling to end, but before I knew it, it was over. The lights didn't fade away, they were just gone, as if a song had come to an abrupt stop. The room felt darker. We turned our heads in vain looking for the light. Michael's voice brought our attention back into focus.

"The solstice!"

Isis rose from her seated position and replaced the necklace around her neck. Michael sat on the edge of his seat as if preparing himself. For the first time since I was with him years ago, I watched his eyes change color. I knew what that meant. This was going to be a very important lecture. I sat back down and made myself comfortable.

"The light is not gone," Michael assured. "It lives inside of you. The colors of the rainbow are sped-up versions of the vibrations you call Music, so the light is with you at all times. It is part of your DNA and always available to you. But remember, to accept the light, you must also accept the dark.

"Humans are an interesting species. Whatever you have, you crave the opposite. If it is cold, you seek the heat. If it is bright, you draw the shades. If you reside in the city, you crave the forest. You see, the farther you are from the opposite, the stronger the pull. There is a great benefit to that. That yearning keeps you moving."

He kept speaking as if we were human and he was not.

He often did things that seemed humanly impossible, but that wouldn't make him beyond human, would it? It's a silly thought, I know, but it didn't stop my mind from going there. Maybe this was just another tactic to keep us questioning. I decided to push it aside, for now, and save the questions for later.

"Phasers seem to know when humans are in the middle, what you might call balanced. It may not mean that you are spiritually centered, it is just that you are satisfied with your current stage of life. That is a vulnerable place to be. That is when you have less desire, less drive, less passion, and more complacency. The Phasers take advantage of that. Right now, at this precise moment, the Earth is at her balance point. The Phasers have no power over the Earth, but somehow, they can use this time to influence you.

"Stay awake. Keep moving. The Earth is round and we live on the surface where the planet moves the fastest. We are not capable of living in the center, so why try? The circus performer on the high wire knows there is no glory in walking straight across. The standing ovation comes only if he loses and regains his balance, so feel free to lose yours. Understand that falling is not the same as defeat."

His serious expression having transformed into a satisfied smile, Michael took a deep breath and looked at me. I sat up straight.

"Victor, although we write Music flat on the page, your vision has shown that she is as fluid as the ocean and always in motion. The clefs are spirals. The ledger lines are also spirals. So, when you see measures and measures of music notated on five lines and four spaces, imagine them spiraling across the page and tell me what you see." Because of my earlier vision, I recognized it right away. Michael confirmed my thoughts. "That's right. You are actually looking at Music's DNA."

Michael came over and stood in front of Seiko. He held both of her hands as he spoke.

"Young dreamer, full of spirit and vision, whom many saw as a deserted seedling, has now proven to be a full-grown flower. Soon you will be a powerful forest, so strong that no one will be able to cut down even one tree."

"That's right!" Seiko responded. "I will hear them coming."

"Even if they make no sound," Ali added.

We all laughed.

"Your understanding of the rhythmic world is well beyond most. With Kiladi's guidance, you have discovered that vibrations are but a physical representation of the spirit that runs through all things. May your valiant intuition continue to guide you as you journey through the 'unified verse,' or as others call it, the universe. It is a wonderful place and so are you!"

Seiko wiped her eyes and took her seat, burying her face in her hands. Knowing that he was next, Ali rose to his feet. Michael turned to face him.

"From birth, your continued quest for knowledge has not only led you to the Elders, but has also led them to you. The care you have poured into Life has also prepared you for becoming an Elder yourself. As the elder of this young trio, you have done well in guiding and protecting them. Your time spent with Essah, along with your experience building and protecting the church, paired with your honest and diligent desire to make the whole world better, has given you amazing abilities that you will soon uncover. I look forward to witnessing it."

Ali's face was bright. He hugged Michael and turned toward Isis, who also hugged him. Tears flowed down his face.

"To all of you . . ." Michael picked up his glass and raised it in the air. "I respect and admire you for carrying forward the tradition of the shaman. Music is indebted to you and so am I."

We drank to that.

It was really good to listen to him speak. It felt like old times when he would stretch my mind and belief systems every day. Having been separated from him for a number of years, I was pleased to be captivated by his words once again, especially with my new friends.

Sifu told us that he would be staying at home with Jonathan tonight. That didn't make me happy. He told us not to worry and that he would still be with us. I wasn't sure what he meant, but it would've put my mind at ease to know he was physically going to be with us.

My mind was full and my body was tired. Michael had already given us a lot to think about, but there was still a lingering question I needed to ask. I finally found the space and the courage.

"Michael, how did you get that woman to reverse her direction and walk over to you? What technique did you use?"

In true Michael fashion, he returned the question back to me.

"You tell me. You did the same thing to the man in the hat."

"I don't know. I just did it."

"Exactly!" he replied.

⊕

"No method is sometimes the best method."

I expected more, but that was enough. It actually made sense.

Michael walked into the kitchen and announced that it was siesta time. Afterward, we would have some snacks and a very light meal. He didn't want any energy wasted on digestion, saying we would need as much as possible for the upcoming events.

Sifu wanted us to spend at least fifteen minutes doing the breathing exercise he'd shown us earlier. It was our choice to do it before or after the siesta, but it had to be done outside while sitting on the ground.

I asked Sifu why my meditation had lasted longer than the others'. He assured me that it hadn't and that all three were the exact same length. That was difficult to believe. I thought I'd been sitting for five minutes, at least. Maybe it was because I'd actually *paid attention.*

Michael exited the kitchen with a glass of water for Jonathan. I stopped him as he walked by, seizing the moment to ask another question.

"Michael, you've spoken a lot about religion over time. I've never asked, but now I'm really curious. What religion are you?"

His answer was not surprising.

"Am I allowed to choose only one?"

"Well, typically, yes," I answered.

"Then, I am not interested. Allow me to choose all of them and I might reconsider."

I nodded. He continued with a question of his own.

"Which style of music is best?"

I quickly responded, "That depends on preference. It's all the same notes."

"Exactly!" He turned and disappeared into the bedroom.

I reclined on the couch and closed my eyes only to find fuzzy bits of information occupying my brain. Although my thoughts were mixed with anticipation of the events to come, I fell asleep rather quickly.

———～～～～～———

I awoke a few minutes later, or so I thought. I'd actually slept a lot longer than I realized. Our departure time was quickly approaching. I hurried to my feet, welcomed by an inviting aroma wafting in from the kitchen. Isis and Ali were preparing a pot of vegetable soup. I was more than ready to eat.

Michael alerted us that we only had an hour before our departure. He wanted to get downtown early so that we could get into our positions. I was aware that my friends and I would be playing together again, but according to Sifu, we'd each be in a separate location, spread out across different parts of the city. Apparently, playing ten paces away from each other was just a warm-up. Michael had neglected to tell us that. To say that I was worried would be a huge understatement. We'd already lost two members of our team. That didn't help my nerves at all. I thought about our new friend from the store.

"What about Brandon?" I asked.

"Brandon is a good one," Sifu replied, "but he hasn't had the training you all have had. He will be an asset but will need to stay with one of you."

"I'll keep him with me," I said.

"Great! Michael told me you would say that. He will meet you on the corner just before midnight."

We were called into the kitchen for dinner. As we gathered around the table, we held hands and took turns expressing our gratitude. Each of us also stated an affirmation for the night. I declared that our collective effort would be enough to beat the Phasers and that Music would be revivified from our love. And because I was going to be the designated driver, I promised to take good care of Sifu's Black Beauty. I silently hoped everything I stated was true and that this was not going to be our last supper.

"Remember," Michael stated, "downbeat is at midnight."

On our way downtown, we found Uncle Clyde under a bridge near Eighth Avenue, exactly where I'd first met him years ago. He'd organized a group of people to help in the night's crusade. I was shocked to find out that many of them, like Uncle Clyde, chose to live a homeless life, working under the radar like real-life superheroes. Apparently, they helped keep the city in balance. I'd thought Uncle Clyde was the only one.

Tonight, he would be taking a group of his people to Fisk University, a historically black university founded in 1866. Known for the famed Fisk Jubilee Singers, the school is rich in musical history.

"Many things been taken from our people," Uncle Clyde said, "but we sho' ain't gonna let 'em touch Fisk. Let's go!"

"Uncle Clyde, do you need a ride?" I asked out of respect, knowing that all of them wouldn't fit in the van.

"Naw, son. Don't you worry 'bout us. We gets there in our own way."

The group sang an old spiritual as they walked north toward Broadway. It was a glorious sound. The remaining men and women dispersed in different directions. I had no idea where they were going. All of them were on foot.

Michael instructed me to drive to West End Avenue. The next stop was Centennial Park, home of the Nashville Parthenon, a full-scale replica of the famed building in Greece. This was where Seiko would be stationed. It was a beautiful sight, but although bright lights lit the large stone stairs that surrounded the building, I wasn't comfortable leaving her there alone. Michael assured us she would be safe. Seiko didn't appear worried at all. She had her drum at the ready and was prepared to play. I was still concerned.

Ali and I walked back to the van as Michael gave her final instructions. We couldn't hear what he was telling her. Ali expressed his concern to me. We hoped we were doing the right thing leaving her all alone.

Suddenly we were startled by a high-pitched screech. A large dark object flew overhead. I looked back at Michael who was holding his right arm out in front of him. A large bird descended and perched on his outstretched arm. *The hawk!* Ali screamed. We were excited.

Michael whispered something to the bird. It immediately flew up, perching high atop the Parthenon. Once settled, the hawk let out another long screech, summoning a band of highly animated birds. I thought owls and bats were the only winged creatures stirring at this time of night, but this vast group descending upon the Parthenon proved otherwise. It was an impressive sight. Silhouetted by the bright lights, the birds took up their positions as guardians. Seiko raised her fist in the air.

Ali and I felt a bit better, but even with winged reinforcements, we were still concerned about Seiko's safety. Michael could sense our apprehension and offered some encouraging words.

"A woman's strength is different than a man's. The sacred gifts she carries within can lift the human spirit higher than any man can lift with muscle alone. Women do not only conceive, carry, and deliver Life, they can endure emotional and physical pain that would make most men crumble. All people have intuition and instinct, but women actually listen. Because they nurture, they are much closer to their true nature. Do not be fooled by Seiko's petite stature. She is a warrior. There is no need to worry about her tonight. Let's go!"

Our next stop was Bicentennial Capitol Mall, a nineteen-acre state park built to commemorate the two hundredth anniversary of Tennessee becoming a state. Two parallel stone walkways line the massive park. The combination of stone and grass forms a 2,200-foot formation, which can only be seen from above. Some say the oblong shape is representative of the staff held in the hand of Athena, a forty-one-foot-tall statue located inside the Parthenon.

On the northern end of the park sits the Court of Three Stars. This circular plaza consists of three large granite stars positioned on the ground in the shape of the state flag. The Court, located at the end of the plaza, can be viewed as the tip of Athena's staff. Surrounding the plaza are fifty limestone towers set in a wide semicircle. On top of the pillars are ninety-five carillon bells that play a popular song every hour.

All sounds that are produced are dramatically amplified when one is standing in the absolute center of the towers. Michael showed Ali where to stand and instructed him to clap his hands. The sound was amazing—bold, rich, and resonant, as though we were standing in a large cavern. The Court of Three Stars is itself a large musical instrument, with the pillars acting as an echo chamber. I was sure that was why Michael chose it as one of the locations.

Ali was instructed to sing from the center of the pillars while slowly rotating in a circle. According to Michael, this would propel the vibrations in all directions. Ali agreed without hesitation. As with Seiko, I was reluctant to leave him there alone. Michael, always a few steps ahead, sang a low G. Eight men and women appeared from behind the pillars, singing in harmony with him. I recognized some of them as part of Uncle Clyde's crew. Incredibly, they'd made it there before us.

Ali was elated and I was relieved. We shook hands and I walked back to the van. Once again, Michael remained to give final instructions. He then caught up with me as I hopped into the van.

"I will see you later," he told me as he began to walk away.

"Wait! What do you mean? Aren't you coming with me?"

"No. I will be elsewhere."

"Where will you be?" I asked.

"Not far away, on Music Row. We cannot afford to lose that place."

"What about Isis?" I asked.

"She will be at the Ryman Auditorium, just a few blocks from you."

"I'm a little scared," I told him.

"Good," he replied. "That means you still have time to prepare. You will not be afraid once you get started. You only have a few minutes. Go!"

My destination was Third and Broadway, the same corner where we'd played the night before. It was nearly ten minutes away.

"But Michael, I don't have enough time and I'll have to find somewhere to park. I'll be late."

"Pay attention. You know what to do."

He turned and walked away. I closed the door and started the van, making a point not to look at the clock. I rolled down the window.

"Michael—"

He interrupted me, speaking over his shoulder as he walked away.

"Regardless of what they do, love them anyway."

His voice faded in the distance.

No "good-bye," "good luck," or even "I'll see you later." I didn't feel good about that. I'd hoped he'd be with me downtown; I always felt secure when he was around, but that would not be the case.

"Be careful," I whispered.

As I put the van into Drive, I heard his voice one more time.

"Your parents named you well."

"My name is Victa," I whispered to myself. For some reason, I heard it in Seiko's accent. It gave me strength. That was what I needed. I drove away full of confidence.

After a short ride, I arrived downtown with three minutes to spare. It was almost game time. Fortunately, my parking space was waiting for me. I stepped onto the sidewalk and listened. Sounds blared from all directions, but my mind was quiet. The streets were crowded, but I was alone. All appeared normal . . .

. . . but I knew it wasn't.

The Second Ending

◈

If at first you don't succeed, fail again.

I stood on the street corner with a four-stringed weapon in hand. I plugged it into my portable amp and took aim, ready to drop a bomb on Music City, one that unites and causes people to feel more love. Tonight, I was Cupid—my bass as my bow and Music as my arrow.

I tuned my bass, starting with the lowest string. Although the volume was down, I could feel my stomach vibrating. I tightened the string, noticing an increased tingling sensation travel throughout my body. Because of the surrounding noises, it was difficult to hear the pitch, but I could feel exactly where it needed to be.

This was not a dress rehearsal and there was no more time to waste. I had one minute until downbeat. Brandon hadn't arrived and Michael wasn't coming. I was alone, just me and my bass guitar. Then, a perfectly timed revelation hit me. I was not alone. Music was here and she is always ready. I breathed a sigh of relief.

I checked the knobs on my bass. *Perfect.* I checked my surroundings. *Normal.* Ten seconds to go: *10, 9, 8, 7 . . .* Showtime! I inhaled and reached for my lowest string just as the lights went out across the street. Merchants, a restaurant and nightclub located on the corner of Fourth Avenue, had suddenly lost all its power. I'd played there many times in the past, but now it sat dark and silent. The Phasers had struck first. I got a chill. This was real.

I struck the lowest note on my bass. Silence. I looked down at my amp. The power was off. I flicked the switch up and down. Nothing! Out of frustration, I kicked it gently. The amp fell over but didn't turn on. Still nothing. Panic was rising but I caught myself. I took another deep breath and traced the path of the power cord with my eyes. It was supposed to be plugged into the extension cord coming from the van, but it wasn't. There was no one to blame but me.

I opened the van door just as a parking officer walked up. I'd forgotten to put money in the meter. I reached in my pockets. *Empty.* The officer pulled out his pad. I reached in the dashboard and grabbed some coins, spilling them onto the pavement. *Wait! It's midnight! Parking on the street is free.* I looked again. The parking attendant was actually a tourist unfolding a map. I was nervous. *Relax!* I left the coins on the street.

The power was still off at Merchants, but the people outside were having a good time. They were obviously oblivious to what was really going on. Maybe I was oblivious, too. I should have been playing.

"PLAY!"

The command was loud and clear. Michael wasn't present, but he didn't have to be. I plugged in my amp and again struck the lowest string. The van door rattled. I felt it and I knew that others did, too, but nothing changed. Everyone and everything appeared normal except that the lights were still off. A few people from the restaurant ventured outside. I wondered if my low E had brought them out. I wasn't sure, since they all seemed to be in a party mood already.

I lined up my sights and aimed a groove straight at the crowd. It was a perfect hit. A couple of them looked in my direction. I kept firing. Then I watched a miracle emerge. First, the drummer began playing with me from inside the dark club. The people standing outside began clapping along, which prompted a vocalist to join in. The voice provided a melody. The drums added rhythm. I held the bottom. The people added energy.

Customers from inside the surrounding venues came out to listen. It was a real live block party. Within a few minutes, the lights inside the restaurant turned back on. Merchants was back in business. We all cheered.

"I did it!" my ego shouted, but the only thing I'd really done was speak too soon.

The flashing red light was visible as he walked out of the restaurant and into the crowd. Everyone was cheering, singing, and dancing except him. He stood motionless, staring in my direction. He didn't look happy, and neither was I.

He walked toward me. Without looking left or right, he stepped into the street. I was reminded of my encounter just a few nights earlier. I held my bass tightly. Music and I were ready.

As he advanced through the four-way intersection, the lights flickered to my immediate right. Third Avenue and Broadway, the corner where I stood, was now being affected. I wasn't sure how, but I was not going to allow the power to go off on my block.

Gruhn Guitars, a popular guitar shop, sat on the corner behind me. Vintage instruments could be seen through the storefront window. That gave me an idea. Using the instruments as reinforcement, I turned and faced my opponent. With complete confidence, I pointed the neck of my bass directly at the Phaser and played with intention. I felt the instruments behind me awaken. Our combined energy did the trick. He halted a half block away. We kept the energy flowing, determined not to allow him any closer.

I could feel his presence and I knew that he could feel ours. He wanted to close the distance, but we weren't budging. He stood in the middle of the street, neither advancing nor retreating. The groove was strong, but I needed more reinforcement. *Brandon, where are you?* As soon as the thought entered my mind, a familiar figure came running through the crowd.

"I'm here. Sorry I'm late. I got stuck in—"

"Brandon. I need you to play! Whatever you brought—play it now!"

I continued playing as I spoke, while also keeping my attention on the Phaser standing in the middle of the street. I was relieved to have Brandon with me but was shocked to see him pull a kalimba out of his bag. I was not happy. The instrument was too quiet, plus he'd only played it once. At least he'd also brought a microphone and a battery-powered speaker. I hoped it would be enough. He set it up quickly and was preparing to play when another familiar figure emerged from the crowd.

"Brandon convinced me to come along. Tell me what to do."

It was Brandon's boss from the store. He'd been running as well, but hadn't been able to keep up. He was sweating profusely and breathing heavily. Fortunately, he had a guitar on his back.

"Play!" I shouted.

"It's been a while since I've played. I'm not sure it'll sound any good."

"Listen," I told him. "Good is not what we need right now. Emotion and honesty are most important. *Not* playing would be a bigger mistake."

"Okay. I'll try. Brandon told me about the Phasers. It was hard to believe at first, but he convinced me. He told me what happened when the lights went out and—"

He was talking too much. I needed him to play. Just as I was about to speak, the lights went out directly across the street. Half of my block sat in the dark. The store manager noticed the man standing in the middle of the street.

"Brandon, is that one of them?" he asked.

"Play!" I yelled, intercepting Brandon's reply.

The manager became agitated. While unpacking his guitar, he dropped it on the concrete. He groaned some inappropriate (or very appropriate) words. He stood there frozen in shock, acting as if he didn't realize there was a battle going on.

Fortunately, Brandon had already started playing, and although new to the instrument, he played beautifully. His arpeggiated chords added the needed harmony to our impromptu composition. Melody, rhythm, and harmony. The trilogy was complete.

The Phaser began a slow retreat. He walked backward through the traffic without looking behind him. Once on the other side, he stepped onto the curb and vanished into the crowd. Instantly the lights came back on. The crowd cheered. I closed my eyes and breathed a sigh of relief.

～～～～～

Seiko had begun playing as soon as we'd left. She felt comforted by the birds perched watchfully overhead. She was having an uneventful time when, at the stroke of midnight, the birds became agitated and began sending out alarms. After a few seconds, all became quiet. Something wasn't right. She listened for footsteps but heard nothing. The air was still, the trees were silent, and there were no cars moving in the distance. Her eyes were even less reliable in the dark, but maybe, just maybe, she saw a flashing red light in the distance.

The large hawk flew down, landing next to Seiko's foot. She followed the hawk's gaze as it stared off into the distance and noticed an unwelcome presence approaching. She couldn't see or hear anyone but recognized the unmistakable feeling. She tried not to worry but could not ignore her instincts.

The hawk ascended to a landing just above Seiko's head and shrieked as the floodlights suddenly went dark. The other birds began chirping wildly. Seiko blinked her eyes, trying to see more clearly. Her feelings were confirmed. Tiny red dots were blinking in the distance. Scared but confident, she readied her drum. It was showtime.

She struck with intention and noticed the vibrations travel away and ricochet back. She hit the drum twice more and felt two returns. The sound reverberated off something. The darkness outside amplified her feelings inside. That gave her an idea. She closed her eyes and smiled.

~~~~~~~~~~

Ali stood on the northern end of Bicentennial Capitol Mall and took stock of his position. He placed both feet on either side of the spot marking the exact center of the pillars. The reinforcements that Uncle Clyde sent were positioned in a semicircle behind him. He looked at each of them and nodded. Their presence was comforting. They stood poised, quiet, and alert.

Various-sized carillon bells attached to the top of each pillar played a familiar Tennessee folk song at the beginning of each hour of the day. Something was different about this hour, though. It was midnight and all was silent. Ali waited. One minute after midnight, silence remained. He knew what it meant when the bells didn't ring.

Ali could see the state capitol, brightly lit, sitting atop a large grass-covered hill in the distance. The beautiful sight calmed his nerves until suddenly the top of the hill became cloaked in blackness. His body tensed.

One by one, the lights illuminating the walkway from the capitol building also began to black out. Ali knew that the Phasers were closing in, and he was determined not to allow the darkness to reach him. He glanced behind him. His team was ready.

Ali widened his stance and prepared to sing, but something didn't feel right. His ears began to clog. He was familiar with that sensation and it wasn't good. Suddenly, out of the silence came an awful sound.

From the top of the pillars, all ninety-five bells began ringing simultaneously. There was no order to the sound, only chaos. The sheer pandemonium was disorienting. Ali's instinct was to cover his ears and run, but he held his ground. His comrades were in disarray. Some of them crouched down and turned away from the noise. Others held their ears.

Ali struggled to maintain control. His mind played tricks on him, flashing back and forth between Tennessee and Africa. He recalled the time at his church when the bells hadn't sounded despite being rung, but now, all the bells were ringing wildly on their own. Both scenarios were unpleasant.

Ali was at a loss. As flashing red lights began to appear, the lights illuminating the walkway were vanishing one by one. That meant only one thing. Complete darkness was approaching. There were no overhead lights where he stood, which meant the only light remaining was a lamppost on the right side of the mall. Ali wasn't afraid of the dark but was determined not to let all the lights go out. He couldn't allow the Phasers to have that much control.

Ali tried to sing. Nothing came out. He tried to rally his choir, but they were startled and confused. He clapped his hands to get their attention. The vibration reverberated forcefully off the pillars. Ali's eyes widened. He clapped again, focusing on the sound. He felt the echo return from all directions. That gave him an idea. He closed his eyes and smiled.

I stopped playing and turned the volume down on my bass. Brandon continued. His hands were shaking. I told him that he could stop but he kept playing. He appeared to be in a trance.

"Brandon! It's okay. You can stop."

"But . . . but . . . what if he comes back?"

"Oh, he'll definitely come back, but we're okay at the moment." I pointed to Brandon's boss.

"Let's get him up and running. We'll need his help."

Brandon's boss was still staring at the guitar lying on the ground.

"It won't help us down there," I told him.

"It's broken," he replied. "The top of the headstock snapped off. Two of my strings are gone. I can't play."

"You still have four strings. That's all I have. You can play . . . if you can play." He looked at me but didn't respond. I continued, "I'm sorry. I don't even know your name."

"Larry," he replied, extending his hand.

I grabbed his hand and pulled him closer. Brandon's eyes widened. Mine narrowed. My tone was serious.

"Listen, Larry! Tonight, we play! And even if we fail, we fail big! We do nothing halfway. Mistakes are part of Life's process. It doesn't mean you are wrong. Treat it as Music pushing you in the direction she wants you to go."

"But I don't want to make a mistake."

◍

"If at first you don't succeed, fail again."

"Okay," Larry said as he picked up his guitar. "I'm a little rusty. Just give me a minute to warm up."

"You're not rusty, you're scared, and we don't have a

minute. It's not *what* we play or *how* well we play, it's *why* we're playing that matters tonight."

Larry still looked frightened. Maybe I was being too tough. I offered a different approach. I placed my hand on his shoulder.

"Larry, don't worry. I'm scared, too. You don't have to play if you don't want to. I'm really happy you're here. Thank you."

He took a deep breath and let it out forcefully. He picked up his guitar and strapped it on with conviction. Two of the strings hung to the ground. He no longer cared. He plugged into Brandon's amp and stood up straight. Brandon and I positioned ourselves on either side of him. We were ready.

~~~~~~~~

Seiko sat on the steps of the Parthenon fueling her rhythms with emotion. She asked Music for help. Gradually, she was able to synchronize her rhythms with the birds, turning their chirps into a giant chorus.

She turned left and right, sending vibrations across the park. With her eyes closed, she could hear the sound bouncing off objects in the distance. Using the echo from her drum, as well as the chatter of the birds, she was able to locate objects in the immediate area—the faster the rebound, the closer the object. If a vibration bounced back the first time but not the second, she then knew the object had moved.

Using different parts of her hands to produce different tones, Seiko realized that each frequency reverberated differently. She was excited about her new discovery. She was also smart. With this information, she was able to hit her targets with pinpoint accuracy.

A soft echo was moving from left to right across the grass. Seiko squinted her eyes. A flashing red light was also moving across the grass. Her drum was round and wide at the top, tapering down to a narrow opening at the bottom. While continuing her rhythm, she lifted the drum with her feet and aimed the open bottom at the moving target. She closed her eyes.

"I can see you," she whispered.

With a rapid slap of her right palm, she hit the drum hard, producing a dynamic pointed tone. The drum, acting like a cannon, sent a powerful vibration directly at her target. *Gotcha!* The echo grew longer as her target moved farther away.

"Yeah, you better run!" she shouted.

A pair of blinking headphones were left lying on the ground. Seiko pointed her cannon and blasted them with a powerful cadence. The red lights faded into darkness.

"One down, more to go. Bring it on!"

Seiko was in control. Repeating the process, she blasted another Phaser, causing the Parthenon's lights to reilluminate. Like deer caught in the headlights, the remaining Phasers stood out in the open, frozen in place. With her eyes closed, Seiko downed two more. The birds alerted her to movement on the opposite side of the building. Following their trills, the Phaser was easy to locate and extinguish. Seiko walked around the building twice more, making sure no blinking lights remained. Her mission was complete. Knowing she had not acted alone, Seiko thanked the birds, Music, and her drum for assisting in her success.

Seiko laid her drum by her side and leaned back against the wall. Although she'd done her job, her insides were still unsettled. The air was calm, but it carried a sense of uncertainty. She closed her eyes and visited the sacred place Kiladi had helped her create. Immediately, she felt her new friends' presence. She knew what it meant.

Seiko summoned Music, and in the back of her mind she could hear a choir singing and bells ringing. Without question she knew who it was. She amplified the feeling and began playing along, aiming her drum in that direction. Benefiting from her lesson the day before, Seiko immediately connected with Ali. Now she completely understood why Michael had had them spend hours jamming on the street corner. Seiko was thankful. She intensified her efforts, sending rhythmic energy in her friends' direction.

Seiko opened her eyes just as the hawk landed nearby. His call alerted her to someone's presence. Seiko wasn't alarmed. She'd heard him coming. His footsteps were a welcome sound.

"Seiko, we must go!"

"Yes, Kiladi. I know."

~~~~~~~~~

The bells continued ringing unharmoniously. Ali listened and found a rhythmic pulse in the apparent randomness of the noise. He began clapping along in an attempt to bring a semblance of order. It was working. He mentally asked Music to accept him.

A faint melody embedded in the bells grabbed his attention. It was the famed hymn "Amazing Grace," the song the bells were supposed to play at midnight. Ali blended his rhythm with the melody. Following Ali's lead, the choir also began clapping. The additional rhythms increased their collective intensity, providing the strength for Music to gradually overtake the chaos.

Almost imperceptibly, a beautiful voice emerged. Ali looked at his group. None of them appeared to be singing. He couldn't discern where the voice was coming from and he didn't really care. The voice gave him hope. It also reminded him of his original assignment.

Ali checked his position and began singing from the center of the pillars. He raised he head, aiming his voice at the bells. He circled his troops, who joined him in harmony. They linked arms and slowly rotated in a circle. Finally, the bells surrendered and began blending with their voices. Together, their united energy swirled out, reaching far beyond the four corners of the mall.

The bells slowly hit a decrescendo and lapsed into silence, but Ali and his choir kept singing. They sang and danced passionately as the chaos totally subsided. Ali looked up at the state capitol building as it sat fully illuminated at the top of the hill. He knew that the Phasers were no longer present. Peace had reclaimed the area.

Ali sat down in the middle of the choir. Like a soloist uplifted by an ardent rhythm section, he was able to use their collective force to heighten his own consciousness. At first, he thought it was his imagination, but in the back of his mind, he sensed a low rumble. The vibrations moved down into his lower abdomen. His instincts were correct.

Along with the rumble, he sensed a powerful rhythm. He was certain of the source. He knew that Victor and Seiko were close. Accessing the lessons from the day before, he connected with his friends. Ali also thought about the voice that had rescued him from the dissonance of the bells.

He realized where it must have come from, but she was at the Ryman Auditorium, nearly a mile away. He knew exactly what to do. Using the energy of the choir and the pillars, Ali sent a mental message:

"Thank you for saving us, Mother Essah. You are beautiful."

Without hesitation, another thought appeared.

"You are very welcome, my child, but your job is not done. Come at once. Your brother needs our help."

"Yes. I know. I am on my way!"

Ali raised his hands in the air. The choir followed.

~~~~~~~~~

Merchants had returned to normal. The customers were back inside and the band was playing their final set. At least thirty minutes had passed with no incidents. My friends and I sat on the curb wondering if we were finished for the night. Although we weren't playing at that moment, a number of people asked if we had a tip jar. I answered in the negative and chuckled at the thought. *These people have no idea what's really going on.*

"My ears feel funny," Brandon commented.

"Yeah, mine too," Larry responded.

Although my ears felt fine, I paid attention. I sat up straight and plucked the lowest string on my instrument. The low rumble reverberated throughout my body.

"What was that for?" Brandon asked.

I didn't reply. I closed my eyes and reached out to Seiko and Ali. I needed their help. I hoped they could feel me.

Suddenly, I felt pressure building as if a storm was approaching, but there was no wind. I rose to my feet and looked in all directions. Everything appeared normal, but my instincts told me it was time to act.

"Saddle up, boys. It's time to play again."

No sooner had I spoken those words when a large explosion occurred at the top of a telephone pole on the corner of Fifth and Broadway—only one block from the Ryman Auditorium. There was darkness as far as I could see. The only light came from a few emergency backup lights and the cars driving down the road. I feared for Isis.

For a short moment, the drummers inside the clubs continued playing, but their sounds soon faded away. For the next minute, all was silent. Cars slowed their pace and people on the street stood motionless. I could tell they could also sense the strangeness. They may not have known what they were feeling, but I did. It was definitely Phasers, numerous Phasers! I'd never felt them this strongly before.

"Play!" I shouted.

I began playing immediately, directing my energy in every direction. I couldn't see any Phasers, but I knew they would feel me if I was genuine.

Brandon and Larry hadn't moved. "Play!" I shouted again.

They hopped up quickly and joined me. It took a few measures for us to find each other but we eventually connected. Brandon's kalimba was powerful, but with only four strings, Larry played too tentatively. I flashed an unsatisfied look. He stopped playing and grabbed his ears.

"I can't do it. The pressure is too much."

I was starting to feel it, too. "Whatever you do, don't stop playing!" I told him.

"I can't. I can barely play this thing anyway and my ears hurt."

He let his hands drop. His head followed. I was having none of that. I urgently motioned for Brandon to keep playing. I walked over to Larry and stood in front of him, my nose almost touching his. In a loud whisper, I gave him something to think about.

"Listen closely. You have no idea what is at stake and I do not have time to explain. If you do not play tonight, we may never play again. It is time to take risks. If you cannot play well, play badly. In any case, play!" I walked away only to turn and offer one last command: "The time is now!"

I took my place and rejoined Brandon. Larry wiped his eyes and joined in as well. It took him a moment, but he eventually figured out a four-note chord. We were playing together, but it still wasn't enough. The pressure in our ears was increasing. Larry grimaced. I asked him to alternate between a G sus and a G^7 chord, hoping the suspended chord would provide us with extra dominance. It was a stretch, but we needed all the help we could get. Because of the darkness inside the venues, more patrons began to filter outside. That gave me an idea.

"We need to get the people involved. Spread out."

Larry started to walk away, pulling his guitar cord out of the amp in the process.

"No! No!" I shouted. "Not physically. Spread your energy. We need to push out with our feelings so that Music reaches the people farthest away." I looked at him. "Don't ask how. Just do it." Larry plugged in and we continued jamming.

"Brandon, we need to pull those two drummers outside.

You grab the one on the right, direct your music at him. I'll get the one on the left."

"Gotcha! I'm on it!"

A half minute later, two drummers from inside the dark clubs began playing with us. That intensified our groove, but we still needed more. We'd only learned the technique the day before, but we needed to be successful at it now.

Almost immediately, the people on our side of the street began clapping along with the drummer on the right. *Perfect!* I imagined my energy as a bubble exploding on top of the crowd across the street. They cheered louder. It was working.

I combined my energy with the excitement of the crowd and poured it into my Music. I closed my eyes and made an imaginary musical lasso. Using it, I pulled the drummer outside. It was an improvised technique, but it worked. The crowd roared. I opened my eyes to find the drummer standing on the sidewalk, playing his snare drum while an audience member held it. The sound of his drum was powerful, exploding outward in all directions.

Brandon's drummer was still inside. I wanted to assist him, but I needed to bring my drummer closer. I told Larry to help Brandon.

"I don't know how," he responded.

"Just do it!" I answered. "You don't have to know how."

Larry nodded, his attitude shifting from complaints to compliance. With the two of them focused in unison, the other drummer quickly exited the club, playing a cowbell. Another band member had a tambourine. Our efforts were taking effect.

Bass, kalimba, guitar, snare drum, cowbell, tambourine . . . and saxophone? Where had he come from? Then I recognized him. He was the guy I'd pulled from across the street the night before. And there were others with him. The addition of extra people and a saxophone complemented our ensemble perfectly. We were having a party and the Phasers were not invited.

Wherever Michael was, I hoped he was having as successful a time as we were. I knew that he would be proud if he were with us. I looked at the people dancing in the street. Everyone was so happy and so unaware of the troubles that had just been averted.

"Victor." It was Brandon's voice.

"What?"

"Rain!"

I was so proud of our achievement that I hadn't noticed the slight drizzle. The rain increased, causing everyone to scatter. The musicians and the crowd took cover under nearby awnings. Some went back inside the clubs, which were still dark. We gathered our equipment and retreated into the van. Except for the rhythm of the raindrops hitting the windshield, all Music had ended.

We were discussing what to do next when Larry pointed out the back window. I looked behind and saw a person standing in the middle of the street one block away. That wasn't too abnormal, but this wasn't just *someone*.

I rolled down my window to get a better look. It was raining where we sat, but dry where the man stood. I looked in front of us and noticed another man standing in the street. It appeared to be dry where he stood also. That didn't make sense. I turned the key in the ignition and checked the radio. Static hissed from the speakers. I turned off the car and opened the door.

"Phasers!" I alerted. "Everybody out!"

"It's raining. We can't bring our amps," Brandon warned.

"Bring your kalimba," I instructed.

We exited the car and hurried into the street. We stood in the middle of the intersection of Broadway and Third Avenue with Phasers positioned east and west of us. Their blinking lights were now visible. Larry grabbed my shoulder and pointed. There were two additional Phasers approaching on Third Avenue from the north and south. We were surrounded.

Fear arrived in full force, and for the first time in my life, I welcomed it. As my father taught me, I was about to grow. I also knew that it meant I still had time. How much time, I didn't know.

The mind is a wonderful creation. It is not bound by time or space. It can speed up, slow down, or freeze time when necessary. The mind can instantly be in any location it chooses and can see things the eyes cannot.

We are often told to quiet the mind, but that is only because our minds are often chattering unsupportive thoughts and fabricating observations incessantly. If we can train it to respond more like cheerleaders to a sports team, who offer encouragement and provide motivation, then we won't need to silence ourselves. Quieting the mind will become a thing of the past. Right then, my mind became my best ally.

I had forgotten Isis's foremost direction. I directed my two friends into the middle of the street where we positioned ourselves into a triangle. The rain continued to fall. I instructed Brandon not to play.

"Love the Phasers," I told him. "We need to love them."

Brandon turned and faced the Phasers without asking any questions. As we began, these words formed in my mind:

There's a higher law we need to turn to and there's no
more time to waste.
We need to sit right down in the middle of the floor
instead of running all over the place.
Open up your mind. It's time. We need to leave those fears
behind.
There's not much time at all. There's a higher law.

I sat down in the middle of the road, realizing that Love is the highest law. Although we weren't playing Music, we filled the space with Love, directing it at each Phaser. Larry let out a slight gasp. The Phasers had stopped their advance. They could feel our energy.

Immediately, the rest of the musicians from the club returned, joining us in the middle of the road. The saxophonist sat next to me, apparently unconcerned that his instrument was getting wet. I wasn't sure if any of them really knew what was at stake, but I was glad they were with us.

Brandon and I sat quietly, but Larry broke the silence. He stood and turned in all directions. He began speaking nervously.

"How am I supposed to love them? They're Phasers and . . . and they have us surrounded."

I tried to ignore him, but he stumbled onto me, knocking me off balance and out of focus. With my attention weakened, fear strengthened. The Phasers resumed their advance. The pressure in our ears begin to increase. I asked Music for help. Again, words appeared.

There's a new sun rising, coming over the hill.
There's no use running. You'd be better off standing still.

And don't keep acting like we have time to kill.
It's time to go higher.

"Play!" I instructed the saxophonist.

He immediately played a melody.

"Higher," I instructed.

He raised his volume.

"Higher!" I repeated with more intensity.

He stood up, lifted the bell above his head, and played a powerful, high squeal. His intensity caused the rest of us to jump to our feet and cheer in celebration. Additional cheers sounded above our heads. We looked up to find dark shadows flying through the air. To our delight, our winged cavalry had arrived, producing loud shrieks as they swooped up and down and circled overhead. The hawk perched on top of our van. I was happy to see him. We'd left him with Seiko. I hoped she wasn't far behind.

The Phasers were powerful. They were giving us everything they had. Somehow they'd caused the power outage and were possibly responsible for the rain. Our group, huddled in a circle, was too small. Together, we held the Phasers at bay, but even with the sound of the birds, we weren't enough. We needed to be stronger. If only the rain would stop, the streets would fill with people again. The Phasers would not be able to handle that. We needed help.

I closed my eyes and entered my sacred place. Seiko's and Ali's markers were just inside my entrance. I sensed my friends up ahead and ran toward them. Music was also present. I soaked in her energy. Next, I shifted my awareness to the Phasers. I'd never encountered four of them at once. They stood still, but their headphones flashed rapidly.

From my vantage point I could sense that the blinking of their headphones in unison helped unify their power. The answer was clear. Our alliance needed to be stronger than theirs.

I visualized myself joining hands with my friends. As soon as I touched Seiko's hand, I heard her drum. Her rhythm was powerful and steady. I grabbed Ali's hand and heard his voice. His African chant surged with energy. Their vibrations blended seamlessly with Brandon's kalimba. That was a good sign.

I opened my eyes, surprised to find four more figures standing in the darkness. They appeared from the four compass points and stood about twenty yards behind each Phaser. At first, panic took over as I thought our troubles had multiplied, but in actuality, my prayers had been answered.

Seiko's unmistakable sound emanated from my right and Ali's powerful voice resonated on my left. Bells in front and a soulful harmonica behind secured my notion that things were about to get much better. With Brandon and the saxophonist playing next to me, combined with the birds overhead, we had our opponents more than surrounded.

My friends had answered my call. Although they were barely visible from where I stood, I could feel their energy. Isis sang an enchanting melody. The radiance of her ankle bracelets pierced the air as she stomped her feet to Seiko's rhythm. Uncle Clyde was behind us. His bluesy harmonica descended upon us as steadily as the rain.

Our adversaries equally captivated my attention. Like a spinning radio dial, my awareness jolted back and forth between the Phasers and my friends. The sounds produced by my bandmates soothed my ears while the static of the

Phasers clogged them. There was an unceasing struggle. Michael had called it a battle, and I understood why.

The intense standoff pushed my endurance to the threshold. Our rivals were on all sides and were not backing down. They took a unified step forward. The walls of failure were closing in. The rain increased, as did my heart rate. The sound of droplets pounding the pavement diminished the sound of Music. Although my bandmates were still playing, I realized that I was not participating. The Phasers had captured too much of my attention. I'd lost my focus and dropped my guard.

Everything would be easier if Michael was with us. He was on Music Row, which was only thirteen blocks away. I hoped he was having an easier time than I was. He'd put his trust in me, and even with my friends' help, I was letting him down. I reached out to him, sending my energy in his direction. I needed him now more than ever. I bellowed a silent scream. *"Michael, we need your help!"*

"Love them!" was his reply.

It was a very simple concept but so easy to forget.

Allowing Michael's words to sink in deeply, I realized that I no longer wished any harm for the Phasers. I just wanted their pursuit to end. But even if they didn't retreat, I could love them anyway. I stood there with my arms open wide, allowing the rain to wash away my fear. In the face of possible defeat, I closed my eyes and opened my heart and sent love to the Phasers in all four directions.

Almost immediately, my ears popped. The pressure inside my head decreased as another sensation took its place. My group stopped playing. The sounds of horns, percussion, and strumming guitars filled the air. We could also hear women and men singing, but the lyrics were in a different language. I turned to look at Uncle Clyde. The Phaser standing between us seemed oblivious to the large group of musicians advancing from behind. At first, I thought Uncle Clyde was also unaware, but then he began dancing. Michael was coming. I knew it, but the darkness made it difficult to see. I closed my eyes to connect with his energy. The energy was different—very different.

As the procession came closer, I noticed a very animated man leading the way. He wore a big brimmed hat and an even bigger smile. He sang in Spanish and danced vigorously as he walked. With a big smile, Uncle Clyde joined their procession. The two of them danced buoyantly as they advanced toward the Phaser in front of them. It was a wonderful sight.

Perhaps realizing the finale was imminent, the Phaser made a desperate move and took a step toward me. I took a giant step toward him. He dropped his headphones on the street and gracefully retreated to the sidewalk, blending into the crowd who had come outside to see the approaching band. It was then that I noticed the rain had stopped. I hurried toward the dancing men.

"Hey there, son," Uncle Clyde said. "Meet my southern brother. He's the Michael of Mexico." I offered my hand. The gentleman grabbed it and twirled me in a circle.

"*Hola, mi amigo. Me llamo Eduardo. Somos de Mexico City. Gracias por llamarme. Es tiempo de festejar.*" (Hello, my friend. My name is Eduardo. I am from Mexico. Thank you for calling me. It's time to party.)

His voice was powerful and robust. I don't speak Spanish but somehow I understood him. He thanked me for calling him. Even if I had, I wasn't sure if a party was the solution. Regardless, I was happy he had come. His energy was infectious. I wondered how he'd found us. As Michael had done many times, he responded to my thoughts.

"Dance first. Think later. That is the way, *muchacho*!"

I let go and allowed Music to control my body. It was a joyous feeling. The sounds of trumpets filled the air with happiness while the percussion propelled us along like the ocean current. The people I'd met with Uncle Clyde under the bridge were part of the parade. The women wore flowing skirts and sang happily as they twirled and promenaded down the middle of the road. Eduardo's hips were his main mode of locomotion. He gyrated, squatted, and wiggled back and forth while pointing his finger to each side of the street.

Then I felt a strong hand on my shoulder. I recognized the forceful touch, but this time it was playful. I turned to find Sifu also dancing down the street—if you choose to call it that. His style was unique, and I feared for anyone who ventured too close. He stepped on the Phaser's headphones, demolishing them as we passed. With the addition of Eduardo and Sifu, I felt secure even though there were still three Phasers remaining.

I looked to Sifu's left and was happily surprised to see Jonathan. I showed it by squeezing him, maybe a little too hard. He tried to break free, but I held on.

"Jonathan! You're here."

"Oh, you really are the bright one," Sifu scoffed.

I should have come up with a better greeting, but I was caught totally off guard and at a loss for words. So, I tried again.

"I'm happy but surprised to see you, Jonathan. I thought you weren't going to make it tonight."

Jonathan wriggled free from my grasp and replied with a smile and an evasive comment.

"It's dancing time, don't you think?"

He danced his way out of my reach and away from further questioning. I let him go and followed his lead. I felt as if I were floating on air as I followed Jonathan down the street.

As Eduardo and the procession passed each building, the lights inside and along the streets magically came back on. He was right: it *was* time to party. With the lights on and the rain gone, hundreds of people filled the streets. Musicians exited the clubs, bringing their instruments with them. The sound was enormous and our emotions were high. The energy multiplied as everyone participated in the high-spirited celebration.

Larry grabbed his guitar from the van and pranced around, uncaring that it wasn't plugged in. He joined the party unabashedly, finally breaking free of his inhibitions.

The remaining Phasers had nowhere to hide. Their lights had stopped blinking completely. Seiko, Ali, and Isis closed the distance, blasting the Phasers with Love and musical vibrations. The Phasers appeared stunned and their movements were no longer synchronized. As if *their* ears were aching, they rapidly removed their headphones and dropped them on the ground. Then, glancing around for the nearest exit, they hurried away in different directions, vanishing into the crowd. I watched my friends stomp on each pair of headphones, crushing them into pieces, guaranteeing that they could never be used again. I threw my hands in the air triumphantly.

Mission accomplished! The Phasers were finished, but the celebration continued. I ran to Isis, Seiko, and Ali and hugged them gratefully. We linked arms and promenaded through the street, meeting up with Brandon, Larry, and the other musicians. Our celebration was jubilant. Isis gestured toward the crowd. The streets were filled with smiles, dancing, and Music. Although the people were unaware of what they had contributed, I sent a mental, heartfelt *"thank you"* to each of them. And although we were separate individuals, I knew that, at that moment, we were all one.

The festivity continued as if it would never end, and I hoped that it wouldn't, but I gradually stopped dancing as I sensed a slight chill in the air. It was similar to the breeze that had originally led me to Jonathan's apartment. The Music faded into silence and the crowd lowered their voices. Uncle Clyde bowed his head and Isis stopped twirling. Eduardo closed his eyes and raised his hands to silence the crowed. A gratified smile adorned his face.

A soft rumbling sounded overhead. The sound intensified as it traveled through the sky toward the east. I turned just in time to see a lightning bolt strike the river. The crowd roared. The sound was deafening and the light glaring. I covered my eyes in reflex. I was stunned, but for some reason, I was not worried.

The echo faded and all became quiet. A peaceful calm remained. Everything moved in slow motion. All the people and even the trees were surrounded in a faint glow. I could read the serenity in everyone's faces as they stared at the sky.

"We could have died tonight," Brandon remarked, breaking the silence.

I placed my hand on his shoulder and nodded.

"From now on," he continued, "we are living in bonus time."

It was an interesting concept.

A large hawk caught my eye as it flew toward the river. I broke away from the crowd and followed it. My walk turned into a run as I crossed First Avenue and continued down the hill to the bank of the Cumberland River. On the opposite edge stood a figure silhouetted in the glow of the rising sun. I knew exactly who it was. I whispered his name. He pointed at me and then raised both hands in the air as if I'd scored a touchdown. I smiled. He cupped both hands over his heart and thrust them out toward me. I felt a warm sensation in my chest. My smile increased.

The hawk soared across the river, swooping low just above my head. A reddish-brown feather floated down through the air. I stretched forward my arm. The feather landed in my open palm. With a loud screech that echoed through the air, the hawk rose up and flew back toward the east.

I followed the bird as it led my gaze back to my teacher standing at the river's edge. His hands were raised to the sky as if in prayer. I shouldn't have been able to hear his whisper, but his voice sang clearly in my mind.

> *I see a rainbow. It is a product of the storm.*
> *As the sun shines down to keep us warm and the winds of change blow,*
> *You might call it a dream, but when I dream, I dream in color.*
> *Keep dreaming.*

I watched him bow slowly at the waist . . . rise . . . turn . . . and disappear into the sunrise. Time seemed to race and stand still at the same time. I knew he was gone. For how long, I didn't know. This time I wasn't sad. I knew that we weren't parting forever. Although a tear ran down my cheek, the emptiness in my stomach had turned to joy. My eyes were open and I knew I would see him again someday. But even if we never met again in the flesh, I knew I would be okay. There is a place we can communicate whenever we want, a place where Michael and Music are always welcome. I know where to find him. He left a marker for me. I held it in my hand.

Thank you, Michael.

A new day was dawning. The lesson was now mine to give. I took a deep breath, turned, and walked toward the west feeling overjoyed.

Like **the second ending** of a great composition, another movement has concluded, but the song is far from over. There is more Music to be written, and I still need your help! You'll know how to find me. I'll leave a marker for you.

Are you with me?

WHO IS MICHAEL?

*It is better to have a question you cannot answer
than an answer you cannot question.*

"Who is Michael?" You are curious about me. I like that. But instead of wondering who I am and if I am real, why not ask yourself who *you* are and if *you* are real. Those are the important questions. When you can answer them clearly and honestly, you will have a better understanding of who I am. But to indulge your curiosity, I will play along (for a little while). Keep in mind, I am a skilled improviser.

Who am I? I am me, and I am much more than that. We are all more than that. The difference between us is that I have remembered. My objective is to help you remember. That is who I am.

Being human is an extraordinary gift, but it also comes with a price. To join the game, we must first agree to forget who we truly are. Think about it: we do not know how we got here, where we came from, or where we are going.

But that is a blessing. Forgetting does not change who we truly are, only who we think we are. Forgetting allows us to choose our song and perform it however we choose. Forgetting allows us to re-create ourselves again and again. Who we are is an extraordinary gift. That is certain!

On the surface, we know the mechanics of how babies are conceived and born into this world. But underneath the surface, all we know is that magic happens! The human result of that magic is you. Life explodes into existence in a way that is just as powerful and miraculous as the big bang! And yet, our best scientists do not actually know what happens before that. Their knowledge is simply based on what occurs once our bodies first appear as tiny detectable cells. Nor do scientists or philosophers know when the mind arrives, where it comes from, or even if it actually exists. The answers to those questions are but theories and arguments.

So, celebrate you. Understand that your birth is a success! You have already completed and won the biggest contest, the biggest lottery, the most important race you will ever enter. That's right! You are the grand prize winner! Think about it: of all possibilities, Life has chosen you. Even if you do nothing the whole time you inhabit this planet, you have already won, and no one can ever take your victory away. As the Beatles have alluded to, you are a magical mystery. Yes! Let us start here. I already know that *I* am Magic.

Life has given you a stamp of approval to signify your triumph. Your personalized stamp is called a fingerprint, but it is more than that, much more. Throughout the existence of humankind—past, present, and future—your print has never been on Earth and will never be on Earth again. That is significant! We recognize them at the end of our fingertips, but in actuality, our whole being is a print. Here is a question for you to ponder: If we are all prints, to whose fingers do we belong?

As humans, we are a part of Life, all of it unique and special. That means we are different *and* the same. Yes! We are both! Opposites! To be good, there must be bad. To move forward, we must push backward. To grow an extraordinarily beautiful flower, we need plain, ordinary dirt. Experiencing both ends of the spectrum is the beauty of Life. Happiness or unhappiness—both lead to oneness. Pay attention, whenever you are happy; notice that you feel connected to something. But just as the seasons come and go, happiness is fleeting. Only through our recognition and acceptance of absolute oneness, inseparableness, and our grand union with *all* Life will we ever experience true and lasting happiness. Is it possible?

We are who we are only because of who we are not. So, bless all the things you strive not to be, for without them, it would be impossible for you to be who you are. Realize this: many things have to go right even to have a bad day. Opposites!

Okay, okay. That is not what you asked for. You want to know about *me*. As I stated earlier, I will play along (for a little while).

I am one who remembers who I am. I also remember who I was, which allows me to remember who I will next be. That is the main difference between you, me, Essah, and Clyde. We are aware of our journeys and adventures, successes and failures. But even our failures are successes. It has nothing to do with the outcomes, but everything to do with the adventure. You see, it is all about what you put into the adventure.

Although I have currently chosen this voyage as a teacher, I do not look upon myself exactly as that. The title is routinely misunderstood and misused. Teachers do not teach, and those who think they do are mistaken. We (teachers) are transmitters of information whose role is to inspire the receivers (students) so that they may teach and learn the information themselves. If the students are having trouble understanding, we must provide the information again, possibly in a different way. If teaching were really in the hands of teachers, all students would learn at the same rate. Realizing this, we must be fluid. Like great jazz improvisers, we must adjust our methods constantly, rapidly, and in surprising ways, depending on the needs of the student.

Is it a mere coincidence that the letters used to make up the word *teacher* can be rearranged to also spell *cheater*? If we are not careful, we risk becoming more invested in our teachings than we are in our students. If this becomes the case, we may be cheating our students into believing in us more than they believe in themselves.

Let us teach in ways that encourage students to recognize and reclaim their inner knowing—the knowledge of Self. One way is through thoughtful questioning. We must be careful not to squash the students' process of thought. Too often, teachers take pride in giving answers when our goal should be to guide students toward their own questions. Misguided teachers do not like to be questioned. It is through questioning, not answering, that one finds her true self.

◈

*It is better to have a question you cannot answer
than an answer you cannot question.*

I was an inquisitive child. I questioned everything. I was
not interested in normal adolescent activities and chose not to
participate in them. Because I was smart, I was teased. Because
teasing didn't bother me, I became an outcast. Because I was
an outcast, I did not squander my time. Because I was focused,
I prevailed. My closest friends were animals, trees, plants, and
other unseen entities who spoke to me because I listened.

Most of my time was divided between shredding the
streets on my skateboard and sitting silent in the woods. To
coerce me to become more social, my parents suggested
music. At first, I totally rejected this—that is, until an old
man, who appeared to be homeless, showed up at the door.

Without a thought, I opened the door, revealing a dark-
skinned man standing silently with his hands folded at the
waist. His face held a sly grin as if he somehow knew I would
answer. We stared at each other for a brief moment. I think
he was waiting for my memories to catch up. Even as a child,
I could feel his greatness.

If there is a word for the combination of knowledge, wisdom, love, and empathy, this man was that. My parents were
not happy that I was so trusting, but when the old man magically produced a small cello, seemingly out of thin air, and
offered free lessons for their young boy, the deal was made
and the song was played. I was eleven years old.

In 1975, I received a Bachelor of Arts in chemistry from
a college in the southeastern corner of the United States.

The degree per se was not important, but I had an urge to explore humans' relationship to the elements and their composition. It was a fruitful time. I could have completed it in less time, but my professor was a slow learner. He had a sincere connection with the information, but zero connection with me or the other students. Plus, he had no conception of chemistry's real relationship with Life and Music. So, I experimented on him using techniques I had learned from my cello teacher, who was a master in the art of teaching without teaching. In the end, my professor confessed that there was much he needed to learn. He turned out to be a good student and so did I. We learned much from each other and have remained friends.

While walking from my teepee to the college graduation ceremony, a large bird swooped down, dropping a feather just above my head. As it landed in my hand, a chill spread throughout my whole body. I felt awakened and alive, as if I had jumped into a cold river.

A beautiful female voice called out to me as it sailed aloft on the wind. Honoring my instincts, I altered my course to follow and track the captivating melody for three and a half miles until I found a very short woman standing on the bank of Jordan Lake. Her outstretched left hand held a small bouquet of wildflowers. Sitting on the rock next to her was a wise-looking old man, who donned a smile I recognized from when I first opened my door years ago to an apparent stranger. Above the two of them sat a red-shouldered hawk, staring at me from his low perch in a tree. Their faint smiles and a unified nod told me that they were expecting me.

Time took an intermission as Essah passed her hand through the water. Immortal memories and animated apparitions danced through the waves in front of us. Teeming with bright vivid colors and intense emotions, the water made it clear that my friends and I had been on previous adventures together. Once the visions ceased and the stillness of the lake returned, my complete memory had been restored. As soon as I recognized them, I was filled with a burning intensity. Meeting Essah and Clyde again brought vividly to life our universal purpose and connection that was formed eons ago.

My true graduation took place right there at the lake, but not a word was spoken. Essah handed me a diploma of flowers and Clyde rose to his feet. They began the procession and I followed, knowing not where we were headed. I knew incontrovertibly that the journey was continuing. And now, this journey has brought me to you. This is real chemistry at work.

You may have noticed that Essah, Clyde, and I stand very close to our pupils. In this way we loan them energy. The energy is actually emotion. Humans remember and learn more fully when emotionally attached to the information. So we stand close in order to create a field of emotion that the student can unconsciously or consciously tap into. Once the student gains enough confidence and awareness of self, we increase the distance. Soon (hopefully) the student will need us no longer.

Jonathan, he is a special one. His brain is wired in a way that allows his thoughts to interact differently with his emotions. He has pushed past his so-called limitations and has become an innovative creator. He is also a convincing performer. Jonathan played a very important role in convincing Victor to realize himself.

I contemplated using Sam, the eleven-year-old boy I sent to Victor's house years ago. He is a very talented kid and a brilliant instructor, but he was away at college and the timing wasn't quite right. Plus, his previous relationship with Victor would have started the tune off on a different beat. Upon seeing Sam, Victor would have immediately assumed himself the student. That would have been a backward step. Plus, with Victor wearing those funny clothes, Sam wouldn't have been able to control his laughter.

You probably thought that I had called upon my friends Clyde and Essah as part of my team, but now you must realize that it was they who recruited me. They have guided and counseled me through numerous cycles around this galaxy. As I am standing close, giving energy to you, they are often standing close giving energy to me. So, in a sense, I am still their student. How did I do?

Now, here's my cadenza, short and sweet. The next movement has already been written. I urge you to make the choice, to re-member, to re-create yourself as whole. That is the magic of the universe. It is also the magic of you.

With your eyes closed or open, I urge you to walk the path. Like a musician playing a song, your part does not increase or diminish who you truly are, but it does allow you to demonstrate who you are. Play every part with your whole being. In this way you will give others the awareness and the courage to do the same.

View your uniqueness as a reminder that your victory can never be erased. Then share the grandness of your victory with the world. The world already has me. The world has Essah, Clyde, and Victor. What the world needs now is You!

You may have journeyed this far alone, but we must continue together. You do not have to know the destination; knowing *why* will get us there. When you start to forget, we will send reminders—one you can see, one you can hear, and one you can feel.

A feather from our winged friends will remind you that we are together. Remember: *A feather/together.* Do not worry; you will see it. Music will sing through the trees, blow with the wind, rise with the sun, and fall with the leaves. *Listen and be silent.* Her vibrations will be clear. Do not fret; you will hear her. She can be found in every sound. *Be still and feel and Music will heal.* That is her way.

Time is of the essence. You are not alone. Whether you see us or not, it's all right; you will know that we are there. You will feel our energy. You are one of us and we thank you. Music thanks you! And if you remember nothing else, remember this, as Isis has already alluded to: Whatever the question, LOVE is the answer!

"Who is Michael?" You have asked and I have answered. I am as real as you imagine me to be. Now! It is time for you to answer the most important question:

Who are you?